Economics of Power Generation, Transmission, and Distribution: A Case Study of Kerala

Economics of Power Generation, Transmission, and Distribution: A Case Study of Kerala

Dr. K.V. Pavithran
Co-ordinater
Department of Applied Economics
Kannur University
Thalassery Campus
P.O. Palayad–670 661

SERIALS PUBLICATIONS
New Delhi

First Published–2005

ISBN: 81-86771-58-1

Published by

Head Office : **SERIALS PUBLICATIONS**
4, B.S.S. Hall, Khyber Pass Market,
Civil Lines, Delhi–110054 (India)
Phone: 23245225
Fax: 91-11-23272135
e-mail: serials@satyam.net.in

Branch Office : *4830/24, Prahlad Street, Ansari Road,*
Darya Ganj, New Delhi-110002 (India)

Printed at :

PRINTED IN INDIA

Foreword

This study on the power system of Kerala using a techno economic analysis by Dr. K.V. Pavithran is a very timely topic relevant for policy makers. I congratulate his efforts to methodically analyze the problem to identify the strengths and weaknesses of the system, and the opportunities and threats that exist.

Inefficient power system affects the poor more than the rich. In this modern age, latest technology driven by efficient power system facilities development and poverty reduction. An inefficient power system obviously widens the gap between the rich and the poor.

Furthermore, although literacy rate is very high in Kerala, several multinational corporations and industrialists tend to locate their operation in the neighboring Karnataka, Hyderabad and Tamil Nadu. Besides the political and labor issues, the inefficient power system in Kerala play a major role. It is imperative to improve the power system to attract foreign direct investment and also to put the large volume of remittances that flow into Kerala for productive uses. This will create more gainful employment leading to poverty reduction.

The strength of the author lies in well conceptualizing the problem and examining it using rigorous methods. Indeed, few studies connect the multi dimensional contributions of various specialists to examine a problem and offer solutions. The author has succeeded in incorporating technical details along side economic factors to examine the issues. This allows both the technocrats and economists to sit together and look at the problem to fix it.

I recommend this book as an essential ready to policy makers, and academics and researchers interested in economic modeling and analysis.

Dr. Geetha Nagarajan, Ph.D.
Director, Microfinance & Alternatives, and
Adj. Professor,
The American University,
Washington DC,
USA.

Acknowledgement

At the outset let me express my deep sense of gratitude to Dr. P. Ibrabim, Professor, and Head of the Department of Economics, Pondicherry University, Mahe Centre, for his sincere and valuable help rendered in the preparation of this work. My sincere thanks are also due to Dr. P.S. Chandramohanan Nair, Professor, Department of Electrical Engineering, College of Engineering Thiruvananthapuram, who took pain to enlighten me on the technical and engineering aspects of power generation transmission and distribution. I also thank Shri. S.B. K. Menon, the then Chief Engineer, Kerala State Electricity Board, who graciously provided me with the details and statistics of the state power system. My thanks are also due to Dr. G. Pavithran, Deputy Chief Engineer, KSEB Thiruvananthapuram for having rendered to me all kinds help for the competition of this study.

I have received a good deal of intellectual input from energy experts like Dr. R.V.G. Menon, and Dr. M.K. Radhakrishnan former Principals Government Engineering College, Kannur, Prof. V.K. Damodaran, former Director, Energy Management Centre, Thiruvananthapuram, I wish to place on record my sincere thanks to all of them.

Dr. G. Subramanian, Professor, and Head, Department of Economics, Madurai Kamaraj University, Dr. M.H. Surya Naarayana Professor of Economics, IGIDR, Dr. S. Harikumar, Reader, Department of Economics, Pondicherry University, Mahe Centre, and others have spared their valuable time in discussing with me some of the important aspects of research work. I remember with gratitude the help and support extended by all of them. I acknowledge with thanks the help and services extended by the Principal and government college of Engineering Kannur, my colleagues in the collegiate education wing, and the professor and lectures working in various engineering branches.

In my endeavor to complete the research work, many members of Energy Conservaiton Society, KSSP, engineering students, staff, friends and well wishers have extended valuable cooperation. It is quite impossible to list down the names of all of them. I am expressing my sincere thanks to all to them. I thankfully acknowledge the services rendered by the office staff members of Mahe Centre of Pondicherry University-Smt. Srikala C.M., (Office Manager) Preman M.P., Vijaya Raghavan K.M., and Stella Fernandez, who were very kind and helpful to me in various ways.

I must also mention a few members of may family without whose help this work would never have come to lime light. I acknowledge with full respect the unfathomable sacrifice and encouragement received from my mother even on her last days, my wife Jayamala, my children-Ashwathy, Revathy, and Yadhunath and other family members who bore with remarkable fortitude my preoccupation with research.

Above all, I thank God, the Beneficent and the Merciful, for enabling me to complete this work in spite of several odds. In spite of the help received from several quarters, I am solely responsible for the errors and shortcomings that may still remain.

Contents

Acronyms

AC	=	Alternate Current
AD	=	Average Demand
APEB	=	Andhra Pradesh Electricity Board
CEA	=	Central Electricity Authority
CERC	=	Central Electricity Regulatory Commission
CL	=	Connected Load
DC	=	Direct Current
DF	=	Demand Factor
Dfr	=	Diversity Factor
ECS	=	Energy Conservation Society
EHT	=	Extra High Tension
EJ	=	Exajoules (10^{18} joules)
GDP	=	Gross Domestic Product
GJ	=	Giga Joule
Gwh	=	Giga Watt Hour
HT	=	High Tension

IGIDR	=	Indira Gandhi Institute of Development Research
IISc	=	Indian Institute of Science
IIT	=	Indian Institute of Technology
KEB	=	Karnataka Electricity Board
KSEB	=	Kerala State Electricity Board
KSSP	=	Kerala Sasthra Sahithya Parished
kV	=	Kilo Volt
KVA	=	Kilo Volt Ampere
kW	=	Kilo Watt
kWh	=	Kilo Watt Hour
LF	=	Load Factor
LRMC	=	Long Run Marginal Cost
LT	=	Low Tension
MD	=	Maximum Demand
MJ	=	Mega Joule
MSEB	=	Maharashtra State Electricity Board
MU	=	Million Units
MVA	=	Million Volt Ampere
MW	=	Mega Watt
NHPC	=	National Hydro Power Corporation
NTPC	=	National Hydro Power Corporation
PGCIL	=	Power Grid Corporation of India Ltd.
PLF	=	Plant Load Factor
SDP	=	State Domestic Product

SEBs	=	State Electricity Boards
T&D	=	Transmission and Distribution
TEDDY	=	Tata Energy Data Directory and Year Book
TERI	=	Tata Energy Reserch Institute
TNEB	=	Tamil Nadu Electricity Board
V	=	Voltage
W	=	Watt

1

Introduction

Introduction

The story of human civilization is the story of how energy resources have been exploited for the use of mankind. For the primitive man at the dawn of history, human energy was the only source of energy. Human muscular power provided the mechanical energy needed at this stage of man's evolution. The invention of fire at a later stage, was a development of far reaching significance in the progress of mankind, as burning wood enabled cooking of food, heating of dwellings and extraction of bronze and iron. This was made possible by harnessing animals for draft purposes. The use of animal power for purposes like ploughing fields, drawing water and thrashing of food grains enhanced agricultural productivity, leading to agricultural surplus and even to the development of cities in several parts of the world. The discovery of the burning property of hard black rocks in the northern England in the 12th century ultimately led to the excavation of vast coal deposits in England. With the invention in the 19th century, of steam engine, which could perform a variety of tasks by burning coal and wood, a new era was opened in the history of energy excavation, and use. Thus coal mining was made on a continuous and ever increasing scale and coal became the major source of energy for industrializing countries in the 19th and early part of the 20th century. The exploration of oil in the latter half of the 19th century and subsequently the invention of the generator to produce electricity revolutionized human history by providing humanity with such means, comforts and facilities of life as could not be dreamt of in the previous centuries. The use of coal, oil and electricity revolutionized the entire gamut of production, consumption and exchange of goods and services in the economies of the world. With this energy came to be regarded as a universal input, a fifth factor of production and energy consumption a major indicator of economic development.

The domineering role of energy in a modern economy is to be sought in various substitutions that use of energy makes possible. Malcolm Slesser[1] succinctly summaries these substitutions or trade off as (1) capital-energy substitutions, (2) time-energy substitution, (3) space energy substitution, and (4) labour energy substitution.

Energy and Economic Development

The *sine quo non* of economic development and human progress during the era of post industrial revolution has been energy. Most scientific endeavors during this period have gone towards effective utilisation of energy in exogenous equipment for man, and progress was formed to be sequentially related to energy and scientific inventions. Statistical data corroborate that the higher the level of income and output of a country, the higher its consumption of energy (Refer Table 1.1).

Table 1.1: Per capita National Income and per capita Energy consumption in selected countries (1966)

Country	Per capita National Income (US $)	Per capita Energy Consumption (kWH)
U.S.A.	3842	6345
Sweden	2732	6484
U.K.	1925	2703
Japan	986	2171
Taiwan	245	593
India	92	75

Source: Tyner Wallace (1978) "Energy Resources and Economic Development in India" – Allied Publishers, Mumbai.

It is also empirically true that the members of a relatively higher economic group consume not only more energy, but qualitatively better and more different variety. World experience shows that countries that had abundant supply of energy have had realised substantially higher economic growth. In view of these facts, economists like Backerman and Bacon[2] consider energy consumption as an index of economic growth.

One can not, however, establish a one to one correspondence between per capita energy consumption and per capita income, (Conventionally considered as a fair index of economic growth) as the exact correlation between energy consumption and economic growth broke down in advanced countries during last two and a half decades. For instance the US consumption of energy in 1991 was only 9% more than 1973, whereas the US economy had grown 51% larger in 1991, as compared to 1973. Between 1973 and 1990 Japan's real GNP grew by 93% while the energy consumption grew by only 21.6%. Similarly the GDP of Great Britain increased by 42% between 1970 and 1990, but the primary demand for energy remained virtually static during the period. In OECD Countries energy intensity dropped at the rate of 2.6% per year during the period 1979-1986.[3]

The scenario in developing countries is, however, different from this. In the developing countries energy consumption has been growing 7 times faster than in OECD countries, the annual rates of growth in the former being 5.3% and in the latter 0.7% during the period 1970-90[4]. It was found in a sample study of 51 countries that the installed capacity and generation of electricity per capita in 90% of these countries was 2 times the real growth of GDP[5]. What accounted for a decline in the energy intensity in the developed countries as compared to their developing counterparts is that in the wake of the oil shock, the former made huge investments in energy saving devices. Apart from this, a country may experience a decline in energy consumption in the process of economic development. The initial stages of economic growth would necessitate building up of infrastructure facilities and basic metal industries, which consume a great deal of energy. Once this stage is over, there develops consumer and service industries, most of which require comparatively less energy.

Though energy intensity has a tendency to decline with economic development and innovation in technology, it is a commonly accepted fact that energy is a universal input and its consumption, a major index of economic development. The popular notion that energy consumption is an index of economic development led to a phenomenal increase in the demand for energy during the post Second World War period, in the major countries of the world (Refer Table 1.2).

Table 1.2: Growth of commercial energy consumption by region (in TW)

Region	1925	1938	1955	1965	1972	1981	1983
Industrialised Countries	1.229	1.317	2.167	3.281	4.531	4.92	4.74
Centrally Planned Economies	0.076	0.228	0.648	1.170	1.633	2.263	2.395
Developing Countries	0.086	0.131	0.331	0.786	1.310	1.914	2.061
World	1.390	1.676	3.145	5.237	7.474	9.097	9.193

Note: TW = Terra Watt

Source: Goldenberg. et. al. (1989) "Energy for sustainable world" – Wiley Eastern, Bangalore. p. 419.

It was this unprecedented increase in the demand for energy, which culminated, in the oil shock of 1973 when the OPEC countries quadrupled their oil prices. In the wake of the oil shock all the oil exporting countries began to experience serious resource crunch. This generated serious debate at the world forums about the sustainability of the present rate and consumption pattern of energy by the world economies. The United Nations Conference on Environment and Development (UNCED) held at Rio-De-Janeiro in 1992 agreed that the existing pattern and utilisation of energy cannot be sustained. The Summit further pointed out that if the world is to control environmental hazards like Global Warming, Green House Effect and Ozone depletion, the world economies have to economize energy use. The exigencies created in the wake of the oil crises prompted many countries to change their production and consumption patterns of energy.

There is a definite relationship between pattern of energy consumption and the state of development of economy. As a country moves from under developed agriculture state, to an industrially advanced one, its rate of increase of energy consumption first lags behind that of gross domestic product, then rises well ahead due to increasing substitution of non commercial and inefficient fuels with good quality ones and setting up of heavy energy intensive industries and finally falls behind once again as light industries become prominent. This is reflected in the energy –GDP coefficient of each nation, which is well below unity in the first stage, increases towards and above unity in the temporal stage and tends back to unity or even falls below it in the final stage. It is this coefficient which determines the degree of impact of an energy crisis on the economy.

Energy: The Global Scenario

Conventionally energy resources are divided into two broad categories, Commercial and non-commercial. Coal, Oil, Natural gas and hydroelectric power constitute the main sources of commercial energy. Among the non-commercial sources the most important are firewood, cowdung and vegetable wastes, together referred to as biomass energy. In developing countries, which represent about 70% of the world population, the dependence on non commercial sources of energy vary from 5% to 98%, the average for the developing world being 43%[6]. The dependence of the developed countries on non-commercial sources, however is very low, about 5%[7] (Refer Table 1.3).

The energy requirement of the industrialized countries is mostly met from fossil fuels like coal and oil. According to an estimate of 1994 the total coal reserve of the world is of the order of 1031.6 billion

Table 1.3: Global distribution of energy use and population (1978)

Variables	Industrialised Countries	Developing Countries	World
Population (Billion)	1.1 (26%)	3.1 (74%)	4.2 (100%)
Energy Use	208EJ (69%)	92EJ (31%)	300EJ (100%)
Commercial Energy	206EJ (80%)	52EJ (20%)	258EJ (100%)
Non Commercial (Biomass)	2EJ (5%)	40EJ (95%)	42EJ (100%)

Note: Figures in parentheses indicate the percentage of total. Exa joule = 10^{18}

Source: Goldenberg et al (1989). "Energy for sustainable world"—Wiley Eastern Ltd. Bangalore. p. 432.

Tonnes, enough to meet the demand requirements for the next 230 years[8]. Coal is the most abundant among the four commercial fuels (Coal, Oil, Gas, and Uranium).

World's oil reserves were estimated to be 1007.475 billion barrels as on 1st January 1997, which is equivalent to 44 times the production level of 1996. 86% of this is held by the developing nations[9].

The global reserve of the natural gas is fairly abundant and as per the latest estimate (January 1996) the reserves are of the order of 140 Billion M^3. Its production is expected to continue without any handicap for the next 60 years. Nevertheless, natural gas at present remains largely a domestic energy resource, because of the serious prospective limitations in the sphere of transporting and distributing gas from the well head to the consumers. The global reserves of the natural gas can be fully utilised only if it can rise to the status of a major commodity in the industrialized market. The indications in this respect are quite encouraging. The reserves position of the major commercial energy resources at the global level is presented in Table 1.4.

Hydropower is one of the first non-animal energy resources harnessed by man. Today nearly all hydropower is converted to electricity. Currently hydroelectric power plants supply 23% of the world's electricity[10]. Global hydroelectric resources considered to be economically feasible under constant conditions are estimated to be of the order of 2.4 million MW of installed capacity[11]. Installed capacity in 1976 was just over 15% of the total hydro potential of the world. The developed countries have already exploited a large share of the feasible hydro sites. The developing countries, which possess a bulk of hydro potential, however have been able to exploit only a small portion of this potential-Africa 5%, Latin America 8%, Asia 9% and China 10%. If the estimated potential capacity was fully utilised, hydropower can contribute 37.5 Exa joules of energy annually, assuming a 50% capacity Utilisation rate[12].

The Nuclear Power

The enormous possibility for producing electricity out of nuclear source had become a reality a couple of years before the detonation of the first atomic bomb in 1945. Soon it became evident that Co_2 free energy would become the major answer to the energy shortage of the world, and what is more electricity generated through this process would be "too cheap to meter". In the years ensuing the Second World War, there took place a progressive switch over to the exploitation of nuclear energy especially by the developed countries. By 1977, the combined capacity of 204 commercial reactors of the

Table 1.4: World energy resources reserves-1996 (Region wise)

	Oil	Natural Gas	Coal	Uranium
Proved Reserves (R)	As of January 1st 1997-1007.48 Billion Barrels	As of January 1st 1996,140 Billion M'	As of the end of 1994, 1031.6 Billion Tonnes	As on January 1st 1995, 4.5 Million Tonnes
North America	27.21 (2.7%)	6.58 (4.7%)	249.65 (24.2%)	0.765 (17.0%)
Central and South America	126.94 (12.6%)	7.7 (5.5%)	11.35 (1.1%)	0.261 (5.8%)
Western Europe	18.13 (1.8%)	4.76 (3.4%)	75.31 (7.3%)	0.139 (3.1%)
Middle East	668.97 (66.4%)	45.36 (32.4%)	0.0 (0.0%)	0.0 (0.0%)
Asia/Pacific	42.31 (4.2%)	9.38 (6.7%)	318.76 (30.9%)	1.08 (24.0%)
Africa	66.49 (6.6%)	9.52 (6.8%)	61.90 (6.0%)	0.747 (16.6%)
Eastern Europe/CIS	58.43 (5.8%)	56.84 (40.6%)	315.67 (30.6%)	1.508 (33.5%)
Annual Production Quantity (P)	As of 1996, 63.38 thousand barrels/day	As of 1995, 2.22 Billion m'	As of 1994, 4.45 Billion Tonnes	As of 1994, 31 thousand Tonnes
Recoverable Year (R/P)	As of 1996, 44.0 Years	As of 1995, 62.9 Years	As of 1994, 231 Years	As of 1994, 73 Years

Note: Figures in parentheses indicate the percentage of total.
Source: "Japan Energy conservation Hand Book" (1997) The Energy Conservation Centre, Japan. p. 5.

world –majority of them in the OECD countries- stood at 95000 MW. The growth of nuclear power generation was so fast that by 1986, electricity from nuclear sources exceeded that from hydro, geothermal and wind. It was then expected that by 2000 AD the combined capacity of the reactors in some 50 countries of the worlds would reach the level of 2 million megawatts. However the growth of nuclear power plants began to slow down after 1986. As against the expectation, the installed capacity in about 520 reactors of the world could rise only to 400,000 MW, generating about 400GW of world's electricity[13]. The tardy growth in the expansion of nuclear power could be attributed to cost concern and the chilling effects of accidents in the Three- Mile Islands [1979] and Chernobyl [1986][14]. After these accidents, the trend through out the world, even in countries like France, with the highest concentration of nuclear power plants has been to shift away from nuclear power.

The major constraint in the nuclear energy supply is the great problem involved in storing low, medium and high level of nuclear waste safely. This has always been a problem for nuclear industry and it seems likely to remain so, largely because of stiff opposition to waste disposal measures. All the same, nuclear power constitutes a major component of global energy. In 1991 it accounted for 6.5%[15] of the total fuel mix. World electricity production from nuclear power plants constituted only 2.1% in 1971, whereas its share increased to 17% in 1991. According to the latest available estimates the proven reserves of uranium is 4.51 million Tonnes, enough to last for 73 years (Refer Table 1.4). As per the estimate, it is the second largest available energy resource, next only to coal. However, the world nations are apprehensive to fully exploit the nuclear potential, in view of the constraints hinted earlier.

Having touched upon the reserve position and the utilisation rates of alternative energy sources at the global level, it may be in the fitness of things to touch upon the approach to energy development. This can be examined in terms of two paradigms, which have been identified by energy experts: (a) supply based development paradigm and (b) sustainable development paradigm. The approach to energy planning till the early seventies was based on what is called the conventional supply based development paradigm. In this paradigm, increased energy use is a necessary condition for increased economic growth, which is measured in terms of GDP. Energy requirement and the corresponding investment required are projected on the basis of the targeted growth rate in GDP, and the supply of electricity is planned to meet the requirement. This approach is subject to the following limitations[16].

- Demand for energy is assumed to be a matter of destiny and not of choice.
- The focus is on energy, per se and not on energy services like lighting, heating, processing, watering etc.
- Increasing energy consumption is the only way of increasing the growth rate.
- It is supply based, taking the demand for energy as given and not amenable for maneuverability.
- It is technologically static as it ignores the possibilities of improving energy efficiency and substitution by alternative sources of energy.[17]

The pursuit of the above paradigm by a large number of countries in the world resulted in 4 types of crisis. (a) Capital crisis, (b) Performance crisis, (c) Equity crisis and (d) Environmental crisis[18]. This state of affairs necessitated the pursuit of an alternative paradigm referred to in the literature as DEFENDUS, an acronym for Development Focused END Use oriented Service directed. This alternative originated in the process of identifying a strategy in the book entitled "Energy for sustainable World" Co-authored by Goldenberg et al. A brief description of "DEFENDUS" is given below. This description is drawn with minor modification from an article by Gladys Sumithra[19].

The development indicator of this Paradigm is the level of energy services and not of energy supply or consumption. It is not the units of energy consumption that matters, but the level of services at minimum cost, and using energy to promote development goals. The "DEFENDUS" strategy consists of planning a rationally determined mix of sources, and thereby achieving a holistic integration of efficiency improvements, decentralized renewable energy sources and clean centralised energy sources. The "DEFENDUS" paradigm crept into energy literature in the wake of energy literature in the wake of persistent scarcity of electricity, experienced by both developing and developed countries.

Development of Electrical Energy

Historically, commercial production of electricity, for the first time began in New York in 1880, following the commissioning of an electric company set up by Thomas Edison in 1878. The successful record of this company resulted in a mushrooming of similar power companies in many parts of the United States in the ensuring years. The United Kingdom also took to commercial production of electricity after a few years, closely following the US. However at the beginning of the 20th century, even in these pioneering countries, gaslights were the dominant means of illumination and steam engines ruled most of factory floors. But within a few years electricity emerged not only as the most popular and convenient form of energy, but also an essential tool of development as well as a symbol of modernity, largely because of its unmatching ability to run a variety of new industrial equipment and household appliances.

In the earlier years, electricity was generated from coal (through coal fired thermal stations). Later electricity came to be produced from other sources such as oil products, natural gas, hydro and nuclear. The world position in regard to production of electricity from alternative sources is presented in the Table 1.5.

Table 1.5: World electricity production-1971 and 1990

Power Sources	1971 (TWH)	% share	1990 (TWH)	% share
Coal	2142	40.3	4645	39.3
Hydro electric	1209	22.8	2142	18.1
Nuclear	111	2.1	2011	17.0
Natural Gas	714	13.5	1578	13.3
Oil	1102	20.8	1385	11.7
Others	32	0.6	67	0.6
World	5311	100	11828	100

Source: World Watch Institute Report on progress towards Sustainable Society (1994) "State of the world—1994". Horizon India Books. New Delhi. p. 64.

In 1971 world electricity production stood at 5311 TWh, which rise to 11828 TWh, within 2 decades, an increase of 122.71% (or an annual increase of 6.14%). The most important source of electricity generation even at present is coal, which accounted roughly for 40%. The

Second largest source of Electricity production is hydro electric. Its relative importance significantly declined during the last 2 decades due to opposition from environmentalists, as well as indigenous population on the grounds of destruction of flora and fauna, destruction of rain forests and displacement of inhabitants. The relative importance of nuclear source increased from 2% to 7%. Several factors accounted for this shift: (1) Nuclear electricity provides Co_2 free clear power. (2) Vast potential for Uranium availability (3) Government subsidies for setting up of nuclear projects, (4) cheapest form of generating electricity, a single gram of Uranium can produce 3800 units of electricity[20].

The Table also shows that the importance of oil in electricity generation declined from 20.8% in 1971 to 11.7% in 1991. The explanation for this lies in the soaring prices of oil in the wake of oil shocks of 1973.

The possibility for generating electricity from multiple sources has propelled electricity production into a gigantic industry in several countries of the world. According to a conservative estimate, the annual revenue from electricity industry is of the order of $800 billion, roughly twice the sizes of the world auto industry[21]. The trends in the generating capacity and in actual generation in selected developed and developing countries are shown with a view to seeing the differential in trends, if any. Data relating to electricity generating capacity and electricity generation for selected countries are shown in the Table 1.6.

In the developing countries both electricity generating capacity as well as actual generation appear to have increased at a faster rate during 1980-1990 as compared to 1970-1980. By contrast in the newly industrialized countries and developed countries the rate

Table 1.6: Generating capacity and Generation of Electricity in selected countries- 1970 to 1990 (MW and MU)

Countries	Electricity Capacity [MW]			% increase of capacity		Electricity Generation (MU)			% increase of Generation	
	1970	1980	1990	1980	1990	1970	1980	1990	1980	1990
Developing Countries										
Bangladesh	-	990	2520	-	154.5	-	2653	8056	-	203.7
India	16271	333000	75995	104.7	128.2	61212	119150	286045	94.7	140.1
Pakistan	-	3518	9137	-	159.7	-	15277	43903	-	187.4
Sri Lanka	281	422	1289	50.2	205.5	816	1668	3150	104.4	88.8
China	24180	67000	137891	177.1	105.8	107000	300600	621200	180.9	106.7
Indonesia	907	2786	11480	207.2	312.1	2300	6981	44255	203.5	533.9
Total	41639	108016	238312	148.6	120.6	171328	446329	1006609	150.0	125.5

(Table Conte...)

Table 1.6: Contd...

Newly Developing Countries										
Malaysia	936	2430	5037	159.6	107.3	3543	10186	24722	187.5	142.7
South Korea	2764	10272	24056	271.6	134.2	9597	39979	118740	316.6	197.0
Singapore	644	1900	3400	195.0	78.9	2205	6940	15620	214.7	125.0
Total	4344	14602	32493	236.1	122.5	15345	57105	159082	272.1	178.6
Developed Countries										
U.K.	62060	73643	73059	18.7	-.79	249016	284937	318976	14.4	11.9
Canada	42826	81999	104140	91.5	27.0	204723	377518	481752	84.4	27.6
U.S.A.	360327	630111	775396	74.9	23.1	1639771	2354384	3031023	43.6	28.7
Sweden	15307	27416	34189	79.1	24.7	60646	96985	146534	59.9	51.1
Japan	68710	143698	197763	109.1	35.5	359539	577521	857347	60.6	48.4
Germany	47540	82585	99750	73.7	20.8	242611	368785	454661	52.0	23.3
Total	**596770**	**1039452**	**1281297**	**74.2**	**23.3**	**2756306**	**4060130**	**5290293**	**47.3**	**30.3**

Source: World Development Report—Infrastructure for Development- 1994. Oxford University Press pp. 140-142.

*1980 total is derived excluding Bangladesh and Pakistan for calculating the percentage increase of capacity and generation.

of increase in capacity as well as generation declined during the late eighties as compared to the seventies. This is because, in these economies, infrastructure development had already made significant headway, as compared to the developing countries, which are yet to develop basic infrastructure facilities

The ratio of generation to capacity is generally considered as an index of energy productivity. Energy productivity of selected countries is shown in the Table 1.7. In newly industrialized countries like Malaysia, South Korea and Singapore, there is a consistent increase in energy efficiency during 1970-1990. Among the developing countries, a consistent increase is observed in the case of China and to some extant in Pakistan. In developed countries, by and large, efficiency appears to have declined. Sri Lanka, Bangladesh and India marked the lowest magnitude of energy efficiency in 1990, the highest figures being in South Korea, Malaysia, Canada and Singapore.

Being considered as a symbol of modernity and development, the demand for electricity began to increase by leaps and bounds in almost all countries. In Industrial countries, electricity demand was growing at an annual rate of 8% during the sixties, but it slowed down to 3% in the mid seventies due largely to higher fuel prices and saturation in the use of several home appliances. This has resulted in a leveling of electricity intensity of industrial economies. In the least developed countries electricity use was growing annually at the rate of 10% during 1970s and 7% during the 1980s[22]. Between 1971 and 1989 electricity production grew at an average annual rate of 6.3% in Africa, 7% in Latin America and 8.3% in Asia as compared with 3.3% in OECD countries[23]. The growth rate of demand for power in the developing countries is generally higher than that of GDP.

Table 1.7: Energy productivity of selected countries 1970-1990 (MU/MW)

Countries	Electricity Capacity' [MW]			Electricity Generation (MU)			Productivity (MkWh/MW)		
	1970	1980	1990	1970	1980	1990	1970	1980	1990
Developing Countries									
Bangladesh	-	990	2520	-	2653	8056	-	2.68	3.20
India	16271	33300	75995	61212	119150	286054	3.76	3.58	3.76
Pakistan	-	3518	9137	-	15277	43903	-	4.34	4.80
Sri Lanka	281	422	1289	816	1668	3150	2.9	3.95	2.44
China	24180	67000	137891	107000	300600	621200	4.43	4.49	4.51
Indonesia	907	2786	11480	2300	6981	44255	2.54	2.51	3.85

Table 1.7: Contd...

Newly Industrialised Countries									
South Korea	2764	10272	24056	9597	39979	118740	3.47	3.89	4.94
Malaysia	936	2430	5037	3543	10186	24722	3.79	4.19	4.91
Singapore	644	1900	3400	2205	6940	15620	3.42	3.65	4.59
Developed Countries									
U.K.	62060	73643	73059	249016	284937	318976	4.01	3.87	4.37
Canada	42826	81999	104140	204723	377518	481752	4.78	4.60	4.63
U.S.A.	360327	630111	775396	1639771	2354384	3031023	4.55	3.74	3.90
Sweden	15307	27416	34189	60646	96985	146534	3.96	3.54	4.29
Japan	68710	143698	194763	359539	577521	857347	5.23	4.02	4.40
Germany	47540	82585	99750	242611	368785	454661	5.10	4.47	4.56

Source: World Development Report—Infrastructure for Development—1994. Oxford University Press pp. 140-142.

Power Sector: Issues the World Over

Till a few decades ago when the supply of electricity power in most countries was confined to a few cities, most people did not have accessibility and the industry itself relied upon relatively small plants, the sector did not throw up many formidable problems. However with rapidly growing demand for power and drastic changes in the technical process of power generation and the rising prices for power inputs, several problems cropped up in the power sector of most countries in the world. These problems can be summed up as:

- Widening demand and supply gap in power capacity as well as energy
- Escalation in the cost of power generation
- Technical loss in the transmission and distribution of power
- Environmental problems like green house gases and global warming
- Depleting inputs like coal, oil and gas
- Financial problems as manifested in the inability of the utilities to make additional investments.

Though varying in their volume and intensity, these problems are common to all economies. However some of the specific problems confronted by the developing economies, merit special mention in this connection.

Specific Issues in the Power Sector of Developing Countries

I. Inadequate tariff and poor revenue collection arising from the historical cost analysis and political tariffing. Studies indicated that normally 30-35% of revenue is backlog in countries like India. The lack of economic approach to costing as well as pricing result in cost-revenue gap, compelling them to borrow funds from foreign sources. According to World Bank sources, 69 out of 111 developing nations, had been caught in a debt crisis by 1990[24].

II. Poor quality of supply of power:- As an example, in many developing countries voltage drops are of the order of 50% to 80% below the rated voltage caused mainly due to higher peak demand, and relatively lesser units of generation.

III. Power system unreliability: In the developed countries supply interruptions are very rare. For example in the USA, the overall system reliability index expressed as the percentage of energy demand met is of the order of 99.98%. But in developing countries interruptions occur several times a day and normally there is no guarantee about power availability. The reasons include inadequate technology, over loaded and over extended lines, over loaded transformers, insufficient sub-stations and above all insufficient system management.

IV. Heavy T and D losses:- System losses- the difference between electricity sent out and electricity billed- are far high in many developing economies. As a matter of fact, any power system will entail technical losses in Transmission and Distribution. But at the present level of technology, experts maintain that these losses can be limited to the range of 7 to 10%[25]. Studies show that in a considerable number of developing countries such losses are in excess of 20%[26].

V. Higher level of energy intensity: Energy intensity expresses the relationship between electricity consumption and gross domestic product. Several studies have revealed that the pattern of electricity use in developing countries are wasteful as a result of poor planning and self-serving development assistance offered by the industrialised countries. There is wide spread recognition that inefficient use in developing countries imposes enormous financial and environmental costs[27]. Per capita energy consumption- rather than increase in energy services-continues to be viewed as the primary energy development measure, in turn promoting wasteful energy investment.

Future decisions on new resources of power for developing countries are bounded by the twin constrains of limited financial resources and the need to contain environment and health damage emissions. This will require a transition to much greater reliance on renewable and much more efficient use of available energy resources[28].

Indian Scenario

India is one of the major developing countries, which has been facing almost all problems listed above, for the last several years. The electricity sector of India during the post independence period had made rapid strides judged in terms of indicators like the quantum of electricity generation, installed generating capacity, per capita consumption of electricity, the number of villages electrified etc. Electricity generation, which was only 41 billion units (kWh) in 1947, had increased to about 351 billion units (kWh) by 1995, the annual compound growth rate being 7.5%[29]. The installed generating capacity during the period had increased sixty folds. The per capita electricity consumption has increased from 15 units to 314 units between 1947 to 1995

Despite impressive growth in these broad indicators, the power sector has been plagued by serious shortages of supply Vs demand. Presently (1995-96) the peaking capacity shortage is of the order of 18.3% and energy shortage of 9.2%[30]. Financial position of the state electricity boards has been steadily deteriorating, the commercial loss incurred by all SEBs having increased by 50% between 1992 and 1995. All the SEBs put together made a negative return of roughly 13.5% during the financial year ending March 1995.[31] The persistent resource crunch of the SEBs have stood in the way of expanding generating capacity, with the result that shortage of power has become very acute in many states.

Kerala: Problems and Characteristics

It is true that the State Electricity Boards, there are 19 of them in the country –have several common problems, most of which we have already mentioned. However all of them are not similarly placed in every aspect. For e.g., in contrast to the general trend of financial loss, at least the SEBs of the two states – Maharashtra and Orissa are making positive returns, marginal though[32]. In most states prices of power is lower than cost of production. But in Maharashtra, Tamil Nadu and Himachal Pradesh, the average unit revenue is higher than average unit cost. The states also differ among themselves in regard to sectoral demand for electricity and also in respect of per capita consumption. Kerala is one of the states, which exhibits several differing characteristics in respect of power sector as compared to other states in the country. Kerala, Himachal Pradesh, Meghalaya and Jammu Kashmir are the only 4 states, which exclusively depend on hydro stations for electricity generation. Kerala has started adding thermal generation only in recent years. Kerala is one of the very few states, which had surplus power, for several years in the past, but began to experience severe power shortage subsequently and where the problem is now more acute than the rest of the states. The state with the lowest per capita consumption of electricity is at present Kerala. But the proportion of per capita domestic consumption and commercial consumption of energy are highest in India. T and D losses are higher than the all India average. T and D losses are not uniformly distributed, over the state, and its magnitude increases as we move northward. The peak demand is above 24%[33] of peak availability. The state's power system has high load factor, which implies lower running cost and hence the system is capable of selling the product at lower price. Kerala State Electricity Board has been consistently loss making since the turn of the eighties, although the cost of production of electricity is one of the lowest in India.

Objectives of The Study

Inspite of such peculiar characteristics and problems, the power sector of Kerala has not been subjected to any systematic and serious study by economists. The only study carried out from an economic perspective pertained to the period, when the state was surplus in power and the nature and dimensions of the problems of the power sector were widely different from what they are today. The present study is a comprehensive analysis of the power system of Kerala from a techno-economic angle. The specific objectives of the study are:-

1. To present an overview of the power scenario of India, with a view to placing the study in a national perspective.
2. To analyze the trends in the supply and demand variables affecting the power system of Kerala.
3. To examine the power system efficiency of the state in terms of load factor, demand factor, transmission and distribution network and tariff structure.
4. To evaluate the performance of the major ten hydel power projects in the state in terms of capacity utilisation factor, plant load factor, and energy productivity.
5. To develop a suitable forecasting model for power demand in the state.

Hypotheses of The Study

The major hypotheses formulated are:-

1. During the post energy crisis period, energy productivity declined in India in contrast to the developed countries.
2. Peak-load shortage in India is to a large extent due to the fuel shift away from hydel stations to thermal stations,
3. Though per capita consumption of electricity in the state has increased, per capita consumption of electricity by actual consumer is on the decline.

4. Supply side variables of the power system of the state grew slower than the demand side variables.
5. The magnitude of Transmission and Distribution loss exceeded the increase in power generation.
6. A high level of voltage drop leading to low voltage profile in the power system of Kerala is due to insufficient HT lines and distribution transformers.
7. It is not the tardy growth in installed capacity, but the operation of multiple factors on both supply and demand side that is responsible for the power shortage faced by the state.

Approach and Organization of The Study

The study is an investigation into the causes of the power shortages experienced by Kerala for the last several years. A shortage in power as in the case of any other commodity is the outcome of an interaction of supply and demand factors. Power is generated and supplied in Kerala by Kerala State Electricity Board, [KSEB] a state monopoly. Therefore the core of the study is a detailed and comprehensive analysis of the growth of various supply and demand factors affecting the Kerala State Power System. (KSPS) The Supply factors considered are, the installed capacity, the maximum system demand, the generation, and total energy sales, energy loss, distribution transformers and the length of distribution lines. The Demand factors are, the number of consumers, the maximum internal demand, connected load, and per capita consumption. Some of the supply and demand factors like installed capacity, maximum demand, (Internal and the System) and connected load are purely technical factors. The incorporation of these factors makes the study a techno- economic analysis.

The study is based upon secondary data collected mainly from the Reports and Publications of Kerala State Electricity Board, the Central Electricity Authority, Southern Regional Electricity Board, Tamil Nadu Electricity Board, Karnataka State Electricity Board, Maharashtra State Electricity Board, Indira Gandhi Institute of Development Research. In addition the study also made use of the materials available from the publications of premier private research organization called Tata Energy Research Institute, [TERI] and the data issued by the, Centre for Monitoring Indian Economy, [CMIE] and those of individual researchers.

The study is presented in **seven chapters.**

The introductory chapter touches on broader aspects like relation between energy and economic development, energy development paradigm, global energy scenario, with particular reference to power sector issues in the developed and developing countries.

Chapter two attempts a review on energy studies undertaken at the global, national, and the state level

The present study is concerned with the problems in the power sector of Kerala. Since electricity is placed in the concurrent list, and overall power planning in the country is vested with Central Electricity Authority, the developments in the state's power system its features and problems are to a large extent influenced by all India patterns. Taking this into consideration, the **third chapter** is set apart to examining Indian energy scenario. This chapter has looked into resource potential, resource availability, and utilisation rates of major energy resources- coal, oil, gas, and hydropower. In addition, this chapter examines the growth of power sector in India, in terms of variables like installed capacity, power generation, connected load, sector wise consumption, number of consumers, etc. As part of discussing growth in demand, demand elasticites have been worked out using log linear regression equation. Dimensions of power deficit and financial status of state electricity boards (SEBs) were also analysed in this chapter.

Chapter four is devoted to examining the development and growth of the power sector of Kerala. This is done by examining the growth in the major power sector variables falling under demand and supply categories. The supply side variables include installed capacity, maximum demand, (System) generation, energy sales, transmission and distribution loss, number of transformers and length of distribution lines. The demand variables considered are, power consumers, internal maximum demand, and per capita consumption. (Units) The trend analysis of per capita consumption, revenue and expenditure were also worked out. The trend growth rates of the system variables were worked out by using semi log linear regression equation.

Chapter five attempts to identify the reasons for power shortage and power unreliability from supply side and demand side angles. The reasons for tardy growth of additional capacity are examined. Performance analysis of ten major hydel projects has been done, in terms of indicators like capacity utilisation factor, plant load factor, and energy productivity. Power system efficiency was analysed using certain technical parameters, namely, the load factor, the demand factor, and the diversity factor, and the transmission and distribution loss.

Chapter six is essentially concerned with forecasting energy demand in Kerala. For this purpose trend growth rates of sectoral consumption of power were worked out on the basis of twenty-five years data using semi log linear regression model. Demand projections for different terminal years were made with the help of the statistical software called "Regression and Time Series" (RATS). The best model for each category of consumers was identified after searching forty-five standard mathematical models available by using the software called "Curve Expert."

Chapter seven sums up the major findings and suggestions.

Notes and References

1. Hill Robert, Keefe O' Phil and Snape Colin (1993) *"The Future of Energy Use"*, Earth Scan Publications, London.
2. Backerman and Bacon (1966) *"International Comparisons of Income Levels"* Economic Journal no. 303. Vol. LXXVI, Sept. 1966 pp. 519-20, quoted in Raiky and Singh *"Energy Consumption in India–Pattern and Determinants"* Deep and Deep Publications, New Delhi. (1992).
3. Balu. V. *"Global Trends in Reduction of Energy-GDP Coupling"* in Dr. R.V.G. Menon and Dr. P.S. Chandramohanan (eds.) *"Lecture notes on Energy Conservation and Management"*, College of Engineering, Thiruvananthapuram, May 1994. pp. 1-9.
4. Meneon. R.V.G. (1993) *"Global Energy Scenario – The Importance of Efficiency"* (1993) Energy Conservation Society, Monograph, p. 5.
5. Ibid. p. 5.
6. Goldenberg, Jose; Reddy. A.K.N. and et. Al. (1988) *"Energy for a Sustainable World"*, Wiley Eastern Ltd., Bangalore, p. 199.
7. Ibid. p. 432.
8. Japan Energy Conservation Centre, (1997) *"Japan Energy Conservation Hand Book"*, Japan. p. 5.

9. Ibid. p. 5.
10. Pandey. G.N. (1994) *"A Text Book on Energy System Engineering"*, Vikas Publishing House, New Delhi, p. 180.
11. Ibid. p. 180.
12. Ibid. p. 180.
13. Balu. V. *"Environmental Impact of Energy Production: Thermal, Nuclear and Hydro Electric Power"* in o.p.c.i.t. (Refer 3) pp. 1-23.
14. Ibid. p. 6.
15. Hill Robert, Keefe O' Phil and Snape Colin (1993) "o.p.c.i.t." [Refer 1] P. 18. World share of primary fuels are- Oil, [38.1%] Solids, [25.6%] Natural gas, [20.9%] Nuclear, [6.5%] others, [8.9%].
16. Sumithra Gladys (1994) *"Economics of Energy Conservation"*, in 'o.p.c.i.t.' [Refer 3] pp. 37-53.
17. Ibid. p. 38.
18. Reddy, K.N. Amulya (1994) *"Electricity Planning in India: Current Approach and Resulting Problems"* in 'o.p.c.i.t.' (Refer 3) p. 1.
19. Sumithra Gladys (1994) *"Economics of Energy Conservation"*, in 'o.p.c.i.t.' (Refer 16) p. 42.
20. Balu. V. (1994) 'o.p.c.i.t.' (Refer 3) p. 6.
21. Brown R. Lester (ed.) (1994), "Reshaping the Power Industry" in the "State of the World", World Watch Institute – Horizon India Books. p. 61.
22. Bhatacharya. S.C. *"Power Sector Privatisation in Developing Countries- Will it Solve All Problems"*, Energy Sources Vol. 17, U.K., 1994. pp. 373-389.
23. Ibid. p. 374.
24. Bernett Andrew. *"The Financing of Electric Power Projects in Developing Countries"*. Energy Policy, April 1992. pp. 326-334.
25. Schramm Gunter *"Issues and Problems in the Power Sectors of Developing Countries"*, Energy Policy, July 1993. pp. 735-747.
26. Ibid. p. 740.

27. Sanhvi P. Arun *"The Economic Cost of Electricity Supply Interruptions"*- Energy Economics, July (1993).

28. Kats Gregory *"The Earth Summit-Opportunity for Energy Reforms"* Energy Policy, June 1992. pp. 546-557.

29. Government of India *"Indian Infrastructure Report 1996"*. Ministry of Finance, New Delhi. p. 54.

30. Government of India *"Annual Report 1995-96'*. Ministry of Power, New Delhi. p. 11.

31. Planning commission (1995) *"Annual Report of the Working of the State Electricity Boards and Departments."* October, New Delhi. p. 1233.

32. Ibid. p. 123.

33. Power Line, August 1997, New Delhi, p. 26.

2

Studies in the Area: A Brief Review

Energy Economics is a relatively recent area of research, a development of the post—1950s. The growth of this branch remained quite slow till the beginning of the seventies, the bulk of the studies in the area being confined to fossil fuels, the basic and the most important source of commercial energy. Studies began to proliferate in this area, in the wake of the energy crises sparked off by the oil price hike of 1973. The energy crisis provoked the advanced countries to institute research centers, whose immediate concern was to develop energy alternatives to costly oil and to invent energy conservation techniques. It was in this background that electricity as a form of energy received priority treatment at the hands of policy planners and researchers, mainly because it is a cheap and clean energy. The notion that electricity is a clean energy has gradually changed as generation of electricity from thermal plants (the dominant method of electricity generation in the West) gave rise to serious problems of pollution in several western countries. Therefore studies in this area in initial years turned to environmental issues from generation. Such studies often lacked economic content.

In the ensuing years, particularly after the eighties the concern of the developed countries turned to technological innovation aimed at improving efficiencies at generation, transmission and distribution points of electricity. Simultaneously economic issues associated with the three segments were also taken up by energy experts in these countries. The developing countries were, on the other hand pre occupied with the problem of meeting the demand supply gap in energy, issues relating to technological improvements seldom figuring in their priorities. However the rising input costs, persisting power shortage and burgeoning revenue deficit of the utilities compelled developing countries to study economic issues of electricity sector.

The pioneering study in the realm of energy economics is usually attributed to Scarlotte and Eugene (1952)[1]. This Study mainly focussed on the reserve potential of major forms of commercial and non-commercial energy, their rate of utilisation, as well past and future trends. Though the scope of the study covered the world as a whole, the authors' examination was largely confined to the developed countries, due to severe data constraints in the underdeveloped world. This work generated considerable interest on the part of economists in examining the contribution of energy to economic growth. Darmstadter's[2] study merits special mention in this context. He found that as GNP increased, energy consumption rose in close conformity. A subsequent enquiry by Fremont Felix[3] using 1961 data pertaining to 153 countries proved the positive correlation between per capita national income and energy consumption.

With continuing economic growth and development, neo dimensions were added to energy related studies. Ford Foundation Energy Policy Project[4] examined at length, aspects related to the interchangeability of energy with other production factors. According to the Project, the rapid increase in energy consumption since the Second World War was mainly caused by systematic substitution of energy for labour, capital, and raw materials. It was in this context, Tanzer[5] referred to energy as the 14th factor of production. As rightly observed by him, just as capital without labour is useless, so too sophisticated labour without energy.

The circumstances mentioned just before also led to proliferation of studies on energy related issues. The growth of studies in demand related issues was so tremendous that, during its formative years, energy economics meant studies in energy demand, as rightly observed by Ramesh Batia[6].

A celebrated pioneering study pertaining to energy demand was that of Hill et al[7]. The importance of this work is that it related to an early period when energy economics had not emerged as distinct branch. In this historico statistical work, the authors give a graphic description of the changing energy scenario of the United Kingdom. The authors have attempted to estimate energy requirement for different time points using simple conventional techniques. As per their calculation per capita energy consumption per day was 88.2 Mega Joule in 1500 AD, 378 Mega Joule at the time of industrial revolution and one Giga Joule in recent years. The chief drawback of this work is that the authors were not able to make use of the modern sophisticated techniques of demand forecasting.

The unprecedented increase in energy consumption across the countries in the wake of the realization that energy consumption is a symbol of development and a virtual factor of production called for studies on energy efficiency. The energy demand analysis carried out from the turn of seventies falls under two categories: at the macro level and at the sectoral level. A convenient method of macro level energy demand analysis is to compute energy GDP ratios over time or across countries or regions for comparison. The conceptual issues in using energy GDP ratios, the problem of measuring energy consumption and GDP, and the problems with cross-country comparisons in this context have been examined at length by Desai[8] Smolik[9] Choe, et al[10] and IBRD[11]

The early works at the macro level category were done within the framework of single equation model. Works of these genera are those of Wolf[12], Siddayao[13] and ESCAP.[14] Later researchers pointed out the limitations in the use of single equation model since it does not consider possible changes in the energy mix over time.[15]

To overcome this deficiency many authors subsequently made use of double log formulation, incorporating variables like population, urbanization, agricultural growth, structure of GDP, relative prices of energy and non energy inputs etc. Such works included in those of Pindyck,[16] Berndt et al,[17] Bohi,[18] Dunkerley et al,[19] Munasinghe and Sehramm[20] and others. In this connection special mention should be made of a study by Rehman[21] using Indian data. His is a thorough analysis of various factors affecting energy consumption and economic growth in a simultaneous framework using macro econometric and computable general equilibrium models.

An easy method that was followed for energy demand analysis at the macro level was to compare the growth rates of energy and GDP. It is a convenient method to see the relation between energy consumption and the level of economic activity. Because the calculation of the two growth rates are very easy, many authors have used this techniques in the early years, and have evinced great temptation to use this measure without going to the factors that might have affected superficial interpretation of the growth rates, often led to wrong conclusions. Bhatia[22] found no stable relation between energy consumption and GDP in the context of India. This method is also very sensitive to the selection of the base and terminal years for estimating growth rates.

The limitations of macro level studies and the problems associated with identifying demand determinants at the macro level have been pointed out by Bhatia[23]. In view of inter regional differences in socio-economic development, Bhatia suggested that demand studies at the sectoral level could be more tractable. Accordingly he estimated energy demand for the four major sectors: Industrial, Agricultural, Transport, and Households- in Indian context.

Regarding energy consumption in the agricultural sector, one of the early important studies is that of FAO (1972). According to this study, the average use per hectare of commercial energy in developing countries was only one tenth of that in developed market economies. However during 1972-80, the estimated consumption of commercial energy in agriculture in developing countries increased by 117%, the bulk of the increase being in fertiliser consumption.

Energy use in the industrial sector has been studied at the aggregate, sub sector industry, or enterprise level, by various researchers. Jankowsky[24] has examined aggregate consumption of energy in the industrial sector for four countries- Brazil, India, Korea and Kenya-taking industrial demand for energy as a function of the absolute size of the industrial sector, the structure of output, and the energy intensity of production. The finding is that in Kenya Industrial demand grew faster than industries; while in Brazil, rapid industrial growth had been accompanied by comparable increases in energy demand despite the greater role of heavy industries in the total. In India, the structure of fuel sources, namely, the high dependence on coal appears more significant in explaining industrial energy demand than does the structure of its output mix.

Available energy studies have analysed aggregate demand for transportation services, energy demand by type of transport service and demand for various transport fuels. (The studies of Divan[25] Pindyck[26] Parikh[27] etc). A review of some of these studies shows that the price elasticity is limited for petroleum products in the short term, especially for gasoline. The demand for these product is income elastic, especially in the long run.

Available studies on the energy demand of the household sector, use both macro level data and data obtained from surveys of household expenditures on energy uses to workout elasticities with respect to income, price, and demographic variables. Studies of Cecelski et al[28] Havrylyshym and Munasinghe[29] Amarullah[30] and others are worth mentioning. The level of detail as well as sophistication of analysis varies from one study to the other. Some studies give bivarite tables, while some others attempt econometric analysis to estimate income and price elasticities.[31]

Raily[32] studied the demand aspects of energy and pointed out that the date on energy consumption do not reflect the demand as such, but rather demand is constrained by the supply factors. Raily suggested to include supply variables in the regression equation to overcome this problem.

Thus far our review covered major economic studies pertaining to energy at large. From now on the review will be confined to economic studies relating to electricity, as the primary concern of the present study is with power.

The study on electricity demand in Costa Rica by Dias-Bandaranaike and Munasinghe[33] explicitly considers the quality of power supply by distinguishing three levels of voltage variation. The results indicated that the quality of supply has a significant impact on demand and thus should be recognized in planned electricity consumption. The residential consumers whose supply of electricity was poor or very poor in Costa Rica consumed only 85% and 70% respectively of the electricity they would have consumed if the supply quality had been medium. A study like this would be highly useful to determine power investment planning to achieve optimal power system reliability. There is relevance for such a study in Indian context.

Goldenberg et. al[34] have suggested DEFENDUS [Development Focussed END Use oriented Service directed.] model to determine electricity demand in a state, based on the end use of services of electricity rather than the volume of electricity consumption. Though the model appears to be a better method of electricity demand projection, the state Electricity Boards in the country are not interested in applying this model. Thus a national level electricity demand analysis based on this model needs to be carried out in the Indian context, so that the actual energy requirements in the economy, the potential for energy conservation, and the thrust area of energy conservation can be identified.

Reddy[35] analysed the pattern of energy carrier consumption in residential sector. The dependence of income on the energy carrier utilized has been established by using a Carrier Dependence index. Using regression analysis, the index verified the impact of different explanatory variables on consumption. The study showed that income played a very important role not only in the selection of energy carrier, but also on the quantity of consumption per household.

In an another research work on the end use pattern of power consumption of the people of the metropolis of Bangalore, Reddy[36] found out that the share of traditional fuels, household energy consumption has been declining rapidly from 67%, in 1953-54 to 35% in 1989-90. In contrast to this, there is a sharp increase in the demand for LPG and electricity. The major finding of this study is that with increase in income, household energy carrier consumption increased in favour of electricity.

Ranganathan[37], in his research work on the application of cost benefit analysis of rural electrification has developed an econometric model for demand forecasting for electrical power sector, to determine high load growth area. He suggested that the high load growth area, which should be electrified first, so that the benefits of electrification are maximized.

The largest electricity demand forecasting model on Indian economy, which was designed for the 6th five-year plan, with an aim to augment input –output model was developed by Parikh[38]. This was one of the major models developed for India to determine energy policies at the national level. In an another study on policy alternatives for Western and Southern power system in India, Parikh[39] developed a model called "INGRID2"- a non-linear optimisation model used to simulate inter connections of two regional grids. The model minimises the total variable costs for the total power system with physical constrains on demand and supply side. This model was basically aimed as an aid to the planners for the 8th five-year plan.

In several countries, it is observed that electricity consumption doesn't reflect the real demand. There are constraints on supplies. Also the Utilities curtail energy demand through load shedding, blackout, power cut, quote allocation etc. Monasinghe[40], Monasinghe and Schramme[41] and Sanghvi[42] have attempted to study the adverse effects of energy constraints on economic activity. It is proved that apart from general inconvenience, power breakdown may result in shutdown of industrial activities. Since shortages may result in undesirable consequences and its impact would differ from one sector to the other, it is necessary to assess where the shortages (or unfulfilled demand) are occurring.

Batia[43] carried out a study on the impact of power shortage on the industrial sector, and observed that power shortages in the industrial sector may lead to captive power generation. Such back up system involves higher unit investment costs, because they lack economies of scale, and use costlier fuel inputs other than coal. In India, there is greater increase in the number of captive power plants yet the economic aspects of captive power, both at the national and the state level are to be researched.

Sectoral demand analysis of power was carried out by scholars like Pindyck[44] and Uri[45]. In their model of study they took industrial output as independent variable. The parameter of these models were determined from time series data for a number of industries and worked out the responsiveness of electrical energy demand to these independent variables.

Nayar[46] attempted to study the problems of power availability in the rural areas. He suggested hybrid energy system, which integrates renewable energy technologies with diesel generators, batteries and inverters to provide highly reliable twenty-four hours grid quality AC power in remote areas. This hybrid system has been applied in Australia for electrification of remote communities. A microprocessor based control system optimises the performance of the system as it meets the site load requirements for any given application. One limitation of this study, we have observed is that, it doesn't mention anything about the cost/kWh generated by renewable and an inter price comparison of hybrid energy system.

Raiky and Singh[47] studied the determinants of energy consumption patter in sectors like household, agricultural and industry. This study was based on the primary data collected from 120 farmers, 74 industrial units and 128 household families. The determinants of energy consumption in the three sectors have been studied through statistical and econometric techniques.

The research work on the demand for energy in Indian industries has been carried out by Joyashree[48] using quantitative techniques. This work contributes to the general trend by estimating elasticity of substitution and price elasticity for three conventional fuel types: coal, oil and electricity for the "energy intensive" manufacturing industries in India with the help of three input translog model. They observed that in the wake of the supply constraints especially in the oil sector, dependence of oil could be reduced by influencing the demand responsiveness of the industrial consumers through price mechanism.

Now let as turn to some of the review of literature available on the pricing aspect of electricity. Munasinghe et al[49] have studied the significance of marginal cost principle in electricity price determination. They do not find any reason to follow average cost pricing, since it used historic data, which proved inadequate for price fixation.

Hill et al[50], in their study on the pricing aspect of electricity stressed the significance of adding the environmental cost as one of the components of electricity pricing. This attempt would help to depend heavily on environmentally benign renewable.

Wee and Li's[51] work on the pricing aspect of electricity supply in China made it clear that in the wake of globalization, tariff restructuring becomes inevitable. They even suggest that power sector reforms in the economy is highly useful to introduce optional pricing policy in this sector. They have appreciated the role of foreign capital in electricity sector.

Pachauri[52], while analysing the role of inputs on production has asserted that like labour and capital, energy shall be considered as one of the inputs of factors of production. Though this point is well known to the manufactures and producers, due to its lowest percentage share on the total cost of production, energy cost is still included in the miscellaneous items. In his explanation, there is an indirect indication to apply partial productivity analysis of energy.

Partial productivity analysis of electricity has been worked out in the research study of Sumanth[53]. In his book on partial productivity, he referred to a study assisted by Du Boff[54] (1966) on the relationship between price of electric power and changes in productivity in American manufacturing industry. He also builds a theoretical framework for measuring the effects of electrical technology on factor costs, i.e. labour, capital and raw materials.

Deshmukh et al[55] studied the pricing aspect of electricity consumption by the H.T industrial units of Maharashtra. It was a techno- economic study to find out how and how much of load can be staggered from the peak load to peak load period, through pricing mechanism.

Scholars in electricity pricing like Reddy[56], Little child and Vaidya[57] Manasinghe[58] Chemberlin[59] have worked on the determination of optimal price for electricity. They do not find any reason to follow average cost pricing, since it used historic data, which proved inadequate for price fixation. They preferred to apply long run and short run marginal cost principle for determining unit cost. For long term planning application, long run marginal cost finds more appropriate than the short run marginal costs.

Korean Electric Power Corporation which is responsible for generation, transmission and distribution of electricity in Korea, has implemented one of the sophisticated tariff structures incorporating long run marginal cost and the time of the Day tariff. The tariff levels are fixed on the basis of the anticipated rate of return on investment. KEPCO's experience in tariff policy led SEBS of developing countries to follow Korean example.

Faruqui and Malko[60] have analysed the sources of time of use Tariff (TOUT) this rate has been tested for the residential and small commercial energy users in the USA, and a review of 12 such experiments found that TOU rates can reduce peak period electricity consumption by up to 30%.

Pont et al[61] has examined the validity of least cost utility planning process in different planning process in difference nations. They reviewed that countries like US, Canada, Australia, Sweden, Jamaica, Thailand and Malaysia have implemented least cost utility planning process in determining the best sources of electricity generation on a priority basis, which takes into account, besides the direct cost, the cost of externalities as well.

Rao Govind et al[62] examined at length the nature, characteristics and the issues found in the power tariff in India. They observed that actual tariffs levied by SEBS are at variance with the broad principles of rational pricing policy, which is incentive compatible and is required to generate resources for reinvestment. SEB have failed to recover cost even when measured in accounting terms, with interest payable on State government loans being highly subsidized and depreciation calculated by historical costs. They have also pointed out that economic consideration do not seem to have dictated the determination of tariff. The tariff on different categories of consumers bears no relationship to marginal cost of supplying electricity to them. In fact, in some case the tariff is inversely related to the average costs under lining the importance of political factors.

Munasinghe[63] examined the significance of demand management and conservation in electricity sector, and has pointed out that the power system should follow the principles of integrated energy planning, which would help to conserve energy. Hastopoulos[64] used various models to identify the cost effectiveness of energy use. A number of technical, economic and financial factors combined to determine the cost effectiveness of investment in energy conservation technologies. Widely used in analysis of engineering economics of projects are the Net Present Value (NPV) the Internal Rate of Return (IRR) and the Gross Pay Back Period (GPBP).

Bose and Anandalingam[65] have studied the different engineering solutions to overcome electricity crisis. They pointed out that there was a lack of general ability to diagnose, design and implement engineering solutions to energy problems. They summarized that lack of technical know-how was the greatest non-economic barriers to energy conservation.

Bhattacharya[66] examined the functioning of public sector utilities in developing countries and argued that the problems being faced by the power sector were diverse and privatization and deregulation cannot solve all of them, though the financial burden of the utilities may be eased. He further argued that privatization may lead to neglect of long term planning of electricity sector.

The studies of Schramm[67] World Bank[68] Bernelt[69] Sanghvi[70] Tenenbaum et al[71] were mainly concentrated on the current issues of power sector in developing countries. They analysed that all the SEBS in developing countries are characterised by factors like structure of the system, growth rate, technical performance, debt crisis, heavy T&D losses, and capital scarcity.

Nadal[72] has examined the scope for and the methods of energy conservation in Indian context. He further suggested that there are 27 ways of efficiency improvement. Through the application of these efficiency measures in industrial, agricultural, commercial and domestic sector, on an average 20-25% electricity consumption could be saved. Cost effectiveness of energy saved per kW and cost of generation per kW by various sources has been elaborated. He recommended that whenever a measure costs less per kW than a new power plant, a measure is likely to be cost effective in Indian context.

Morris[73] critically examined the recent policy changes, especially as regards the Independent Power Producers (IPPs) and revealed that there are many disfunctionalities in this policy, particularly the enormous and quite unnecessary burden it places on the balance of payments. He has also pointed out several constraints to the healthy growth of the power sector. These constraints include the inability of the state sector to discipline its management and work force, large-scale corruption and leakages, load and system imbalances, brought about by inadequate investments in distribution system, and in hydel capacities etc. Recently the bulk of industrial consumers being increasingly left to fend themselves through captive power generation as also the political inability to raise tariff and thus contributed to the structural weakness of State Electricity Boards.

Reddy and Sumithra[74] analysed Karnataka's power sector- the present situation, and the trends of electricity demand and supply, the financial problems, the import ant policy and technical milestones in the development of power sector. A number of realistic and small measures are suggested, both on the demand side and the supply side to over come present power shortages. These measures include- (1) Demand side measures like (a) efficient lighting, (b) use of solar water heaters (c) efficient irrigation pump sets, (d) efficient motors, (2) Supply side measures like (a) environmentally sound hydro electric power projects (b) reducing T&D losses (c) captive power generation, (d) cogeneration (e) small hydel, wind, and solar and (3) a new energy paradigm- the solution for the long term like the shift to the new energy paradigm, giving thrust up on energy services, rather than energy consumption. Besides the above short and long term measures to make the power system efficient, viable, and dependable, the authors stressed the need to develop a sustainable energy future. However one of the limitations of this research work is that the economic contents of power shortages have not been properly looked into.

The review attempted in the forgoing sector covers the major works in the power sector carried out within the country and abroad. In this review, studies directly concerning the performance of State Electricity Boards have figured but rarely, for the simple reason that such studies are few and far between in India. The present study is concerned with an exhaustive analysis of the power system of Kerala, from technical and economic angle. Therefore a brief look at the works already done in the context of Kerala would be in order.

The first and perhaps the only comprehensive economic study about the power system of Kerala is that of Pillai.[75] The author examined supply and demand aspects of the Kerala Power System during 1957-58 to 1976-77, using econometric techniques. The major findings of the study include (1) Aggregate demand for electricity consumption grew at an annual compounded rate of 10.4% during the period 1957-76. (2) The income elasticity of demand in the short and long run are 1.63 and 1.363 respectively and estimated price elasticities- 0.633 and –0.813 respectively. The income elasticity of demand for electricity in Kerala has been much higher than those prevailing in other developed countries like USA, USSR, UK, France or West Germany, but less than that at the all India level.

Many of the findings of the study have however become irrelevant as the work was carried out in the seventies when the State was surplus in electricity production. The continuing deficit occurred since 1982 have thrown out several issues in the power sector of the State, which the author could not foresee. Inspite of such visible limitations found in his work, the methodology followed, the observations derived, the major suggestions put foreword have valuable relevance even today.

Parameswaran[76] examined the reasons for severe power and energy shortages in Kerala since 1979 and strongly recommended introducing super power thermal station in the central part of Kerala to meet power demand for the next few decades. But it is observed that the Kerala Power System did not install thermal alternative till 1997. In another work he[77] observed that the power potential of the state was limited due to inter-state disputes over hydro sites, and the serious environmental objections raised against hydro projects. Menon[78] studied the attractiveness of the unexploited hydel projects, in comparison with thermal power projects based on coal to be transported from eastern coalfields of Orissa.

Pavitharan, G.[79] Examined the demand and supply gap in energy and pointed out that the gap has been growing at an exponential rate. The situation took a worse turn beyond 1986 when "Blackout" and "Brown outs" became regular phenomena in the state.

The causes and the characteristics of power crisis in the context of Kerala have been examined by

Pavithran, K.V.[80] and observed that the internal peak demand and the system peak supply has been widening over the years, particularly from 1990 onwards. Some of the causes of power shortages mentioned are- (1) insufficient installed capacity, (2) neglect of hydel alternatives, (3) unexploitation of mini, micro, and small hydel projects, (4) poor energy conservation programme. (5) relatively low tariff structure, and (6) lack of measures to reduce heavy T&D loss in the state.

Unnikrishnan[81] examined the reasons for power shortages in Kerala and observed that (1) the energy policy of the Central government (2) the stand of environmental fundamentalists, (3) the cost over run and time over run of hydel projects, (4) corruption in the project construction and (5) lack of central investment in the power sector in Kerala, have been responsible for the present power crisis. However such issues have not been examined in analytically rigorous manner by the above authors.

KSSP[82] studied the problems of power sector confined to the district of Kannur and pointed out that the most of the power problems in the district are just the continuation of the State level problems. However some of the problems peculiar to the districts of north Malabar are- (a) abysmally low voltage during the peak hours, (b) insufficient transmission lines leading to high level of voltage drop, (c) over loaded connections per transformer, (d) inadequate sub stations, (e) lack of 220 kV lines, (f) centralized store purchase, and lack of energy conservation awareness. This study recommended to use renewable like mini/micro/small hydel potential to meet energy demand during the peak hours. It also suggested using solar water heaters, and automatic lighting. One of the important suggestions of this study is to install at least 100 MW thermal power project in the district of Kannur.

Menon[83] studied at length the merits and demerits of a nuclear power project in Kerala in the wake of acute power shortage. He stressed that nuclear power projects in the state were not to be encouraged due to health and environmental considerations. He was of the view that the present energy crisis was the direct result of the heavy appetite for energy by the EHT and HT industrial units. Most of the large-scale industrial units in Kerala are highly energy intensive. To reduce the energy demand and supply gap, industrial restructuring giving importance to energy light, and employment-oriented industries is suggested.

ECS[84] prepared a draft report on the alternative energy strategy for Kerala and the main proposals are – to introduce renewables in the energy sector, adopt an environmentally and economically sustainable energy policy, and involvement of voluntary agencies and people movements in energy conservation and other energy related issues.

Jyothis[85] carried out a study on the economic aspects of environment friendly technology in the power sector of Kerala. Alternative energy option available in the state has been verified and observed that even if the existing cost per unit of solar energy is relatively higher, by harnessing technological advancements, the cost per unit can be significantly reduced, and solar photovoltaic system may complement the existing hydel generation, particularly during summer. It is observed from the analysis of this study that sufficient attention has not been given to cover up the technical aspects of environment friendly technology.

Devi's[86] Study on the energy perspective of Kerala economy examined the reasons for present power shortage in Kerala. The main findings of her study included:- (a) internal energy resources of Kerala are inadequate to meet energy requirements of the state in future, (b) The T&D losses are quite high by comparable standards, (c) energy policies of the state have not considered properly the possibilities for energy conservation. To meet power requirement for the next decade, two pronged approaches have been suggested, (1) to develop non-conventional energy on a significant scale, and (2) enhance technical efficiency in both generation and consumption of energy, together with ceaseless efforts to conserve energy.

Isac et al[87] studied the pattern of power consumption at the micro level. This study merits special significance due to the obvious reason that a similar study of this kind was not conducted in the state. This study covers major aspects like (1) Pattern of energy consumption (2) Energy demand for the Panchayat (3) End use analysis of power consumption (4) Power line mapping to determine load concentration (5) Levels of voltage to the consumer end during peak hours (6) Scope for integrated energy planning at the micro level. This pioneering study has now become the base for energy studies at the local level.

IRTC[88] conducted a detailed study on the electricity demand in seven major sub divisions in the State. These seven areas belong to seven districts chosen on the basis of the voltage problem and similar other considerations. The demand analysis was held using end use analysis (DEFENDUS Model). One of the major findings of this study was that the power consumption of higher income group is much higher due to the use of various types of domestic electrical appliances. The impact of gulf boom on the demand for power in the domestic sector has also been observed. It followed two methods of end use analysis called (1) Appliances approach and (2) Engineering approach. Based on this analysis, it recommended following energy conservation techniques like the use of CFL (Compact Fluorescent Lamp) in the State liberally which would help to bring down energy demand by 400 MW.

Pavithran, G.[89] examined the different aspects of T&D set up in the state and recommended introducing drastic measures to curb energy loss and also to improve the voltage level during the peak hours. The major findings of this study are – (1) Poor ratings of power lines and transformers, (2) Insufficient reactive compensation (3) Value of power factor below the expected minimum (0.90) (4) Over loaded transformers and (5) Over extended HT&LT lines. His recommendations included (1) Load staggering (2) Installation of additional transformers (3) Setting up of additional substations of various ratings and (4) Replacement of old and weak transformers.

Krishanan and Pavithran[90] analysed the problems and remedies of huge T&D in the State is due to the low priority in the allocation of financial and managerial resources required for the power system. The technological advancements in the electrical engineering in West countries helped them to curb energy loss below 15%. Such technological developments including equipments and software packages are rarely used in the context of Kerala. The measures suggested to curb energy loss are (1) Energy auditing (2) Load survey (3) Network reconductoring and reconfiguration (4) Reactive compensation (5) Use of more shunt capacitors and (6) Underground cables. The investment on T&D improvement will be paid back within a few years.

Mohanan[91] worked on the technical and non-technical aspects of energy conservation potential in the State, particularly in the industrial sector. The motor drives used in most of the industrial units are induction type and if it could be replaced by variable speed motors, about 20% of energy consumption could be saved. However in the context of Kerala such a move is yet to take place.

Hydari[92] conducted a Delphi study on energy efficiency and energy conservation in the context of Kerala. Non availability of sufficient data on different aspects of energy conservation prompted him to make an expert opinion study namely Delphi. Energy auditing is commended as a policy measure to promote energy conservation in the State. Another point suggested by him is to promote less energy intensive industries like electronics to conserve much energy. Experts have a convergent opinion that increased energy consumption leads to environmental problems and hence each should be accounted in the assessment of energy efficiency. This study though covers many aspects of Kerala Power System, excluded major areas like the causes of power shortage, demand projections and sectoral demand for energy.

Late eighties witnessed a phenomenal increase in the research work on the power system – both at the National and State levels, due to persistent power shortage and power system unreliability. However one of the limitations observed in many of such studies is that the economic content of power crisis has not been exposed much. When individual researchers find hard time to work on the economic aspects of electricity, institutions like IISc, IGIDR, IIT Delhi, and TERI and similar energy research institutions have carried out extensive research work on the power system, giving special attention to both technical and economical aspects. Some of the area in which special attention has been given are:- (1) Power demand and supply gap (2) Causes of system unreliability (3) Production and value loss due to power shortage and system unreliability (4) Impact of power deficit on value addition and employment, (5) The economics of inter-fuel substitutions (6) Marginal cost pricing (7) Cost benefit analysis of power alternatives like capital power, generators, inverters etc. (8) Integrated energy planning (9) Economic cost of renewable and (10) The energy demand and price modeling. But none of such institutions have taken up for enquiry problems faced by the power system of Kerala.

The forgoing review of major works done on the Kerala power system indicates that most studies are technical in nature and content, economic studies being rather scanty. By virtue of its nature, a meaningful study of power system would dictate a techno- economic approach, which is totally lacking in Kerala context. The present exercise is a techno- economic study of Kerala power system covering such aspects like installed capacity, power generation, maximum demand, pattern of energy consumption, sectoral demands for electricity, and revenue and tariff structure.

Notes and References

1. Scaelott and Eugene (1952) *"Energy Sources—the Wealth of the World"* Mc Graw Hill. New York.

2. Daemstadter, J. et. al. (1971) *"Energy in the World Economy: A Statistical Review of Trends in Output, Trade and Consumption Since 1925"* John Hopkins Press.

3. Fremont Felix in Tyner Wallace, E. (1978) *"Energy Resources and Economic Development in India"* Allied Publishers, Mumbai.
4. Ford Foundation Energy Policy Project in *"Energy and Development"*—World Watch Institute Paper 15, January 1976. p. 51.
5. Tanzer, Michal in 'o.p.c.i.t.' (refer 4)
6. Batia, Ramesh (1990) *"Energy Demand Analysis in Developing Countries"* in Ashok, V. Desai (ed.) *"Energy demand Analysis, Management and Conservation"* Wiley Eastern Ltd.
7. Hill, Robert et al. (1991) *"The Future of Energy Use"* Earth scan Publications, London. U.K.
8. Desai, Ashok. V. (1978) *"Development and Energy Consumption"* Oxford Bulletin of Economics and Statistics. 40 (3) pp. 263-272.
9. Smolik J. (1978) *"The Use of Input–Output Analysis for International Energy Comparisons"* in Dunkerley (ed.) "International comparisons of energy consumption, Washington.
10. Choe, B.J. et al (1981) *"Global Energy Prospects"* World Bank working paper, 489. IBRD.
11. IBRD (1981) *"Energy Pricing in Developing Countries: A Review of Literature"* IBRD.
12. Wolf, et al (1981) *"Oil and Energy Demand in Developing Countries in* 1990 Energy Journal 2 (4) pp. 1-24.
13. Siddayao, C. (1982) *"Demand for Energy and Economic Growth: Some Measurement and Computational Issues"* Hawaii, USA. East West centre.
14. ESCAP (1981) Short term economic policy aspects of energy situation in ESCAP regions" Bangkok, Thailand.
15. Batia Ramesh (1990) *"Energy Demand Analysis in Developing Countries"* in Ashok V Desai (ed.) o.p.c.i.t. (Refer 6).
16. Pindick, J. (1979) *"Structure of World Energy Demand"* MIT Press.
17. Berndt, E.R, et. al. (1981) *"Dynamic Models of Energy Demand—An Assessment and Comparison"* in Berndt, E.R

and Field, B., (eds.) Modelling and Measuring Natural Resources Substitution" MIT Press.

18. Bohi D.R. (1981) *"Analysing Demand Behaviour-A Study of Energy Elasticities"* John Hopins University Press.
19. Dunkerley, et al (1981) *"Factors Affecting the Composition of Energy use in Developing Countries"* USA, Resources for the Future.
20. Munasinghe, Mohan. And Schramm, G. (1983) *"Energy Demand Analysis and Forecasting"* in Munasinghe, M and Schramm, G (eds.) "Energy Economics, Demand Management and Conservation Policy" Toronto, Canada. VNR and Co. pp 213-259.
21. Rehman, S.H. (1982) *"Econometric Modelling of Energy Eçonomy Interactions in Oil Importing Developing Countries—A Text with Indian Data"* Polo Alto. EPRI, USA.
22. Bhatia, Remesh 'o.p.c.i.t.' (refer 6).
23. Ibid p. 18.
24. Jankowsky, J. (1980) *"Industrial Energy Conservation in Developing Countries"* Washington Dc, USA. Resources for the Future.
25. Divan, Ramesh (1978) *"Energy Implications of India's Economic Development"* Journal of energy Development 3 (2) pp 318-327.
26. Pindick, J. (1979) 'o.p.c.i.t.' (refer 16).
27. Parikh, Jyothi K (1980) *"Modelling Approach to the Long Run Energy Demand and Energy Policy Implications."* Government of India. Planning commission. New Delhi.
28. Cecelski et al (1979) *"Household Energy and the Poor in the Third World Countries"*. Washington, DC, USA, Resources for the Future.
29. Havrylyshym, O, and Munasinghe m. (1980) *Interactions Among the Alternative Modes of Energy Production;* empirical care study for Srilanka. IBRD.
30. Amarullah, M (1984) *"Electricity Demand in Indonesia: An Econometric Analysis"*. Jakartha, Indonesia, Pusat Penyelidikan Masalah Kelstanikan.
31. Iqball (1984) *"Residential Energy Demand: A Case Study of Pakistan"*. Journal of Economic Studies, 11 (1), pp. 40-48.

32. Raily, J. (1982) *"Energy Demand Analysis in Developing Countries"*. USA.

33. Dias-Bandaranaike, R and Munasinghe, M. (1983) *The Demand for Electricity Services and the Quantity of Supply.* Energy Journal, 4 (2), pp. 49-71.

34. Goldemburg et al (1989) *"Energy for Sustainable World"* Wiley Eastern. Bangalore.

35. Reddy Sudhakara, B (1995) *"Econometric Analysis of Energy use in Urban Households"*. Energy Sources Vol. 17. pp. 359-371. U.K.

36. Reddy Sudhakara. B, (1990) *"The Energy Sector of The Metropolis of Bangalore"* Ph.D. thesis (Unpublished) IISC, Bangalore.

37. Ranganathan. V, (1977) *"An Application of Cost Benefit Analysis of Rural Electrification"*- Ph.D. thesis, IISC, Ahamedabad.

38. Parikh, Jyothi.K (1981) *"Modelling Energy Demand for Policy Analysis"*, Planning Commission, Government of India, New Delhi.

39. Parikh. J.K. (1992) *"Policy Alternatives for Western and Southern Power Systems in India"*- IGIDR working paper.

40. Mohasinghe, Mohan (1980) *"Costs Incurred by Residential Electricity Consumers Due to Power Failure"*- Journal of Consumers Research 6 (4) pp. 361-69.

41. Mohasinghe M and Schramm G (1983) *"Energy Demand Analysis and Forecasting"*, Energy Economics, Demand management and Conservation Policy. Toranto-Canada.

42. Sanghvi A P (1983) *"Optimal Electricity Supply Liability Using Customer Shortage Costs"* Energy Economics. 5 (2) pp. 129-36.

43. Batia Ramesh (1990) *"Energy Demand Analysis in Developing Countries"* in Ashok V Desai (Ed) Energy Demand, Analysis, Management and Conservation. ERG Series, Wiley Eastern.

44. Pinck, J (1979) o.p.c.i.t. (refer 16).

45. Uri, N D. *"The Demand for Electrical Energy in Korean Industry"* Energy Conservation Management, 23 (4) pp. 201-210.

46. Nayar C.V. (1994) *"Stand alone Wind/Diesel/Battery/ Hybrid Energy System"* Energy Environment Monitor 11 (1) pp. 41-46.

47. Raikhy, P.S. and Singh Parminder (1990) *"Energy Consumption in India – Pattern and Determinants"* Deep and Deep Publications. New Delhi.

48. Roy, Joyashree (1992) *"Demand for Energy in Indian Industries-A Quantitative Approach"*. Daya Publishing house New Delhi.

49. Munasinghe, M, et al (1992) *"Efficient Management of Power Sector in Developing Countries"* Energy policy (20) 2 pp. 94-103.

50. Hill, Robert et al. (1993) *"The Future of Energy Use"*, Earth Scan Publications, London, U K.

51. Wee, Kang and Li, Binsheng (1995) *"Energy Development in China–National Policies and Regional Strategies"* – Energy Policy Vol. 23 (2) pp 167-178, UK.

52. Pachauri, R.K. (1980) *"Energy Policy for India- An Interdisciplinary Analysis"*, Macmillan and Co., New Delhi.

53. Sumanth, David. J. (1985) *"Productivity Engineering and Management- Productivity Measurement, Evaluation, Planning and Improvement in Manufacturing and Service Organisations"*, McGraw Hill Book Company.

54. Du Boff R.B. (1966) *"Electrification and Capital Productivity: A Suggested Approach"* in Sumanth, J. (ed.) "Productivity Engineering and Management- Productivity Measurement, Evaluation, Planning and Improvement in Manufacturing and Service Organisations", McGraw Hill Book Co.

55. Deshmukh, S.J. et al (1991) *"HT Industries Survey"* IGIDR. Working paper D.P. No 43

56. Reddy Sudhakara B. (1995) *"Electricity Pricing and Load Management for Maharashtra"*. Energy sources Vol. 17 pp 337-357, U.K.

57. Little child S.C and Vaidya, K.G (1992) *"Energy Studies for the U.K."* George Allen and Unwim Winchester.

58. Manasinghe M (1992) *"Efficient Management of Power Sector in Developing Countries"* Energy Policy 20 (2) pp. 94-103.

59. Chemberlin C.H. (1985) *"Pricing and Incentives"* in proceeding of IEEE 73 (10).

60. Faruqui A, and Malko, J.R. (1983) *"The Residential Demand for Electricity by Time of Use – A Survey of 12 Experiments with Peak Load Pricing.* Energy (pp 8-10)

61. Pont, DU, P. et al (1991) *"Demand Side Management Master Plan for Thailand's Electric Power System"* Report Submitted to International Institute for energy conservation Bangkok, Thailand. October

62. Rao Govind, M et al (1998) *"The Economics of Electricity Supply in India"* Macmillan Ltd.

63. Munasinghe, Mohan (1990) *"Policy Issues in Energy Demand Management and Conservation"* in Ashok V. Desai (ed.) Energy Demand, Analysis, Management and conservation. Wiley Eastern. ERG series.

64. Hastopolulos, G.N. et al (1978). *"Capital Investments to Conserve Energy"*. Harvard Business Review 56 (2) pp. 111-112.

65. Bose and Anandalingam G.C (1983) *"Barriers to Industrial Energy Conservation in India"* TERI working paper, New Delhi.

66. Bhattaracharya, Subhash c (1994) *"Power Sector Privatisation in Developing Countries-will it Solve all Problems"* Energy Sources (17) pp. 373-389. U.K.

67. Schramm, G. (1993) *"Issues and Problems in the Power Sector of Developing Countries"* Energy Policy (July) pp. 735-747.

68. World Bank (1993) *"The World Bank's Role in Electrical Power Sector"* IBRD.

69. Berneit (1993) *"Aid Donor Policies and Power Sector Performance in Developing Countries"* Energy Policy Feb pp. 110-113.

70. Sanghvi A.P. (1991) *"Power Shortage in Developing Countries-Impacts and Policy Implications"* Energy Policy (June) pp. 425-440.

71. Tenenbaum et al (1992) *"Electricity Privatisation – Structural, Competitive, and Regulatory Optionals"* Energy Policy (December) pp. 1139-1160.

72. Nadal Steven et al. (1991) *"Opportunities for Improving End Use Electricity Efficiency in India"* Nov. USAID.

73. Morris, Sebastain (1996) *"Political Economy of Electric Power Development in India"* EPW vol. 31, no. 20 May 18th and 25th.

74. Reddy, Amulya, K.N. and Sumithra, Gladys, D. (1997) *"Karnataka's Power Sector-some Revelations"* EPW Vol. 32, No. 12. March 22-28. pp. 585-900.

75. Pillai. P.P. (1981) *"Dynamics of Electricity Supply and Demand- A Micro Econometric Analysis of Kerala"* Agricole Publishing Academy, New Delhi.

76. Parameswaran. M.P. (1990) *"Kerala Power Predicament – Issues and Solutions"* EPW Vol. 25 No. 37, Sept. 15th.

77. Parameswaran. M.P. (1990) *"Priorities in Energy Planning" in "Energy Debate"*, Kerala Sastra Sahithya Parishad, Kozhikode.

78. Menon. R.V.G. (1994) *"The Pooyamkutty Project and Kerala's and Kerala's Power Crisis"* Sastragathy, the Monthly Journal of KSSP. Vol. 28. No. 2. May Trichur.

79. Pavithran, G. (1991) *"Voltage Improvement and Actual Energy Demand Projection by Load Shedding"* Hydel, Vol. 36 No. 1 Thiruvanadapuram.

80. Pavithran, K.V. (1996) *"Power Crisis"* in Deshabhimani Weekly, March 24-30. Kozhikode.

81. Unnikrishnan, K.R. (1996) *"Basic Causes of Power Crisis in Kerala"* in Deshabhimani Weekly, May 5-11 Kozhikode.

82. KSSP (1996) *"Electricity Problems of Kannur District"* in the District Development Seminar Compendium, March 9-10.

83. Menon, R.V.G. (1991) *"Why Should not a Nuclear Poer Project at Peringome"* in Sastragathy, (the journal of KSSP) August, pp. 10-16.

84. Energy Conservation Society (1997) *"ECS Bulletin- Special"* July 8th. Thiruvanandapuram.

85. Jyothis, S. (1995) *"Environment Friendly Technology in Energy Sector"* – M.Phil. Dissertation, University of Kerala, Thiruvanandapuram.

86. Devi, Ganga, S. (1995) *"Energy Perspective of Kerala"* M.Phil. Dissertation, Pondicherry University, Mahe.

87. Iasc, Thomas, T.M, et al (1995) *"Power Consumption in Kalliasseri Panchayat"* in Centre for Development Studies (ed.) "Kerala Research Programme on Local Level Development" (KRPLLD) Thiruvanandapuram.

88. Integrated Rural Technology Centre (IRTC) (1996) "Exercises for Integrated Resource Planning for Kerala: End Use Analysis- An Empirical Study" Technical Report-I [Un published]

89. Pavithran. G. (1991) *"Kerala Power System-Yesterday Today and Tomorrow"* 25th Annual Souvenir, Kerala State Electricity Board Engineers Association, Thiruvanandapuram.

90. Krishnan, Ananda and Pavithran, G (1994) *"T&D Losses Problems and Remedies"* in Hydel Vol. 40 No. 3 Sept. Thiruvanandapuram.

91. Mohanan, Chandra Nair, P. S (1995) *"Industrial Energy Conservation-Principles of Energy Management and Energy Planning"* in "ECS Year Book-1995" Thiruvanandapuram.

92. Hydari, Aneez K.P. (1994) *"Energy Efficiency and Conservation in Kerala- A Techno Economic Policy Analysis"* M.Phil. Dissertation (unpublished) University of Kerala, Thiruvanandapuram.

3

Power Development in India: A Historical and Statistical Analysis

Introduction

At the time of independence, Indian economy was characterised by a highly backward agricultural sector, an under developed and lopsided industrial sector and an ill grown service sector. Economic planning was introduced in 1951, with a view to modernising and expanding the production sectors and thereby accelerating the overall growth of the economy. The strategy followed was a sort of forced industrialisation, in which the pride of place was accorded to the development of strategic and basic industries, which included power industries as well.

From the second five-year plan, Indian plans had provided for huge investments in the energy sector. This was dictated by the perception on the part of the planners that power, being a universal input, the growth of the rest of the sectors was contingent on power availability. This resulted in the steady increase both in the number of power plants, installed capacity and generation of power. However, persistent power famine has been a recurring phenomenon in the country for the last several years, both official and unofficial. The recent policy changes introduced in the sector as a part of the liberalisation drive were to address to these problems. However the problems in this sector continue to remain almost unchanged. In this circumstance, a brief review of the developments in the power sector is attempted in this chapter with a view to identifying the problems in the sector and their solution.

Review of Energy Development

On the eve of the launching of economic planning, the energy sector of India remained in a primordial state. The nation depended mainly on non-commercial energy sources such as firewood, agricultural waste and animal dung. The total energy consumption was limited in terms of its magnitude. In 1953-54, the earliest year after independence, for which the published data are readily available, the consumption was of the order of 60.4 Million Tonnes of coal replacement (MTCR)[1], 67.6% of which was in the form of non-commercial energy. Power generation and consumption at this time remained abysmally low. Installed capacity was only 1713 MW and power generation only 51077 MU[2] in 1950. The per capita consumption of electricity remained a low 15.6 kWh[3]. The number of villages electrified stood at 3061, roughly 0.54% of total villages. The above figures eloquently point to the poor state of energy development in India during the early fifties.

Energy planning is a component of overall economic planning and is aimed at a rational and integrated utilisation of various energy sources with a view to achieving a balanced and sustained economic growth. Central to energy planning is the identification of potential energy resources pertaining to alternative sources. Since the concept of resources in any economy is dynamic, the estimates of resources potential are found to change with the time.

Energy Resources

The energy resources are traditionally divided into two categories-Commercial and Non-commercial. Coal, oil, gas, electricity and nuclear fuel constitute the main sources of commercial energy. The non-commercial sources are firewood, vegetable wastes and cowdung. Among the non-commercial sources, firewood occupies the most important place, being the major source of energy for rural households and a supplementary source even to the urban households.

Though no precise estimate about the firewood consumption is available questimates put it at 130Mt. However the importance of firewood as an energy source has been on the decline in the wake of large-scale denudation of forests throughout the country[4].

Table 3.1: Proven energy resources

Items	Units	World	India	
			Quantity	% of world
Coal	Bt[a]	1078.1	59.0	5.47
Oil	Bbbl[b]	1009.2	5.91	0.59
Natural Gas	Tcu.m[c]	119.2	0.73	0.61
Hydro Power	GW[d]	NA	94.0	NA

Note: a= Billion Tonnes, b= Billion Barrels, c= Terra Cubic Meters, d= Giga Watt ('000 MW)

Source: TERI (1995) "Environmental Considerations and Option in Managing India's Long-term Energy Strategy (ECOMILES). New Delhi, p. 9.

India is relatively well endowed with exhaustible and renewable energy sources. In the following table is presented the proven energy resources of India Vs the world.

1. Coal

Coal is the major exhaustible resource of the country and has a life expectancy of over 200 years. However on a per capita basis, the coal reserves would be well below the world average. Identified deposits of coal occur in 44 major coal-fields located in various states. According to the most recent estimates, the total geological resources of coal stand at 192.4 Bt[5], of which more than 90% are in the central and eastern parts of India. The geographical concentrate of this reserves makes it necessary to transport it over long distances to the consuming centers scattered all over India. Coal resources have generally been classified according to the extent of exploration, degree of certainty, convenience of mining and quality in use.

Depending up on the degree of certainty, total reserves are classified as mineable and recoverable[6],

Table 3.2: Geological, Mineable and Recoverable Reserves of Coal (1-1-1991)

Items	Units	Geological	Mineable (upto 600m)	Recoverable (upto 600m)
Prime Coking	Bt	5.3	2.2	1.10
Medium coking and Blendable	Bt	323.9	43.1	7.5
Non-coking	Bt	163.2	125.7	60.3
Total	Bt	192.4	171.0	68.8

Bt = Billion Tonnes
Source: TERI "ECONOMILES" – 1995. New Delhi, p. 10.

which are related to the probability of extracting coal from different seams. This is illustrated in the following Table 3.2 given below.

Coking coal reserves are only 15% of the total coal reserves of the resources of non-coking coal, only 12% are superior grade and bulk of the coal reserves (73%) are inferior grade non-coking coal occurring in thick inter banded seams and located in coal fields like Singrauli, Talcher, North Karanpura, Korba etc.

2. *Oil and Gas*

The reserves of oil and gas that fall in the recoverable category are only 5.88 Bt, as of January 1991. The total area of sedimentary basins in India is of order of 1.72 million km^2, comprising 1.4 million km^2 on shore and 0.32 million km^2 off shore within the 200-m. Isobath line[7]. The prognosticated resources of oil and oil equivalent of gas were estimated at 5.6 Bt. in 1964, increased to 12.8 Bt. in 1975 and to 15Bt. in 1982. The most recent estimates reported by the Ministry of Petroleum and Natural Gas in 1992 stood at 21.31 Bt of oil and oil equivalent of gas.

3. *Hydro power*

The annual hydro electric potential in the country is placed at 600 TWh of which more than ¾ is confined to the northern and northeastern region. A regional break-up of hydro potential as per the preliminary estimates is given in the Table 3.3 and chart 3.1.

Apart from this, the CEA has undertaken extensive studies to identify the sites for the development of pumped storage schemes. The result indicates that the 56 sites identified thus far offer a potential of 94000 MW[8] of which only 20% (18800) had been developed until

Table 3.3: Hydro power potential in TWh

Region	Potential	% share
North Eastern	239.3	40
Northern	225.0	38
Western	31.4	5
Eastern	42.5	7
Southern	61.8	10
All India	600.0	100

Source: TERI "ECOMILES" – 1995. New Delhi. P. 12

Chart 3.1
% Share of Hydro Power Potential

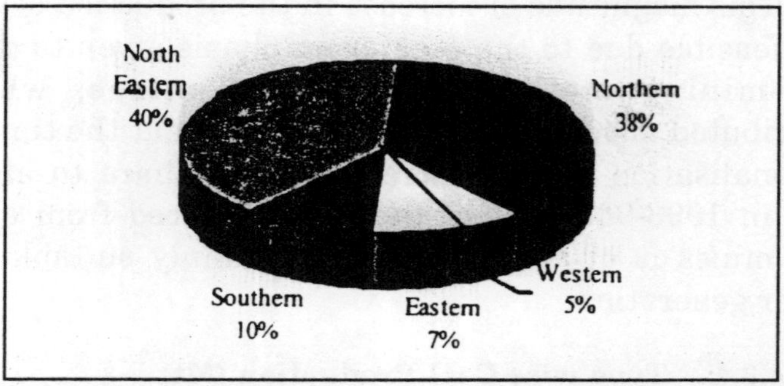

1990-91. There exists approximately another 5000 MW of potential, for exploitation through mini/micro hydel schemes along nearly 1000 sites. About half of these are concentrated in the Southern states (Andhra Pradesh, Tamil Nadu and Karnataka) where the potential was placed at 2000 MU of energy per annum.

Energy Supply

Commercial sources of energy account for nearly 60% of the total energy supplies, while non-commercial sources make-up the balance. Given large resources of coal, it is obvious that, coal dominates the commercial energy profile.

(a) Coal

The establishment of National Coal Development Corporation in 1956 was the first step in the planned development of coal industry. However it was not until the nationalization of coking coal mines in 1971 and of new coking mines in 1973, that a comprehensive programme for development of coalmines was launched. Coal production has registered an annual growth rate of about 6% during the last 2 decades, steadily increasing from a level of 77 Mt in 1972-73 to about 246 Mt in 1993-94.

This magnitude of increase in the production of coal was feasible due to the greater emphasis given to open cast-mining methods. Open cast mines, which contributed about 28% of total production at the time of nationalisation (1973), increased their share to about 70% in 1993-94. Most of the coal produced from open cast mines is of an inferior grade mainly suitable for power generation.

Table 3.4: Type wise Coal Production (Mt)

Year	Coking	Non-coking	Total
1970-71	17.8 (26.41)	55.1 (75.6)	72.9 (100)
1980-81	26.8 (23.6)	87.2 (76.4)	114.0 (100)
1992-93	45.4 (19.0)	192.9 (81.0)	238.3 (100)

Source: TERI (1996). "ECOMILES"—New Delhi, p. 14.

Only 21% of the total coal produced in India have coking properties and largely used for steel manufacturing and in foundries. The non-coking coal is mostly used for power generation and steam generation by industries.

There are no washeries for washing non-coking coal as yet in the country. In 1998 the Ronghe Committee appointed by the Planning Commission had recommended that coal to be supplied to new power stations located more than 1000 kilometers away from the coal fields should be beneficiated to reduce the ash content to about 34%. Based on the recommendations, the Government sanctioned 5 non-coking coal washeries.

(b) Oil and Natural Gas

With acceleration in exploratory and development drilling, there has been a substantial increase in the production of crude oil and natural gas. Production of crude oil rose from 6.8 Mt in 1970-71 to 33 Mt in 1990-91. Natural Gas production, on the other hand, increased from 1445 Million cubic meters to 17998 million cubic meters over the same period.

This increase in production has largely been due to an accelerated production from Bombay High offshore basin. In 1990-91, Bombay High accounted for 64% of crude oil produced in the country and 78% of natural gas (associated and free) production.

Power Sector: Evolution and Growth

The commencement of electricity production in India can be traced to 1880s when a small 130 kW hydroelectric power plant was commissioned at Darjeling[9]. The second important landmark in electricity production was the setting up of a thermal power plant based on coal in Calcutta in 1897. The initial ventures in the power sector in pre-independence India were almost completely confined to private enterprise. The power system during this period was managed according to the Indian Electricity Act of 1910[10]. On attaining independence the need for integrating power development with the development of other sectors of the economy was keenly felt. Accordingly in 1948 the Electricity (supply) Act was passed by the Parliament[11]. As per this act a number of State Electricity Boards (SEBs) and Electricity Departments (EDs) started functioning in various states and union territories. From the very beginning, the independent India placed Electricity in the concurrent list of the Seventh Schedule of Indian Constitution[12]. Electricity was put under the control of Ministry of Energy (including coal and non-conventional form of energy) till 1992, when an independent Ministry of Power (MoP) was formed

The Industrial Policy Resolution (1956) of the Government of India placed electricity industry under schedule 'A' i.e. in the category of industries, the future development of which would be exclusively in the public sector. Since then all future investments (except those by existing licencees) in power generation, transmission and distribution were made under public Sector. (This system continued until 1991 when the Government of India introduced privatization as part of its new economic policies).

With the increase in the number of power projects all over the country, mainly under State governments initiative, the need for a regulatory body at the national level arose. The Central Electricity Authority (CEA) was thus setup in 1950[13], with a view to evolving sound and uniform national power policy, formulating appropriate plans for power development and coordinating the activities of planning agencies in respect of control and utilisation of national power reserves.

The CEA, which was initially a part-time statutory body, was made a full time body in 1973[14]. At present the CEA helps the Ministry of Power in all technical, financial and economic matters. On the recommendation of CEA, for implementation purpose of power projects, the Government of India floated a few of power sector undertakings like National Thermal Power Corporation (NTPC), National Hydro Electric Power Corporation (NHEPC), Rural Electrification Corporation (REC) Ltd., Power Grid Corporation Ltd. And Central Power Research Institute (CPRI). Some of the major power projects set up under the patronage of these undertakings are[15].

Sl. No.	Name	State	Capacity (MW)
1.	Singrauli [Thermal]	Uttar Pradesh	2000
2.	Ramagundam [Thermal]	Andhra Pradesh	2100
3.	Farakka [Thermal]	West Bengal	2100
4.	Talcher [Thermal]	Orissa	1000
5.	Korba [Thermal]	Madhya Pradesh	2100
6.	Salal I and II [Hydro]	Jammu and Kashmir	345
7.	Uri [Hydro]	Jammu and Kashmir	500
8.	Tanakpur [Hydro]	Utter Pradesh	120
9.	Chamerra-I [Hydro]	Himachal Pradesh	540

Source: Ministry of Power (1997) "Annual Report-1995-96" Government of India, New Delhi, p. 33 and 34.

The launching of five-year plans marked concerted efforts at power development by the country. In Table

3.5 is shown the growth of outlay and expenditure on the power sector. The outlay on power sector recorded an increase of Rs. 791959 million at current prices between the first plan and the 8th plan periods. However the relative share of the Power Sector in total outlay doesn't appear to have undergone any perceptible change during the plan period. In fact till the 6th Five-Year Plan, the relative share of power sector outlays remained below that of the first Five-Year Plan.

Taking the entire plan period, we find that plan outlay of the power sector remained roughly at 18.55%. During the sixth plan, the percentage share on power sector was 20.13% of total outlay, but spent only 16.74%. Investment in this crucial sector appears to have remained more or less stagnant in relative terms even during the Post energy crisis period.

Coming to the actual expenditure, we find that expenditure on this sector exceeded the total outlay during the major part of the plan periods (except during the first plan and the sixth Five Year Plan) which in itself is a desirable trend. However, the near stagnancy in the outlay of the power sector is not a healthy trend, in view of the close dependence of the growth of other sectors on power availability. Part of the explanation for the present power famine in the country could be sought in the inadequate investment in the power sector during the previous plans (refer chart 3.2).

Capacity Addition During Plan Periods

Closely related to investment and expenditure, the targets and achievements are to be examined. Table 3.6 presents the plan wise targets of installed capacity as well as the corresponding achievements. The table indicates that till fifth five-year plan the targeted values of installed capacity remained low (below 10,000 MW).

Table 3.5: Plan-wise outlays and expenditure (Rs. Million)

Plans	Outlays			Expenditure		
	Power Sector	All Sector	% Share of Power Sector	Power Sector	All Sector	% Share of Power Sector
1951-56	3934	20687	19.02	2600	19600	13.26
1956-61	4269	48000	8.89	4455	46000	9.68
1961-66	10197	80945	12.60	12523	85765	14.60
1969-74	24476	159022	15.39	29397	157789	18.63
1974-79	72939	392875	18.56	73995	394262	18.77
1980-85	192654	957000	20.13	182987	1092914	16.74
1985-90	342735	1800000	19.04	378953	2182960	17.36
1992-97	795893	4341000	18.33	795890(P)	4349126(P)	18.30
Total	1447097	7799529	18.55	1480800	8328416	17.78

P = Provisional.

Source: Planning Commission (1996) "Annual Report of the working of State Electricity Boards and Electricity Departments"—New Delhi, p. 16.

Chart 3.2

Outlays and expenditure-power sector and all sectors

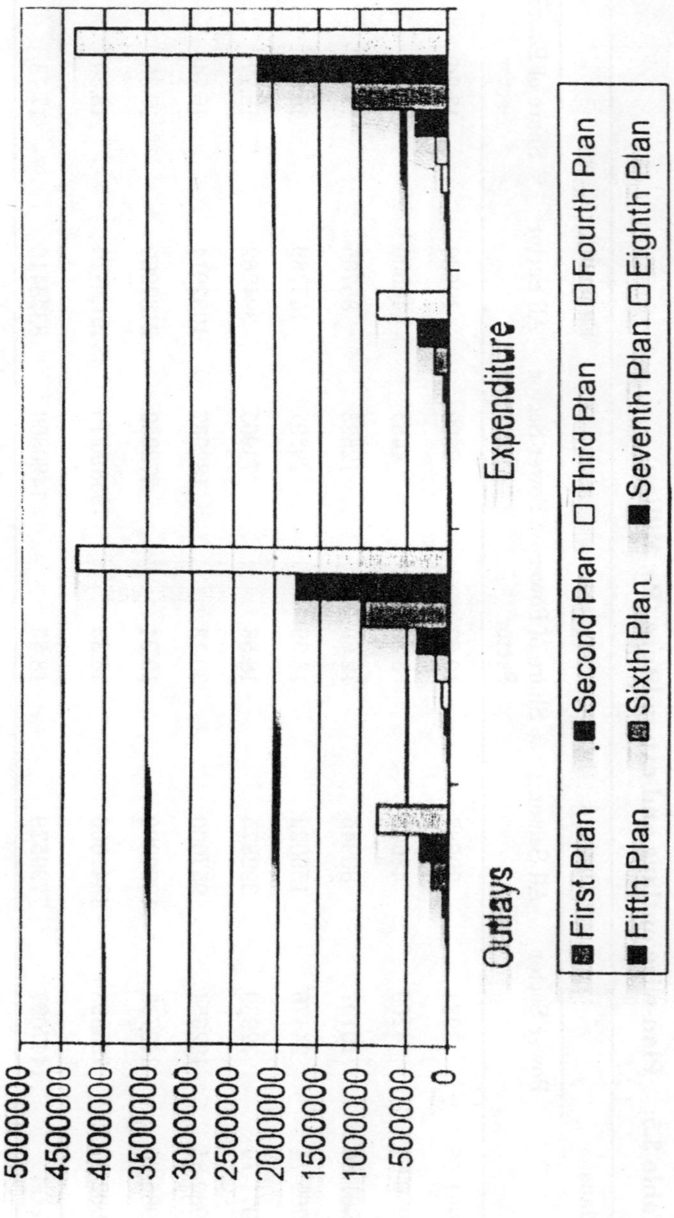

Table 3.6: Plan wise slippage in additional installed capacity (M.W)

Plan Periods	Target	Achievement	Slippage	Slippage %
First Plan (1951-56)	1300	1100	200	15.38
Second Plan (1956-61)	3500	2250	1250	35.71
Third Plan (1961-66)	7040	4520	2520	35.80
Annual Plan (1966-69)	5430	4120	1310	24.13
Fourth Plan (1969-74)	9264	4579	4685	50.57
Fifth Plan (1974-79)	12499	10202	2279	18.38
Annual Plan (1979-80)	2945	1799	1146	38.91
Sixth Plan (1980-85)	19666	14226	5440	27.66
Seventh Plan (1985-86)	4460	4223	237	5.31
1986-87	3396	2625	771	22.70
1987-88	4916	4981	(+) 65	(+)1.32
1988-89	4495	NA	NA	NA
1989-90	4596	NA	NA	NA
1990-91	2450*	1615	835	34.08•
Annual Plan 1991-92	2979*	2365	614	20.6•
Eighth Plan 1992-93	3537*	2805	732	20.7•
1993-94	4539*	4643	(+) 104	2.3•
1994-95	4599*	4810	(+) 211	4.6•

NA = Not Available

Sources: *(i)* Monga G.S. et al (1994) "India's Energy Prospects" Vikas Publishing House. New Delhi, p. 93.

(ii) •CMIE (1995) Centre for Monitoring Indian Economy, "Current Energy Scene in India" Mumbai.

(iii) *Ministry of Power, (1997) Annual Report- 1995-96. New Delhi, p. 3.

One reason for this was the relatively low importance accorded to power, as, during the pre energy crisis period, power was largely used for lighting purposes, the dominant forms of energy then being coal and oil. Power targets began to go up from the fifth five-year plan, when the pinch of power crisis began to be felt the world over. The actual achievement in relation to the targeted values remained very low, over the major part of the plan period. More importantly, the extent of shortage which was only 15.4% during the first plan almost progressively increased reaching the 50% level on during the fourth plan.

Though the position in regard to achievement slightly improved during the fifth plan (the extent of slippage having fallen to 18.4) in the ensuing years, the situation worsened, the extent of shortage being 39% during 1979-80 and 27.7% even during the sixth plan which had accorded priority to electricity production in view of power crisis in the country. Things began to improve slightly from the onset of the seventh five-year plan. Perceptible improvement in achievements began from the turn of the 90s when the slippage tended to become very small or even negative.

In order to get better insights into the slippage; it is necessary to go into a more desegregated analysis of the relevant variables like installed capacity, power generation and operational efficiency of power plants [kWh/kW]. The growth of installed capacity over the plan period has been presented in Table 3.7. Growth of installed capacity increased from 1713 MW from the beginning of the first five-year plan to 16664 MW by the end of the fourth five-year plan, registering an increase of 14951 MW or 873 percentage over a period of 24 years. Installed capacity registered largest increase during the second and third five-year plans (73% increase and 94% increase) as could be seen from the Table 3.7. During this phase the increase in installed capacity was the highest in the hydel sector.

Table 3.7: Growth of installed capacity during plan periods. (M.W)

Plan Periods	Hydro (MW)	Thermal (MW)	Nuclear (MW)	Total (MW)
1950-51	559.00	1154.00	0.00	1713
First Plan (1951-56)	939.48 (68)	1755.34 (52)	0.00	2694.82 (57)
Second Plan (1956-61)	1916.66 (104)	2736.39 (56)	0.00	4653.05 (73)
Third Plan (1961-66)	4123.74 (115)	4903.28 (79)	0.00	9027.02 (94)
Annual Plan (1966-69)	5906.91 (43)	7050.36 (44)	0.00	12957.27 (44)
Fourth Plan (1969-74)	6965.30 (18)	9058.26 (29)	640	16663.56 (29)
Fifth Plan (1974-79)	10833.07 (56)	15206.99 (68)	640	26680.06 (60)
Annual Plan (1979-80)	11383.97 (5)	16423.86 (8)	640	28447.83 (7)
Sixth Plan (1980-85)	14460.02 (27)	27029.70 (65)	1095 (71)	42584.72 (50)
Seventh Plan (1985-90)	18307.63 (27)	43763.71 (62)	1565 (43)	63636.34 (50)
Annual Plans (1990-92)	19194.31 (5)	48085.88 (10)	1785 (14)	69065.19 (9)
Eighth Plan (1992-97)	21811.00 (14)	62120.00 (29)	2225 (25)	86156.00 (25)

Note: Figures in brackets indicate the percentage increase.

Sources: *(i)* CEA (1994) "Public Electricity Supply – All India Statistics- General Review-1992-93" – New Delhi, p. 6and7

(ii) Power Finance Corporation Ltd. (1997) "Power Sector Reforms" New Delhi, p. 27.

No investments had been made in nuclear power during the first three five year plans. Nuclear source has been utilised since the fourth plan. Capacity addition marked a big jump during the fifth five-year plan, being pressed by the exigencies of the world energy crisis of 1973. This is partly due to shift of certain industrial loads from conventional commercial fuels to electricity. Capacity addition increased by 50% each during the 6th and 7th plan periods. The increase during the eighth plan, as compared to the preceding annual plan was 25%. Between fifth plan and the eighth plan, the increase in installed capacity was of the order of 59474 MW or an increase of 222.92%. It implies that the growth in installed capacity after the fifth five-year plan has been slower than during the first four five year plans. During the post 1974 period, the highest growth rates in installed capacity were recorded in thermal source and the lowest growth rates in hydro power, the nuclear source holding an intermediate position. We have also attempted to compute the growth rate of installed capacity of each source, and the total installed capacity for the entire period ranging from 1950 to 1996-97 (47 years). As the nuclear source came to be utilised for power generation from fourth plan (1969-70) onwards, the growth rates for the period 1969-70 to 1996-97 were also worked out. Growth rates were worked out by fitting semi log linear model[16] of the form: $\ln Y=\beta 1+\beta 2\, X_t+U_t$, as it gave better fit compared to simple linear regression model[17]. The results are given in table 3.8 and Table 3.9.

The tables shown above explain that the annual compound rate of growth of installed capacity of different power sources and the total installed capacity varies in the 2 cases. In both Case-I and Case-II, the growth rate of thermal source is the highest. In the post energy crisis period, there has been a decline in the percentage

Table 3.8: Trends in installed capacity using semilog linear model (Case-I)

Variables	Constant	Coefficient	R2	P. Value	Case-I (1950-96)	Growth Rate
Hydro	6.8830 (0.13365)* (51.50)+	0.07499 (0.004914)* (15.26)+	0.84	0.0000	47 years	7.79
Thermal	7.1428 (0.11143)* (64.10)+	(0.004097)* (20.80)+	0.91	0.0000	47 years	8.90
Total	7.7167 (0.01153)* (66.93)+	0.08227 (0.004239)* (19.41)+	0.89	0.0000	47 years	8.57

*= Standard Error, += Student's T.

Table 3.9: Trends in installed capacity using semilog linear model (Case-II)

Variables	Constant	Coefficient	R2	P. Value	Case-I (1969-96)	Growth Rate
Hydro	8.7044 (0.02831)* (307.49)+	0.05074 (0.001706)* (29.75)+	0.97	0.0000	28 years	5.20
Thermal	8.7597 (0.02537)* (345.32)+	0.08664 (0.001528)* (56.69)+	0.99	0.0000	28 years	9.05
Nuclear	5.9683 (0.03885)* (153.64)+	0.06510 (0.002340)* (27.82)+	0.97	0.0000	28 years	6.73
Total	9.4331 (0.02124)* (444.09)	0.07362 (0.001280)* (57.53)	0.99	0.0000	28 years	7.64

*= Standard Error, += Student's T

increase of installed capacity and this has been reflected in its rate of growth too. The difference in growth rates of hydro capacity in both the cases is primarily due to the changes in the installed capacity mix.

The share of hydel capacity in the power source mix declined by 18 points within a span of two decades and a more than commensurate increase has been noted in the share of thermal sector. (See Table 3.10).

Table 3.10: Changes in power source mix (Percentage) 1969-70 to 1995-96

Years	*Hydro*	*Thermal*	*Nuclear*	*Total*
1969-70	43.50	53.52	2.98	100
1975-76	42.07	54.75	3.18	100
1980-81	39.02	58.13	2.85	100
1985-86	33.08	64.08	2.84	100
1990-91	28.38	69.25	2.37	100
1995-96	25.20	72.10	2.70	100

*Author's Calculation.

Source: *(i)* CEA (1994) "Public Electricity Supply – All India Statistics- General Review-1992-93" – New Delhi, p. 6and7

(ii) Power Finance Corporation Ltd. (1997) "Power Sector Reforms" New Delhi, p. 27.

Experts are not categorical about an ideal ratio of the mix. But some maintain that the optimal mix between Hydro and Thermal in Indian condition is something like 40:60. The declining trend in the hydropower capacity would possibly be due to the following reasons. The time and cost over runs are unduly high as compared to thermal and hence SEBs evince greater interest in the case of the latter which are easy to start up and generate. Further people's resistance to hydel projects is also quite formidable, as the construction of dams would cause destruction of forests, submergence of land under water and often-ecological imbalances.

The current trend in favour of thermal stations based on diesel, gas or naphtha and against hydel stations may portend certain ominous trends. As the major inputs like diesel and naphtha are largely imported, the fluctuations in the international market would render the functioning of thermal plants highly volatile and uncertain. Further the environmental problems in the form of Co, Co_2, So_2 and No_x emitted from thermal stations have already become a major concern, as these toxic substances contributed to global warming and green house effect. In the increasing switch over to thermal stations, we are also losing sight of some of the patent benefits of hydel stations. A pronounced advantage of hydel stations is that giant turbines can be switched on or off at momentary notice, unlike in the case of thermal and nuclear stations. In India, many of the hydel stations are generally operated as peaking stations. The peak load shortage (this problem will be taken up for discussion shortly) experienced across the country could be partly explained in terms of the tardy growth of the installed capacity in the hydro sector.

Power Generation

Power generation is directly dependent on installed capacity. However the two variables need not always move commensurately as variations can occur in generation depending upon changes in input availability, (Water in the case of hydel power, coal, gas or diesel, in the case of thermal), plant load factor[18] and plant availability factor**.

** Plant Availability Factor (PAF)= % of hours the plant is in operation in a year

Power generation from all sources increased by 61582 million units or by 1206% between 1950 and 1974. During this period the growth of generation from hydel projects lagged behind that from thermal stations as could be seen from the table 3.11.

Table 3.11: Growth of power generation (MU) (1950 to 92/97)

Plan Periods	Hydro	Thermal	Nuclear	Total
1950	2519.17	2586.93	0.00	5107
First Plan (1951-56)	3742.24 (48.55)	4850.21 (87.48)	0.00	8592 (68.24)
Second Plan (1956-61)	7836.58 (109.41)	9100.43 (87-63)	0.00	16937 (97.13)
Third Plan (1961-66)	15224.67 (94.28)	17765.15 (95.22)	0.00	32990 (94.78)
Annual Plans (1966-69)	20722.67 (36.1)	26710.98 (50.36)	0.00	47434 (43.78)
Fourth Plan (1969-74)	28971.84 (39.8)	35320.83 (32.23)	2396.36	66689 (40.50)
Fifth Plan (1974-79)	47158.86 (62.77)	52593.12 (48.9)	2769.68 (15.61)	102523 (53.73)
Annual Plan (1979-80)	45477.55 (-3.56)	56273.12 (7.0)	2876.59 (3.84)	104627 (2.05)
Sixth Plan (1980-85)	53948.25 (18.62)	98836.3 (75.6)	4074.83 (41.64)	1568.59 (150.0)
Seventh Plan (1985-90)	62116.09 (15.1)	178696.45 (80.87)	4625.38 (13.49)	245438 (56.47)
Annual Plans (1990-92)	72757.09 (17.13)	208747.1 (16.82)	5524.4 (19.4)	287029 (16.95)
Eighth Plan (1992-97)	72513.0 (-0.34)	299606.0 (43.53)	7965.0 (44.19)	380084 (32.42)

Note: Figures in brackets indicate the percentage increase over the previous period.

Source: *(i)* CEA (1994) "Public Electricity Supply – All India Statistics – General Review 92/93" – New Delhi, p. 8-9.

(ii) CEA (1997) "Electric Supply Industry, Salient Data – 1997/98" – New Delhi, p. 68.

Generation from the thermal stations increased faster than the growth in their installed capacity, (see Table 3.7) whereas the trends in hydel stations are the other way. It implies that the operational efficiency of thermal plants has increased and that of the hydel plants have decreased between 1950 and 1974. During the Second phase beginning with fifth five-year plan and extending over the eighth plan, the trend observed in the first five year plan was repeated with minor changes. During this phase as noted earlier, nuclear generation also set in and has been increasing at a rate faster than hydel power, but slower than thermal. The growth of hydel power generation during certain years of this period became even negative. We have attempted to compute the trends of power generation using the semilog linear equation of the form: $\text{InY}=\beta 1+\beta 2\ X_t+U_t$. This model is specifically fitted to determine the annual compounded rate of growth of power generation for two cases, - Case-I from 1950-51 to 1996/97 (47 Years), and the case-II, from 1969-70 to 1996/97 (28 Years). The significance of these two cases has already been explained elsewhere.

The rate of growth of power generation worked out using the semi log linear regression equation for the two cases are shown in Table 3.12 and 3.13. During the entire plan period (1950 to 1996-97) the annual rate of growth of hydro generation is 7.84%. However in the second case, the annual rate of growth of hydro generation is 4.34% only. It implies that from fourth five-year plan onwards, generation from hydro stations is comparatively slower than the first phase of generation upto fourth five-year plan. Moreover we observe that the compound rate of growth of hydro installed capacity and hydro generation are almost equal (7.79 and 7.85). But during the second phase, the growth rate of hydel capacity is comparatively higher than that of hydro generation (5.20 and 4.34). The rate of growth of hydro generation is less than half of that of thermal power (See table 3.13). The annual rate of growth of nuclear capacity is a little more than that of the rate of growth of nuclear generation (6.73 and 6.20). There is an annual increase 9.79% of power generation from all sources in the economy during the entire plan period. This rate of increase is higher than that of total installed capacity in both case-I and case-II (Refer Table 3.8 and 3.9).

As power generation depends on installed capacity, it may be useful to workout gneration elasticity with respect to installed capacity. This elasticity has been worked out for different power sources fitting the log linear regression model of the form: InYt=b1+b2 InXt+Ut where

Y_t = power generation;

β_1 and β_2 = Parameters;

X_t = installed capacity

Elasticity coefficient for the alternative situations are given under:

The value of the coefficient, β2 measure the elasticity of power generation with respect to installed capacity, i.e. the percentage change in power generation for a percentage change in installed capacity. Generation elasticity for hydel source is 0.93; for thermal 1.11; and for the sector as a whole 1.06 (See Table 3.14). In the case-II, the elasticity coefficient for hydro is 0.84, for thermal 1.08, for nuclear 0.90 and for the sector as a whole, 1.03. (Refer Table 3.15.) Thus hydel, thermal and total generation follow the same pattern as in case-I, of course with marginal differences.

Table 3.12: Trends in power generation using semilog linear model—Case-I

Variables	Constant	Coefficient	R^2	P. Value	Cases	Growth Rate
Hydro	8.1658 (0.091756)* (88.99)+	0.075589 (0.003328)* (22.71)+	0.92	0.0000	47 Years	7.85
Thermal	7.9723 (0.03570)* (223.29)+	0.10201 (0.001295)* (78.77)+	0.99	0.0000	47 Years	10.74
Total	8.7108 (0.051228)* (170.04)+	0.09344 (0.001852)* (50.29)+	0.98	0.0000	47 Years	9.79

*= Standard Error, += Student's T.

Table 3.13: Trends in power generation using semilog linear model—Case-II

Variables	Constant	Coefficient	R^2	P. Value	Cases	Growth Rate
Hydro	10.127 (0.044048)* (229.71)+	0.042512 (0.002656)* (16.01)+	0.91	0.0000	28 Years	4.34
Nuclear	7.2772 (0.085347)* (85.27)+	0.060186 (0.0051419)* (11.71)+	0.84	0.0000	28 Years	9.82
Thermal	10.034 (0.030511)* (328.86)+	0.093649 (0.001838)* (50.95)+	0.99	0.0000	28 Years	6.20
Total	10.753 (0.02005)* (536.33)+	0.076241 (0.001208)* (63.12)+	0.99	0.0000	28 Years	7.92

*= Standard Error, += Student's T.

Table 3.14: Elasticity coefficient of generation – Case–I

Variables	Constant	Coefficient	R^2	P. Value	Case-I
Hydro	1.8926 (0.10292)* (18.39)+	0.9364 (0.011815)* (79.25)+	0.993	0.0000	47 Years
Thermal	0.25227 (0.12356)* (2.04)+	1.1130 (0.013401)* (83.06)+	0.994	0.0000	47 Years
Total	0.77042 (0.08198)* (9.40)+	1.0563 (0.008438)* (125.18)+	0.997	0.0000	47 Years

*= Standard Error, += Student's T, All Significant at 5% level.

Table 3.15: Elasticity coefficient of generation—Case–II

Variables	Constant	Coefficient	R^2	P. Value	Case-II
Hydro	2.8152 (0.39750)* (7.08)+	0.8398 (0.042067)* (19.96)+	0.94	0.0000	28 Years
Thermal	0.60554 (0.20593)* (2.94)+	1.0769 (0.020509)* (52.51)+	0.99	0.0000	28 Years
Nuclear	1.9213 (0.56549)* (3.40)+	0.90113 (0.081567)* (11.05)+	0.83	0.0000	28 Years
Total Generation	1.0334 (0.18728)* (5.52)+	1.0304 (0.017807)* (57.90)+	0.99	0.0000	28 Years

*= Standard Error, += Student's T, All Significant at 5% level.

Energy Productivity [MU/MW]

Juxtaposing generation and capacity figures, the efficiency of the power sector can be gauged. The efficiency figures worked out for the 3 power sources are given in Table 3.16. Efficiency of energy productivity of

Table 3.16: Trends in operational efficiency of power plants (kWh/kW)

Plan Periods	Hydel	Thermal	Nuclear	Total	PLF*
1950	4504 (51.41)	2243 (25.61)	0	2982	34.04
First Plan (1951-56)	3983 (45.46)	2763 (31.54)	0	3188	36.39
Second Plan (1956-61)	4089 (46.68)	3326 (37.97)	0	3640	41.55
Third Plan (1961-66)	3692 (42.15)	3623 (41.36)	0	3654	41.17
Annual Plan (1966-69)	3508 (40.05)	3789 (43.25)	0	3661	41.79
Fourth Plan (1969-74)	4159 (47.48)	3899 (44.51)	3744 (42.74)	4002	45.68
Fifth Plan (1974-79)	4353 (49.69)	3459 (39.49)	4338 (49.52)	3842	43.86
Annual Plan (1979-80)	3995 (45.61)	3426 (39.11)	4495 (51.31)	3678	41.99
Sixth Plan (1980-85)	3731 (42.59)	3657 (41.75)	3721 (42.48)	3683	42.04
Seventh Plan (1985-90)	3393 (38.73)	4083 (46.61)	2956 (33.74)	3857	44.03
Annual Plans (1990-92)	3791 (43.28)	4341 (49.55)	3095 (35.33)	4156	47.44
Eighth Plan (1992-97)	3325 (37.96)	4823 (55.06)	3480 (40.87)	4412	50.37

*Author's Calculation

Note: Figures in bracket indicates the PLF of each Power Source.

*= Average Plant load factor.

Source: (i) CEA (1994) "Public Electricity Supply – All India Statistics- General Review-1992-93" – New Delhi, p. 6 and 7.

(ii) Power Finance Corporation Ltd. (1997) "Power Sector Reforms" New Delhi, p. 27.

the thermal stations has been steadily increasing during the entire period. Such a trend is not observable in the case of hydel stations. Hydel stations recorded highest productivity rates during the fourth and fifth five year plan periods and has been showing a general declining tendency since then.

Nuclear stations recorded high and increasing productivity rates during their initial periods (Fourth and fifth five-year plans) and have been showing a fluctuating trend in the ensuing years. We shall now advance certain plausible explanations for the observed trend in favour of thermal power stations.

Most important reason for this trend is technical. The performance efficiency of a power station (irrespective of the nature of source) depends primarily on plant load factor. A generating station is said to operate at 100% efficiency if the plant load factor is 100%. However 100% efficiency is only a theoretical possibility, as in the real world power generation depends on several factors. Especially the hydro power stations are not able to achieve a plant load factor of 100; as hydel power generation depends on (i) availability of sufficient quantities of water, (ii) planned maintenance shut down, (iii) reserve shut down (iv) forced outages and (v) evacuation of surplus power. In countries like India, the normal situation in the case of hydro station is a plant load factor of 60% and generation forecast is made assuming this norm.*

On the other hand thermal stations are free to a large extent from several such constrains, as they

---

* Central Electricity Authority works out energy demand based on 60% PLF. For details see "Infrastructure Report", Ministry of Finance, Government of India, 1996.

require lesser maintenance days and can be operated round the cloth. Obviously the plant load factor of thermal plants is well above the hydro stations (See Table 3.16). Due to these obvious advantages a pronounced tendency to shift to thermal station is observable all over the country. The movement in favour of thermal stations seems to have accelerated in the wake of the technological improvements in the thermal sector. For instance till 1969, all the thermal sets imported into the country were in 30 to 60 MW[19] range. During the last few years, Bharath Heavy Electricals Limited (BHEL) started producing thermal sets much bigger in size and capacity, ranging from 250 to 500 MW. Consequently the thermal plant load factor has jumped up from 40% in the earlier years[20] to almost 80%[21] at present. Further developments in thermal technology, such as fluidized bed combustion technology and integrated combined cycle power plants, appear to have further contributed to efficiency by increasing the plant load factor, leading, in turn to higher power generation. There are regional differences with regard to PLF. The PLF in Southern region (These five regions, as classified by the CEA for the better co-ordination of Indian power system) is 76.6% while the Western region, it was 69.7% and in Northern region 67.1%. The Eastern region is adversely affected because of the difficulties in evacuating surplus power. (The PLF of North-Eastern region is also relatively lower).

Another determinant of efficiency is the plant availability factor[22]. PAF refers to the percentage of days a plant is operational in a year. The average PAF in Indian conditions works out to 76.6%[23]. If the maintenance days, reserve shut down, forced outages etc. can be reduced to the minimum PAF can be enhanced. In the case of hydel generating stations, this is technically near impossible due to the reasons already explained. In the case of thermal plants this factor is relatively more favourable. Thus both plant load factor and the plant availability factor are favorable for the thermal sector and hence the shift.

Power Consumption

Power is demanded for consumption by domestic, commercial, industrial and agricultural sectors and for the use of traction, public lighting and public water works. On the eve of planning (1950) the energy demand in the country remained at 4157 million units, which increased to 280637 million units by the end of Eighth Five Year Plan recording an increase of 276480 units during the entire plan periods. The highest percentage increase in consumption took place in the agricultural sector, followed by the domestic sector (refer Table 3.17). A casual glance at the table shows that the pattern of consumption demands for power appears to have changed over the plan period. Coming to the domestic sector the highest increase in consumption demand occurred during the 6th and 7th five-year plans (84.5% and 90.8% respectively).

Energy demand by the commercial sector registered a hefty increase (94.64%) during the second five-year plan, but in the subsequent plans the rate of increase continued to decline almost steadily. Energy consumption by the industrial sector having increased by 104% and 96.95% during the second and third five year plan respectively, tended to show declining rates of increase during the successive plan periods. In the case of agriculture the rate of increase in power consumption during the second plan period was phenomenal (226.9%). Very high rates of increase were noticed during the fifty (103.2%) and seventh (110.2%) plan also.

Table 3.17: Trends in Energy Consumption (Million Units) during the plan periods—Category wise (1950 to 1995-96)

Periods	Domestic	Commercial	Industrial	Traction	Agriculture	Others	Total
1	2	3	4	5	6	7	8
1950	524	309	2604	308	162	249	4157
First Plan (1951-56)	850 (16.2)	514 (66.6)	4698 (80.4)	403 (30.8)	255 (57.6)	390 (56.6)	7111 (71.1)
Second Plan (1956-61)	1492 (75.5)	484 (64.8)	9584 (104.0)	454 (12.6)	833 (226.9)	629 (61.3)	13840 (94.6)
Third Plan (1961-66)	2355 (57.8)	1650 (94.6)	18876 (97.0)	1057 (132.8)	1892 (127.1)	905 (43.9)	26735 (93.2)
Annual Plans (1966-69)	3184 (35.2)	2126 (28.8)	25891 (33.0)	1247 (18.0)	3465 (83.9)	1439 (59.0)	37352 (39.7)
Fourth Plan (1969-74)	4645 (45.9)	2988 (40.5)	32481 (25.4)	1531 (22.8)	5918 (70.8)	2004 (39.3)	50246 (34.5)
Fifth Plan (1974-79)	7576 (63.1)	4331 (45.0)	47728 (46.9)	2186 (42.8)	12028 (103.2)	3446 (72.0)	77293 (53.8)

Table 3.17: Contd...

1	2	3	4	5	6	7	8
Annual Plan (1979-80)	8402 (10.9)	4657 (7.5)	45956 (-3.7)	2301 (5.3)	13452 (11.8)	3316 (-3.9)	78084 (1.02)
Sixth Plan (1980-85)	15506 (84.5)	6937 (49)	63019 (37.1)	2880 (25.2)	20960 (55.8)	4765 (43.7)	114068 (46.1)
Seventh Plan (1985-90)	29577 (90.8)	9548 (37.6)	80694 (28.1)	4070 (24.4)	44056 (110.2)	7474 (57.1)	175419 (53.8)
Annual Plans (1990-92)	35854 (21.2)	12032 (26.0)	87289 (8.2)	4520 (11.1)	58557 (32.9)	9374 (25.42)	207645 (18.4)
Eighth Plan (1992-97) (4 Years)	49431 (37.9)	12925 (7.4)	99609 (14.1)	5955 (31.7)	81802 (40.0)	30915 (229.8)	280637 (35.2)
Average % Change.	53.18	42.53	42.77	32.50	83.65	62.56	49.22

Note: Figures in brackets show the percentage increase of consumption.

Source: (*i*) CEA "Public Electricity Supply – All India Statistics General Review", 1992/93. P. 10 and 11.

(*ii*) CEA "Electricity Supply Industry Salient Data – 1997. P. 65 to 68.

Plan wise analysis of power consumption by the industrial sector indicates that during the first three five year plans all the major consumption sectors had recorded very high rates of energy consumption increase. Such a break through in power consumption doesn't seems to have occurred at any stage in subsequent planning. The average percentage increase of energy consumption is the highest (83.64%) in the agricultural sector. The category "Others" (Public lighting, public waterworks and Miscellaneous consumption) show a relatively higher rate of average percentage increase (62.56%), on account of some duplication contained in the energy statistics pertaining to this sector for the year 1996.97. The average percentage increase during the entire plan period was 53.17% for the domestic sector. There is an average increase of 49.2% of the power consumption in the country over the entire plan periods. Thus analysis of average percentage increase of energy consumption substantiates that the energy demand in the agricultural and domestic sectors is relatively higher.

We shall now attempt to work out annual rate of growth of energy demand by different categories of consumers for the period 1950-1996-97. This is done by fitting the un-weighted least square semilog linear regression equation. The annual growth rates presented in the Table 3.18 reinforce our earlier observations regarding the trends in energy consumption by major sectors. The aggregate demand for energy increased at an annual rate of 9% during the last half a century of planning. The higher growth rate over the plan period (15%) was recorded by the agricultural sector (Refer Table 3.18). The domestic demand for power grew at an annual rate of 10.5%. The commercial demand for energy (8.74%) increased at a rate marginally higher than that for industrial purposes (8%).

Table 3.18: Growth of energy consumption during the plan period (1950-1996-97)

Variables	Constant	Coefficient	R^2	P. Value	Cases	Growth Rate
Domestic	6.1619 (0.00080)* (278.61)+	0.09962 (0.00080)* (124.17)+	0.99	0.0000	47 Years	10.48
Commercial	5.8579 (0.05098)* (114.91)+	0.08379 (0.001849)* (124.17)+	0.98	0.0000	47 Years	8.74
Industrial**	8.3056 (0.08312)* (99.93)+	0.07697 (0.003015)* (25.53)+	0.94	0.0000	47 Years	8.00
Agriculture	5.1438 (0.06361)* (80.86)+	0.14021 (0.002307)* (60.77)+	0.99	0.0000	47 Years	15.05
Traction	5.6787 (0.9601)* (59.15)+	0.06508 (0.003483)* (18.69)+	0.89	0.0000	47 Years	6.72
Total	8.5363 (0.14436)* (59.13)+	0.08586 (0.005237)* (16.40)+	0.86	0.0000	47 Years	8.97

* = Standard Error. += Student's T.

** = The category "Industrial includes both Low Tension and Medium Tension and high Tension and Extra High Tension industrial consumers. The CEA adds together the energy consumption of these sub groups and that the trends in the rate of group of industrial sector consists of all these sub groups.

Analysis of Sector wise Consumption

The differential growth rates of energy consumption by individual sectors are reflected in changes in the relative shares of individual sectors in power consumption. Between 1950 and 1997, the relative shares of power consumption by the domestic sector increased from 12.62% to 17.61%. The share of energy consumption by the agricultural sector jumped from 3.89% to 29.15% during the entire plan period. The share of industry on the other hand showed a sharp decline from 62.64% to 35.49%. Commercial sector also suffered a decline from 7.43% to 4.60% during the corresponding period (See Table 3.19).

From the Table it could be found that the relative share of the industrial sector reached the highest figure of 70% during the third five-year plan, after which it tended to decline continuously. The share of agriculture remained below 10% till the fourth five-year plan period, but has been steadily increasing, so much so that by the end of 8th Plan, the share of agricultural consumption reached 29%. The very high share of agricultural consumption has serious financial implications. Power tariff for agricultural purpose is highly subsidized in all states (In certain states like Tamil Nadu, the tariff is virtually nil). This is said to be one of the major reasons for the heavy financial loss incurred by several SEBs in the country.

There are concrete reasons for the differential trends in the power consumption by individual sectors. The very high increase in power consumption by the agricultural sector is largely due to green revolution and technological developments. The improvement in the economic position of the agriculturists in the wake of green revolution enabled them to purchase modern

Table 3.19: Trends in the relative share of power consumption (%) 1950-1996/97

Plan Periods	Domestic	Commercial	Industrial	Traction	Agriculture	Others	Total
1950	12.62	7.43	62.64	7.42	3.89	6.0	100
First Plan (1951-56)	11.96	7.23	66.07	5.67	3.58	5.48	100
Second Plan (1956-61)	10.78	6.13	69.25	3.28	6.01	4.55	100
Third Plan (1961-66)	8.80	6.17	70.60	3.95	7.10	3.38	100
Fourth Plan (1969-74)	9.24	5.95	64.60	3.10	11.78	3.99	100
Fifth Plan (1974-79)	9.80	5.60	61.75	2.82	15.56	4.46	100
Sixth Plan (1980-85)	13.59	6.08	55.25	2.52	18.38	4.18	100
Seventh Plan (1985-90)	16.86	5.40	46.00	2.32	25.11	4.26	100
Eighth Plan (1992-97)	17.61	4.60	35.49	2.12	29.15	10.97	100

*Author's Calculation.

Source: 1. CEA (1994) Public Electricity Supply- All India Statistics, General Review-1992/93" p. 10-11.
2. CEA (1997) "Electricity Supply Industry- Salient Data" pp. 65 to 68.

agricultural implements and inputs. The rural electrification policy pursued by the power ministry for a long time particularly favored the agriculturists, as they were given priority in connections and allowed concessions in installation charges and power tariffs. Naturally this enhanced the accessibility to as well as the demand for power by the agricultural sector. In addition to this there is an accounting factor for the hefty increase in agricultural consumption. Normally the State Electricity Boards include under the category of agricultural consumption, those energy units, which cannot be accounted in any other head. Another plausible reason for higher energy consumption in the agricultural sector is the heavy transmission loss, which occurs when power lines are extended to remote villages without sufficient substations and transformers. Thus there are economic, accounting and technical factors for the big rise in the share of power consumption by the agricultural sector.

The decline in the relative share of energy consumption by the industrial sector could be explained partly in terms of the changes in the industrial structure. Generally bulk demand for power arises from heavy and basic industries, fertilizer and heavy engineering units. The growth of this category of industries slowed down after the third five-year plan. The industries, which came up in the ensuing years, were less power intensive.

A proximate reason for the declining share of the industrial sector could be sought in the power system unreliability and inadequacy. EHT and HT units in the whole of India (with the exception of eastern region) have been facing severe power and energy cut due to system's inadequacy to meet peak load demand. Added to it are the power interruptions. Frequent power failures and low voltage cause equipment damage and breakdown of machines. With a view to protecting against such eventualities, many of the industrialists have setup their own captive power plants (ranging 1 to 5 MW). Normally power generated from those captive plants are not metered, though technically, it will have to be added along with the grid consumption. The power consumption data provided by the SEBs is thus incomplete. Under the present situation one is led to presume that the higher the decline in the relative share of energy consumption from the main gird by the industrial sector, the greater the increase in the energy generation from captive power plants.

The reason for the increase in the share of the domestic sector includes increase in per capita income, living standards and urbanization[24]. Studies relating to pattern of usage of different energy carriers have convincingly concluded that households prefer electricity as the most convenient form of energy[25]. Under these circumstances a shift in favour of domestic consumption is understandable.

Demand Elasticities

Having examined the differential trends in consumption by individual sub-sectors, it may be worthwhile to estimate the elasticity of power demand by these sub groups. We shall confine the estimate to three-sub groups namely domestic sector, industries and agriculture. The explanatory variables considered for the domestic sector are per capita income at constant price and population. For the industrial sector the independent variable is gross value added in manufacturing, mining and quarrying at constant prices. Similarly we have taken gross value added in the agricultural sector as the explanatory variable pertaining to the agricultural sector. Time series data for 45 years (1950 to 1994-94) are considered for the analysis. Demand elasticities worked out for the three sectors on the basis of log linear regression equation are presented in the Table 3.20 along with the necessary details.

In the case of all the 3 sectors the independent variables considered are able to explain more than 90% of the changes in the dependent variables. All elasticity coefficients pertaining to the three sectors are positive. In the case of domestic sector the income elasticity is higher than the population elasticity, which means that it is the increase in income which exerts greater influence on domestic consumption of power than population growth.

The elasticity coefficient of the industrial sector is 1.5, which means that 1-% increase in industrial output would lead to 1.5-% increase in industrial energy consumption. In the agricultural sector the value of elasticity coefficient is 5.45. It suggests that 1-% increase in agricultural output lead to 5.45% increase in power consumption by agricultural sector. The explanatory variables considered as determining the total consumption of power in this study are per capita income at constant prices as well as population. The elasticity coefficient works out to 3.09 with respect to population and 0.68 with respect to per capita income. Obviously population is a more important determinant than per capita income. These two determinants are able to explain 99% of the variation in the total demand for electrical energy.

Sector wise Per capita Consumption, Consumers and Connected Load

In order to get better insight into the trends in the total energy consumption, it is necessary to look into

Table 3.20: Sector wise Demand Elasticities

	Constant	Coefficient	Coefficient	R^2	F. Value	P. Value	Case	Durbin Watson
Domestic	-25.853 (0.72874)* (-35.48)+	+2.092 (population) (0.10947)* (16.11)+	+2.9065 (per capita income) (0.18040)* (19.11)+	0.99	4947	0.000	45 Years	1.27
Industrial	-4.6630 (0.58333)* (-7.99)+	+1.5119@ (0.05962)* (25.36)+	-	0.94	643.1	0.0000	45 Years	-
Agriculture	-48.789 (2.2597)* (-21.59)+	+5.4458# (0.215113)* (25.31)+	-	0.94	640.8	0.0000	45 Years	-
Total	-13.568 (0.64644)* (-20.99)+	+3.0934 (population) (0.09711)* (31.86)+	+0.6836 (per capita income) (0.16003)* (4.27)+	0.99	5300	0.0000	45 Years	0.46

Significant at 5% level, *= Standard Error. += Student's T.
@= (Value added in mining manufacturing and quarrying) at constant price.
#= (Value added in agriculture sector) at constant price.

changes in per capita consumption, number of consumers and connected load. The per capita consumption of power in India still remains one of the lowest in the world[26] (319 units). However the per capita consumption has increased impressively during the post plan period (from 15.6 units in 1950-51 to 319 units in 1994-95). The changes in per capita consumption, sector wise and total are shown in the Table 3.22. Between 1970-71 and 93-94, the total per capita consumption increased to 233%. Considering sector-wise, the highest increase appears to have occurred in agricultural sector (144%). The consumption by the industrial sector is found to have declined absolutely (39%). What is more distressing is that the decline in industrial consumption started right from the seventies. Consumption for domestic purposes recorded an increase of 64%, whereas commercial consumption showed a decline of 7.4% during 1970-71-1993-94 period. Per capita consumption of "others" has increased by 69.51% during the period under review.

During the period 1970-71 to 1993-94 the total number of consumers in the country went up from 14665 thousands to 82312.0 thousand in 1993 i.e. increase of 461% between 1970-71 and 1993-94. The Table given below shows the increase in the number of various categories of consumers during the period 1970-71 to 1993-94. The Table indicates that the number of agriculture consumers rose faster (535%) than the rest of the consumers. The lowest increase occurred in the number of commercial consumers (299%) and that of industrial consumers (331%). The category "others" (consists of public lighting, public water works, traction and Miscellaneous) has risen to 645% during the years between 1970-71 to 1993-94.

Connected load is considered as the basis of energy consumption since the units of energy consumption

Table 3.21: Trends in per capita energy consumption – kWh (Sector wise)—1970/71-1993/94

Consumers	1970-71	1975-76*	1980-81	1985-86	1990-91	1993-94	1970-71 to 1993-94 (% change)
Domestic	378	396 (4.76)	414 (4.6)	514 (24.2)	635 (23.6)	621 (-2.20)	64
Commercial	1116	1069 (-4.2)	1022 (-4.4)	1189 (16.3)	1397 (17.5)	1033 (26.06)	-7
Industrial	55464	48631 (-11.8)	41799 (-14.0)	41422 (-0.90)	40543 (2.12)	33849 (16.5)	-39
Agricultural	2846	3135 (10.2)	3423 (9.2)	3862 (12.8)	5830 (50.95)	6956 (19.3)	144
Others	23488	18468 (-21.4)	13447 (-27.2)	4570 (-66.0)	16032 (251)	39814 (148)	70
Per capita Consumption	89.80	109.95 (22.4)	132.34 (20.4)	177.98 (34.5)	252.77 (42.02)	299 (18.3)	233

*= Average value of 1970-71 and 1980-81

Note: Figures in brackets show the percentage changes.

Sources: (i) CEA: All India Statistics 1992/93. New Delhi, p. 11and12.

(ii) TERI: "TEDDY- 1996-97" – New Delhi, p. 122.

Table 3.22: Trends in the growth of consumers (in thousands) (Sector wise) 1970/71-1993/94

Consumers	1970-71	1975-76*	1980-81	1985-86	1990-91	1993-94	1970-71 to 1993-94 (% change)
Domestic	10165.2	16251.4 (59.8)	22337.6 (37.5)	33569.3 (50.3)	50389 (50.1)	6.193.3 (19.5)	492
Commercial	2305.7	3443.9 (49.4)	4582.1 (33.1)	6130.8 (33.8)	8002.1 (30.5)	9209.2 (15.08)	299
Industrial	542.3	846.15 (56.0)	1260.0 (48.9)	1617.2 (28.3)	2077 (28.4)	2337.1 (12.5)	331
Agricultural	1570.9	2901.85 (84.7)	4232.8 (45.9)	6064.6 (43.3)	8631.0 (42.3)	9971.1 (15.5)	535
Others	80.8	174.8 (116.3)	268.8 (53.8)	1087 (304.4)	533.4 (-30.9)	601.6 (12.8)	645
Total	14665	23618.1 (61.05)	32571.3 (37.9)	48468.9 (48.8)	69632.8 (43.7)	82312 (18.2)	461

*= Average of 1970-71 and 1980-81.

Note: Figures in bracket show the percentage changes.

Sources: TERI: TEDDY 1996-97 New Delhi, p. 122.

depend upon connected load and the number of hours current is utilised. Assuming average hours of current consumption as constant, an increase in connected load implies an increase in energy consumption. Table 3.23 gives the changes in the connected load of the various categories of consumers.

The very large increase observed in the connected load of domestic and commercial sectors have serious consequence in view of the fact that energy consumption by these two sectors are mainly responsible for the peak load shortages experienced by the power system all over the country. It also points to the scope for energy conservation through energy efficient lighting and fixtures in these two sectors as a part of energy management. Similarly the very high increase in the connected load of agricultural sector has serious economic implications. The power tariff for agricultural consumption in almost all states are nil or nominal and such huge subsidies in the face of ever growing power consumption have landed the State electricity Boards in progressive financial deficit.

Demand Supply Deficit

From the foregoing discussion relating to demand and supply factors of power, we have found that the demand for energy increased at an annual rate of 8.9%, whereas the supply (generation) of power increased at the rate of 9.6% per annum during 1950-1996-97. Available evidences show that the problem of power shortage has remained persistent after the turn of the eighties and the problem has become worse over time. In Table 3.24 is given the demand and supply position of power capacity and energy generation from mid eighties till the mid nineties. The deficit in energy has increased on an average from 18 billion units during 1985-1990 to 26 billion units during 1991-1996.

Table 3.23: Trends in the rate of growth of connected load (MW) 1970/71- 1993/94

Consumers	1970-71	1975-76*	1980-81	1985-86	1990-91	1993-94	1970-71 to 1993-94 (% change)
Domestic	5985.9	9532.3 (59.2)	13078.6 (37.2)	21218.5 (62.0)	32051.2 (51)	4925.5 (54)	723
Commercial	1911	3202.5 (67.6)	4494 (40.32)	6071.8 (35.0)	8340.8 (37.0)	11799.9 (48.0)	517
Industrial	10944.2	17894 (63.5)	24844 (45.2)	34209.3 (26.0)	42946.7 (9.4)	52438 (11.65)	379
Agricultural	6224.8	11357 (82.45)	16489.2 (45.2)	22605 (37.0)	32511.5 (44.0)	38556 (19.0)	519
Others	1164.30	1828.5 (57.04)	2492.7 (36.3)	3841.7 (54.1)	5051.0 (31.48)	6893.8 (36.48)	492
Total Connected Load	26230.2	43814.3 (67.0)	61398.3 (40.1)	87946.5 (43.0)	120901.2 (37.0)	158942.7 (31.0)	506

*= Average of 1970-71 and 1980-81.

Note: Figures in bracket show the percentage changes.

Source: TERI: TEDDY·1996-97 New Delhi, p. 122.

Table 3.24: All India demand and supply of electricity—1985-95

	Power			Energy		
Year	Power Demand (Peak) (MW)	Power Supply (Available) (MW)	Deficit (MW)	Energy Demand Peak (BU)	Energy Supply (BU)	Deficit (BU)
1985-86	30908	27033	3875 (12.5)	170.7	157.3	13.4 (7.9)
1986-87	33132	29206	3926 (11.8)	192.4	174.3	18.1 (9.4)
1987-88	35681	31933	3748 (10.5)	211.0	188.0	23.0 (10.9)
1988-89	39354	34822	4532 (11.5)	223.2	205.9	17.3 (7.8)
1989-90	41902	35175	6727 (16.1)	247.8	228.8	19.6 (7.9)
1990-91	44005	37171	6834 (15.5)	267.6	246.4	21.0 (7.8)
1991-92	48035	39520	8515 (17.7)	289.0	266.4	22.6 (7.8)
1992-93	52805	41948	10821 (20.5)	278.0	254.6	23.4 (8.4)
1993-94	54875	44830	10045 (18.3)	323.3	299.5	23.8 (7.4)
1994-95	57530	48066	9464 (16.5)	352.3	327.3	25.0 (7.0)
1995-96	60981	49836	11145 (18.3)	389.7	354.1	35.6 (9.1)

BU= Bullion Units

Note: Figures in bracket show the percentage of deficit

Source: *(i)* Centre for monitoring Indian Economy (1995) "Current Energy Scene in India" June, Mumbai. CMIE.

(ii) EPW. Vol. XXXII No 3. August '97. Mumbai, p. 96

(iii) Ministry of Power (1996) "Annual Report 1995-96". New Delhi, p. 11.

Table explains that the power capacity deficiency has increased from 12.5% to 18.3% during 1985-95 period. Likewise energy shortage has increased from 7.9% to 9.1% during the same period. These figures point to the fact that inspite of an increase in power capacity over the years; the rate of deficit could not be brought down.

A close scrutiny further shows that the problem of power deficit is widespread problem, which has afflicted all the states in India (Refer Table 3.25). The recent studies carried out show that future demand for energy is likely to grow at rapid rate. For example the estimates of 14th Electric Power Survey by the Central Electricity Authority shows that Electricity demand will grow at an annual rate of 8.3% during 1993-2002 A.D[27]. To meet this requirement, according to some studies, the additional installed capacity has to be raised from 90,000 to 1,63,000MW during the next 15 years[28]. However with Demand Side Management (DSM) option it would be possible to bring down the figure to 1,23,000MW.

The power deficit that has been persisting in the country is not merely due to insufficient installed capacity addition, but the outcome of a combination of factors which include (1) High transmission and distribution loss, (2) Energy inefficiency, (3) Low plant load factor and (4) Inadequate investment in power sector, due to the poor financial position of SEBs.

Transmission network is said to be the artery of a power system. Poor transmission and distribution network has the risk of frequent tripping, transformer burning, melting of conductors' short circuits etc. all of which would result in system failure. Indian power system is notorious for its high T and D loss (see Table 2.6). On an average 23%[29] of energy is lost between

Table 3.25: State-wise power requirement, supply and deficit surplus: 1991/92 to 1994/95

State	Peak (megawatts)				Energy (million kilowatt hours)			
	1991/92	1992/93	1993/94	1994/95	1991/92	1992/93	1993/94	1994/95
1	*2*	*3*	*4*	*5*	*6*	*7*	*8*	*9*
NORTHERN REGION								
Haryana								
Requirement	1,820.0	1,930.0	2,000.0	2,000.0	10,326.0	11,340.0	11,745.0	11,695.0
Availability	1,452.0	1,625.0	1,808.0	1,925.0	10,123.0	11,079.0	10,640.0	11,139.0
Surplus (+)/Deficit (–)	-368.0	-305.0	-192.0	-75.0	-203.0	-261.0	-1,105.0	-556.0
Surplus (+)/Deficit (–) (per cent)	-20.2	-15.8	-9.6	-3.8	-2.0	-2.3	-9.4	-4.8
Himachal Pradesh								
Requirement	365.0	390.0	410.0	440.0	1,456.0	1,531.0	1,616.0	1,842.0
Availability	285.0	310.0	365.0	440.0	1,446.0	1,531.0	1,619.0	1,842.0
Surplus (+)/Deficit (–)	-80.0	-80.0	-45.0	0.0	-10.0	0.0	0.0	0.0
Surplus (+)/Deficit (–) (per cent)	-21.9	-20.5	-11.0	0.0	-0.7	0.0	0.0	0.0

(Table Conte...)

Table 3.25: Contd...

1	*2*	*3*	*4*	*5*	*6*	*7*	*8*	*9*
Chandigarh								
Requirement	120.0	135.0	140.0	140.0	657.0	628.0	676.0	729.0
Availability	101.0	102.0	135.0	140.0	657.0	628.0	676.0	724.0
Surplus (+)/Deficit (–)	-19.0	-33.0	-5.0	0.0	0.0	0.0	0.0	-5.0
Surplus (+)/Deficit (–) (per cent)	-15.8	-24.4	-3.6	0.0	0.0	0.0	0.0	-0.7
Delhi								
Requirement	1,640.0	1,840.0	1,850.0	1,850.0	9,347.0	10,158.0	11,045.0	12,205.0
Availability	1,509.0	1,549.0	1,603.0	1,846.0	9,255.0	10,098.0	10,884.0	12,076.0
Surplus (+)/Deficit (–)	-131.0	-291.0	-247.0	-4.0	-92.0	-60.0	-161.0	-129.0
Surplus (+)/Deficit (–) (per cent)	-8.0	-15.8	-13.4	-0.2	-1.0	-0.6	-1.5	-1.1
Jammu and Kashmir								
Requirement	725.0	820.0	825.0	825.0	3,345.0	3,640.0	3,700.0	4,045.0
Availability	498.0	482.0	491.0	600.0	2,984.0	2,932.0	2,971.0	3,296.0
Surplus (+)/Deficit (–)	-227.0	-338.0	-334.0	-225.0	-361.0	-708.0	-729.0	-749.0
Surplus (+)/Deficit (–) (per cent)	-31.3	-41.2	-40.5	-27.3	-10.8	-19.5	-19.7	-18.5
Punjab								
Requirement	3,285.0	3,520.0	3,550.0	4,000.0	17,238.0	18,165.0	18,780.0	20,035.0
Availability	2,919.0	3,026.0	3,153.0	3,463.0	16,177.0*	17,506.0	18,181.0	19,259.0
Surplus (+)/Deficit (–)	-366.0	-494.0	-397.0	-537.0	-1,061.0	-659.0	-599.0	-776.0
Surplus (+)/Deficit (–) (per cent)	-11.1	-14.0	-11.2	-13.4	-6.2	-3.6	-3.2	-3.9

Table 3.25: Contd...

1	2	3	4	5	6	7	8	9
Rajasthan								
Requirement	2,100.0	2,300.0	2,550.0	2,660.0	13,220.0	14,317.0	16,070.0	17,000.0
Availability	1,979.0	2,228.0	2,425.0	2,412.0	13,030.0	14,081.0	15,089.0	16,080.0
Surplus (+)/Deficit (–)	-121.0	-72.0	-125.0	-248.0	-190.0	-236.0	-981.0	-920.0
Surplus (+)/Deficit (–) (per cent)	-5.8	-3.1	-4.9	-9.3	-1.4	-1.6	-6.1	-5.4
Uttar Pradesh								
Requirement	5,750.0	6,520.0	6,550.0	6,550.0	31,540.0	32,415.0	33,735.0	37,195.0
Availability	4,725.0	4,715.0	4,993.0	5,042.0	28,280.0	29,118.0	30,476.0	32,652.0
Surplus (+)/Deficit (–)	-1,025.0	-1,805.0	-1,557.0	-1,508.0	-3,260.0	-3,297.0	-3,259.0	-4,543.0
Surplus (+)/Deficit (–) (per cent)	-17.8	-27.7	-23.8	-23.0	-10.3	-10.2	-9.7	-12.2
NORTHERN REGION								
Requirement	14,390.0	15,765.0	15,860.0	16,950.0	87,129.0	92,194.0	97,370.0	104,746.0
Availability	11,935.0	13,381.0	12,793.0	14,290.0	81,954.0	86,973.0	90,536.0	97,068.0
Surplus (+)/Deficit (–)	-2,455.0	-2,384.0	-3,067.0	-2,660.0	-5,177.0	-5,221.0	-6,834.0	-7,678.0
Surplus (+)/Deficit (–) (per cent)	-17.1	-15.1	-19.3	-15.7	-5.9	-5.7	-7.0	-7.3

(Table Conte...)

Table 3.25: Contd...

1	*2*	*3*	*4*	*5*	*6*	*7*	*8*	*9*
WESTERN REGION								
Gujarat								
Requirement	4,365.0	4,835.0	4,980.0	5,410.0	25,505.0	26,500.0	29,860.0	31,985.0
Availability	3,568.0	3,907.0	4,327.0	4,734.0	24,417.0	25,712.0	28,502.0	30,678.0
Surplus (+)/Deficit (–)	-797.0	-928.0	-653.0	-676.0	-1,088.0	-788.0	-1,358.0	-1,307.0
Surplus (+)/Deficit (–) (per cent)	-18.3	-19.2	-13.1	-12.5	-4.3	-3.0	-4.5	-4.1
Madhya Pradesh								
Requirement	3,665.0	4,085.0	4,360.0	5,080.0	21,115.0	22,439.0	23,945.0	27,840.0
Availability	2,885.0	3,134.0	3,695.0	3,970.0	19,942.0	20,675.0	22,791.0	25,805.0
Surplus (+)/Deficit (–)	-780.0	-951.0	-665.0	-1,110.0	-1,173.0	-1,764.0	-1,154.0	-2,035.0
Surplus (+)/Deficit (–) (per cent)	-21.3	-23.3	-15.3	-21.9	-5.6	-7.9	-4.8	-7.3
Maharashtra								
Requirement	68,630.0	7,420.0	7,800.0	8,310.0	42,070.0	43,970.0	44,895.0	49,525.0
Availability	6,235.0	6,385.0	7,014.0	7,357.0	40,166.0	41,387.0	43,514.0	48,558.0
Surplus (+)/Deficit (–)	-595.0	-1,035.0	-786.0	-953.0	-1,904.0	-2,583.0	-1,381.0	-967.0
Surplus (+)/Deficit (–) (per cent)	-8.7	-13.9	-10.1	-11.5	-4.5	-5.9	-3.1	-2.0
Goa								
Requirement	145.0	155.0	165.0	166.0	683.0	776.0	876.0	965.0
Availability	135.0	155.0	162.0	166.0	683.0	776.0	873.0	965.0
Surplus (+)/Deficit (–)	-10.0	0.0	-3.0	0.0	0.0	0.0	-3.0	0.0
Surplus (+)/Deficit (–) (per cent)	-6.9	0.0	-1.8	0.0	0.0	0.0	-0.3	0.0

Table 3.25: Contd...

1	2	3	4	5	6	7	8	9
WESTERN REGION								
Requirement	14,460.0	15,880.0	16,810.0	18,235.0	89,373.0	93,685.0	99,576.0	110,315.0
Availability	12,675.0	13,822.0	14,748.0	15,601.0	85,208.0	88,550.0	95,680.0	106,006.0
Surplus (+)/Deficit (–)	-1,785.0	-2,058.0	-2,062.0	-2,634.0	-4,165.0	-5,135.0	-3,896.0	-4,309.0
Surplus (+)/Deficit (–) (per cent)	-12.3	-13.0	-12.3	-14.4	-4.7	-5.5	-3.9	-3.9
NORTH-EASTERN REGION								
Arunachal Pradesh								
Requirement	44.0	53.0	54.0	55.0	0.0	161.0	157.0	157.5
Availability	32.0	33.0	29.0	36.0	0.0	111.0	107.3	118.4
Surplus (+)/Deficit (–)	-12.0	-20.0	-25.0	-19.0	0.0	-50.0	-49.7	-39.1
Surplus (+)/Deficit (–) (per cent)	-27.3	-37.7	-46.3	-34.5	0.0	-31.0	-31.7	-24.8
Assam								
Requirement	420.0	466.0	486.0	500.0	0.0	2,424.0	2,368.0	2,437.1
Availability	357.0	365.0	275.0	345.0	0.0	2,040.0	2,098.3	2,231.3
Surplus (+)/Deficit (–)	-63.0	-101.0	-211.0	-155.0	0.0	-384.0	-269.7	-205.8
Surplus (+)/Deficit (–) (per cent)	-15.0	-21.7	-43.4	-31.0	0.0	-15.8	-11.4	-8.4
Manipur								
Requirement	66.0	73.0	74.0	75.0	0.0	290.0	298.4	337.2
Availability	66.0	73.0	70.0	59.0	0.0	258.0	285.1	287.0
Surplus (+)/Deficit (–)	0.0	0.0	-4.0	-16.0	0.0	-32.0	-13.3	-50.2
Surplus (+)/Deficit (–) (per cent)	0.0	0.0	-5.4	-21.3	0.0	-11.2	-4.5	-14.9

(Table Conte...)

Table 3.25: Contd...

1	2	3	4	5	6	7	8	9
Meghalaya								
Requirement	68.0	69.0	79.0	79.0	0.0	289.0	304.4	342.8
Availability	68.0	69.0	79.0	79.0	0.0	283.0	304.4	342.8
Surplus (+)/Deficit (–)	0.0	0.0	0.0	0.0	0.0	-6.0	0.0	0.0
Surplus (+)/Deficit (–) (per cent)	0.0	0.0	0.0	0.0	0.0	-2.0	0.0	0.0
Mizoram								
Requirement	38.0	39.0	41.0	43.0	0.0	104.0	115.2	139.5
Availability	38.0	36.0	41.0	31.0	0.0	87.0	109.9	122.9
Surplus (+)/Deficit (–)	0.0	-3.0	0.0	-12.0	0.0	-17.0	-5.3	-16.6
Surplus (+)/Deficit (–) (per cent)	-0.0	-7.7	0.0	-27.9	0.0	-16.2	-4.6	-11.9
Nagaland								
Requirement	31.0	30.0	32.0	33.0	0.0	143.0	144.9	136.7
Availability	26.0	29.0	27.0	26.0	0.0	121.0	136.6	116.7
Surplus (+)/Deficit (–)	-5.0	-1.0	-5.0	-7.0	0.0	-22.0	-8.3	-20.0
Surplus (+)/Deficit (–) (per cent)	-16.1	-3.3	-15.6	-21.2	0.0	-15.4	-5.7	-14.6
Tripura								
Requirement	61.0	66.0	73.0	82.0	0.0	276.0	273.1	311.2
Availability	41.0	54.0	47.0	45.0	0.0	231.0	245.4	271.9
Surplus (+)/Deficit (–)	-20.0	-12.0	-26.0	-37.0	0.0	-45.0	-27.7	-39.3
Surplus (+)/Deficit (–) (per cent)	-32.8	-18.2	-35.6	-45.1	0.0	-16.3	-10.1	-12.6

Table 3.25: Contd...

1	2	3	4	5	6	7	8	9
NORTH-EASTERN REGION								
Requirement	695.0	740.0	805.0	840.0	3,382.0	3,687.0	3,661.0	3,862.0
Availability	484.0	633.0	542.0	620.0	3,083.0	3,132.0	3,287.0	3,491.0
Surplus (+)/Deficit (–)	-211.0	-107.0	-263.0	-220.0	-299.0	-555.0	-374.0	-371.0
Surplus (+)/Deficit (–) (per cent)	-30.4	-14.5	-32.7	-26.2	-8.8	-15.1	-10.2	-9.6
All India								
Requirement	48,055.0	52,805.0	54,875.0	57,530.0	288,974.0	305,266.0	323,252.0	352,260.0
Availability	39,027.0	41,984.0	44,830.0	48,066.0	266,432.0	279,824.0	299,494.0	327,281.0
Surplus (+)/Deficit (–)	-9,028.0	-10,821.0	-10,045.0	-9,464.0	-22,542.0	-25,442.0	-23,758.0	-24,979.0
Surplus (+)/Deficit (–) (per cent)	-18.8	-20.5	-18.3	-16.5	-7.8	-8.3	-7.3	-7.1
SOUTHERN REGION								
Andhra Pradesh								
Requirement	4,160.0	4,690.0	4,800.0	5,100.0	24,015.0	26,085.0	28,180.0	31,245.0
Availability	3,504.0	3,693.0	3,836.0	4,177.0	22,415.0	24,281.0	26,924.0	28,757.0
Surplus (+)/Deficit (–)	-656.0	-997.0	-964.0	-923.0	-1,600.0	-1,804.0	-1,256.0	-2,488.0
Surplus (+)/Deficit (–) (per cent)	-15.8	-21.3	-20.1	-18.1	-6.7	-6.9	-4.5	-8.0

(Table Conte...)

Table 3.25: Contd...

1	2	3	4	5	6	7	8	9
Karnataka								
Requirement	3,730.0	4,080.0	4,150.0	4,200.0	20,350.0	21,665.0	22,070.0	23,280.0
Availability	2,668.0	2,635.0	2,910.0	3,325.0	15,550.0	16,050.0	17,235.0	19,280.0
Surplus (+)/Deficit (–)	-1,062.0	-1,445.0	-1,240.0	-965.0	-4,800.0	-5,615.0	-4,835.0	-4,000.0
Surplus (+)/Deficit (–) (per cent)	-28.5	-35.4	-29.9	-23.0	-23.6	-25.9	-21.9	-17.2
Kerala								
Requirement	1,575.0	1,700.0	1,750.0	1,760.0	7,440.0	7,700.0	7,990.0	8,902.0
Availability	1,286.0	1,362.0	1,403.0	1,594.0	7,197.0	7,416.0	7,836.0	8,831.0
Surplus (+)/Deficit (–)	-289.0	-338.0	-347.0	-66.0	-243.0	-284.0	-154.0	-71.0
Surplus (+)/Deficit (–) (per cent)	-18.3	-19.9	-19.8	-9.4	-3.3	-3.7	-1.9	-0.8
Tamil Nadu								
Requirement	4,100.0	4,550.0	4,650.0	5,000.0	23,210.0	24,490.0	26,495.0	29,570.0
Availability	3,417.0	3,541.0	3,778.0	4,145.0	22,086.0	24,060.0	25,466.0	28,730.0
Surplus (+)/Deficit (–)	-683.0	-1,009.0	-872.0	-855.0	-1,124.0	-430.0	-1,029.0	-840.0
Surplus (+)/Deficit (–) (per cent)	-16.7	-22.2	-18.8	-17.1	-4.8	-1.8	-3.9	-2.8

Table 3.25: Contd...

1	*2*	*3*	*4*	*5*	*6*	*7*	*8*	*9*
SOUTHERN REGION								
Requirement	12,880.0	14,260.0	14,495.0	15,130.0	75,015.0	79,940.0	84,735.0	92,997.0
Availability	10,280.0	10,651.0	11,340.0	12,335.0	67,248.0	71,807.0	77,461.0	85,598.0
Surplus (+)/Deficit (–)	-2,600.0	-3,609.0	-3,155.0	-2,795.0	-7,767.0	-8,133.0	-7,274.0	-7,399.0
Surplus (+)/Deficit (–) (per cent)	-20.2	-25.3	-21.8	-18.5	-10.4	-10.2	-8.6	-8.0
EASTERN REGION								
Bihar								
Requirement	1,395.0	1,545.0	1,555.0	1,675.0	7,415.0	8,220.0	8,645.0	9,410.0
Availability	785.0	778.0	778.0	1,028.0	5,215.0	5,243.0	5,583.0	6,295.0
Surplus (+)/Deficit (–)	-610.0	-767.0	-777.0	-647.0	-2,200.0	-2,977.0	-3,062.0	-3,115.0
Surplus (+)/Deficit (–) (per cent)	-43.7	-49.6	-50.0	-38.6	-29.7	-36.2	-35.4	-33.1
West Bengal								
Requirement	2,265.0	2,490.0	2,600.0	2,670.0	11,140.0	11,835.0	12,695.0	13,540.0
Availability	1,558.0	1,572.0	2,100.0	2,313.0	10,140.0	11,196.0	12,056.0	12,708.0
Surplus (+)/Deficit (–)	-707.0	-918.0	-500.0	-357.0	-1,000.0	-639.0	-639.0	-832.0
Surplus (+)/Deficit (–) (per cent)	-31.2	-36.9	-19.2	-13.4	-9.0	-5.4	-5.0	-6.1

(Table Conte...)

Table 3.25: Contd...

1	*2*	*3*	*4*	*5*	*6*	*7*	*8*	*9*
Damodar Valley Corporation								
Requirement	1,435.0	1,500.0	1,500.0	1,520.0	7,455.0	7,495.0	7,730.0	7,970.0
Availability	883.0	890.0	1,014.0	1,030.0	6,087.0	5,767.0	6,982.0	7,392.0
Surplus (+)/Deficit (–)	-552.0	-610.0	-486.0	-490.0	-1,368.0	-1,728.0	-748.0	-578.0
Surplus (+)/Deficit (–) (per cent)	-38.5	-40.7	-32.4	-32.2	-18.4	-23.1	-9.7	-9.3
Orissa								
Requirement	1,575.0	1,760.0	1,850.0	1,875.0	8,065.0	8,210.0	8,840.0	9,420.0
Availability	1,199.0	1,078.0	1,160.0	1,480.0	7,499.0	7,156.0	7,909.0	8,723.0
Surplus (+)/Deficit (–)	-376.0	-682.0	-690.0	-395.0	-566.0	-1,054.0	-931.0	-697.0
Surplus (+)/Deficit (–) (per cent)	-23.9	-38.8	-37.3	-21.1	-7.0	-12.8	-10.5	-7.4
EASTERN REGION								
Requirement	6,210.0	6,785.0	7,295.0	7,320.0	34,075.0	35,760.0	37,910.0	40,340.0
Availability	4,350.0	4,360.0	5,045.0	5,766.0	28,940.0	29,362.0	32,530.0	35,118.0
Surplus (+)/Deficit (–)	-1,860.0	-2,425.0	-2,250.0	-1,554.0	-5,134.0	-6,398.0	-5,380.0	-5,222.0
Surplus (+)/Deficit (–) (per cent)	-30.0	-35.7	-30.8	-21.2	-15.1	-17.9	-14.2	-12.9

*includes Pondicherry

Source: Centre for Monitoring Indian Economy Private Limited (CMIE). June 1994. Current Energy Scene in India. P. 51-53. Bombay: CMIE.

Table 3.26: State-wise transmission and distribution losses (in percentage) in state electricity boards and departments: 1980/81 to 1993/94

Region and State	Transmission and distribution losses including unaccounted commercial losses					
	1980/81	1985/86	1990/91	1991/92	1992/93	1993/94
North						
Haryana	22.6	20.1	27.5	26.8	26.8	25.0
Himachal Pradesh	19.3	22.4	21.0	19.2	20.0	18.8
Jammu and Kashmir	48.1	39.0	43.0	50.1	48.1	46.4
Punjab	19.6	18.3	19.3	21.8	19.6	19.7
Rajasthan	26.6	26.2	25.8	23.1	22.7	24.9
Uttar Pradesh	15.6	21.1	27.1	26.1	24.7	24.4
West						
Gujarat	19.8	25.1	23.4	23.6	22.2	20.8
Madhya Pradesh	22.3	19.6	18.0	25.8	22.5	21.8
Maharashtra	16.2	15.7	18.3	18.6	18.5	17.8
Goa	[?]	20.1¨	25.0	23.8	21.9	24.5
Daman and Diu	[?]	0.0	16.9	15.9	15.7	22.3

(Table Conte...)

Table 3.26: Contd...

South						
Andhra Pradesh	22.6	22.3	22.9	20.3	20.7	20.2
Karnataka	24.6	24.2	20.2	19.3	19.6	19.5
Kerala	14.9	25.8	22.4	22.5	22.8	20.5
Tamil Nadu	19.1	18.5	18.0	18.4	17.3	17.0
Lakshadweep	[?]	20.0	18.6	17.4	18.7	17.0
East						
Bihar	22.1	15.8	16.5	18.3	17.2	15.1
Orissa	19.2	24.0	25.8	25.3	25.9	23.1
Sikkim	[?]	[?]	24.5	25.9	22.6	22.6
West Bengal	13.7	19.3	17.7	19.7	17.5	16.0
North-east						
Assam	19.3	24.3	24.1	22.7	21.4	22.4
Manipur	[?]	51.5	28.0	24.4	22.4	23.9
Meghalaya	9.1	10.7	11.5	11.7	11.6	17.9
Nagaland	[?]	15.9	26.1	23.1	27.3	33.5
Tripura	[?]	30.5	29.6	32.0	30.6	30.5
Mizoram	[?]	43.7	29.6	34.9	29.0	31.9
Arunachal Pradesh	[?]	34.1	20.0	28.2	32.3	42.0
All India (utilities)	[?]	21.7	22.9	22.8	21.8	21.4

*the lower transmission and distribution losses in Meghalaya are due to bulk sale of energy at HT (high-tension) level to neighbouring states

**also included Daman and Diu

Source: Central Electricity Authority (CEA). 1995. Public Electricity Supply, All India Statistics, General Review, 1993/94, p. 117. New Delhi: CEA. 214 pp.

transmission and distribution. This figure is unacceptably high by international standards. (China loses only about 7%, Thailand about 10%, Argentina about 12%[30] and Korea below 8%). The World Bank standard is below 8%. The expert opinion is that the existing T and D loss can be reduced by 50%. In the year 1995-96 the average percentage of energy loss was 19% and the gross generation 379776MU[31] (loss=72157). A one-% reduction in T and D is supposed to add 722MU of electrical energy to the power system. For generating additional units of 722 MU and investment of nearly Rs. 5500 Million is required. *(722MU/5.256 (@60% PLF)= 137MW. 137MW □ Rs. 40 million/MW= 5500 Million.) Thus any investment below Rs. 550 Crores for T and D renovation would be cost effective if 1-% T and D loss could be thereby reduced. Power experts view investment in T&D renovation, as equivalent to investment in power generation sans environmental degradation. Inspite of its importance, the power authorities in India have been reluctant to make any worthwhile investment in this area.

Today there exists enormous scope for saving energy consumption through energy conservation and enhancement of energy efficiency[32]. The neglect of energy conservation aspect (through energy efficient methods) by the power planners, has, among other things, contributed to decline in energy efficiency. While in all the developed countries energy efficiency has been on the increase, during the post energy crisis period, in India it has been a steady decline (see Table 3.27).

---

*PLF = kWh × 100/kW × 8760

Assuming a PLF of 60% = $722 \times 10^6 \times 100/\text{kW} \times 8760$

kW = $722 \times 10^6 \times 100/60 \times 8760 \times 10^3$

MW@137

Table 3.27: Energy GDP relationship during the plan periods 1950-1996

Plan Periods	Energy Consumption (MU)	GDP (At constant Price) (Million Rupees)	GDP/Energy
1950	4157	428710	103.13
First Plan (1951-56)	7111	511730	71.96
Second Plan (1956-61)	13841	629040	45.45
Third Plan (1961-66)	26735	721220	26.98
Annual Plan (1966-69)	37352	808410	21.64
Fourth Plan (1969-74)	50246	951920	18.95
Fifth Plan (1974-79)	77293	1205040	15.59
Sixth Plan (1980-85)	114068	1504330	13.19
Seventh Plan (1985-90)	175419	2014530	11.48
Eighth Plan (1992-97) (4 Years)	265380	2742090	10.33

Source: *(i)* CEA. (1994) "Public Electricity Supply – All India Statistics – General Review 1992/93". New Delhi, p. 10and11.

(ii) Economic and Political Weekly Research Foundation (1997) "National Accounts Statistics of India- 1950-51 to 1995-96". Mumbai, p.7.

(iii) CEA. (1997) Electric Supply Industry – Salient Data. 1995-96". New Delhi, p. 73. Annexure 3.33.

GDP Energy Relationship

Gross domestic production (at constant prices) per unit of energy that remained at Rs. 103/- in 1950, declined to Rs. 16/- during the fifth plan and further down to Rs. 10/- at the end of the eighth five-year plan. To obtain a better insight into GDP – Energy relationship we worked out energy – GDP elasticity for the period 1951 to 1995-96, using log linear regression equation. The regression results are given below:

In GDP =	7.0439	+	0.41799	R^2=0.96
	(0.13683)*		(0.012810)*	P=0.0000
	(51.48)+		(32.63)+	Case=45 Years.

*= Standard Error, += Student's T, Significant at 5% level

The elasticity coefficient works out to 0.42, which is less than 1. (In China the energy elasticity coefficient is 0.56[33]). It means that one percentage increase in energy consumption has been able to contribute only 0.42% of GDP. It may be noted in this connection that in most of the advanced countries, a 1% increase in energy consumption contributed above 1% increase in GDP (Energy GDP Elasticity is greater than one). The low value of elasticity coefficient and the steady declining value of GDP energy ratio are eloquent evidences to the inefficiency of Indian power system.

Financial Status of State Electricity Boards (SEBs)

The State Electricity Boards in India by and large have been in the red for the past several years. Th net cumulative loss of all the State Electricity Boards in India stood at Rs. 16480 Million in 1984-85. It rose to Rs. 41160 Million in 1992-93[34] and further to 74200 Million in 1996-97[35].

The financial status (net profit and loss) on State Electricity Boards from 1984-85 to 1992-93 is given in Table 3.28. The trend shows that the net cumulative loss

Table 3.28: Financial Position of SEBs: 1984-1992 (Rs. in Crores)

State	Cumulative Profit/Loss Up to 1984-85	Net Commercial Profit/Loss During the Year							Cumulative Profit/Loss Upto 1992-93
		1985-86	86-87	87-88	88-89	89-90	90-91	91-92	92-93
Andhra Pradesh	76.3	14.3	9.0	29.3	16.8	2.5	81.0	161.5	314.4
Bihar	-129.2	-121.1	4.2	-25.7	-191.0	-247.7	-364.0	-57.8	-1003.1
Gujarat	7.8	-1.7	13.4	24.2	13.9	-203.4	-444.8	622.8	24.4
Haryana	-312.6	-61.5	-61.2	-80.9	-52.1	-56.8	-82.4	-550.1	-945.0
Himachal Pradesh	-93.1	-35.9	-40.8	-16.7	71.7	-5.9	6.1	-90.4	-111.8
Karnataka	135.6	-26.7	-74.5	-104.5	-50.6	-84.3	-132.4	313.6	-159.4
Kerala	7.6	-3.3	-4.9	-56.6	-14.3	-11.6	-51.8	2.9	-139.5
Madhya Pradesh	-50.8	65.0	94.4	45.6	80.0	76.2	-117.5	3.3	277.1
Maharashtra	-62.4	51.6	64.4	73.3	39.5	14.5	85.5	24.9	353.7
Orissa	-63.5	-10.2	-3.7	-45.6	-24.7	18.2	28.2	-27.0	-64.8
Punjab	-96.1	-6.4	-19.8	-5.0	-59.1	-57.8	-68.4	-93.4	-309.9
Rajasthan	-161.7	-45.5	-24.2	-65.9	-57.2	-147.8	-158.1	-185.1	-683.8
Tamil Nadu	90.4	27.9	31.0	N.A.	41.3	58.2	72.2	174.2	407.6
Uttar Pradesh	-603.9	-104.6	54.0	40.8	1.1	42.0	119.2	-546.8	-394.3
West Bengal	-187.3	-29.9	-8.2	-26.7	-38.8	-45.3	-102.6	-279.5	-531.0
Assam	-178.8	-59.8	-99.0	-96.5	-121.1	-227.7	-257.2	-274.9	-1131.3
Meghalaya	-26.1	-2.4	-0.5	-2.4	-1.5	1.1	-3.6	-17.3	-18.8
Total	-1647.8	-350.2	-97.5	-343.1	-870.6	-1390.6	-1390.6	-788.6	-4115.9

Source: TERI. (1995) "Tata Energy Data Directory and Year Book- 1994-95) p. 122.

of SEBs has been on the increase. The major reason for such huge loss is the subsidized tariff on agricultural and domestic consumption of power. The average tariff for agricultural energy consumption was 21 Paise kWh, that for domestic consumption paise 65/kWh, while overall tariff was Paise 83 kWh in 1992-93[36]. The average tariff for agricultural and domestic sectors increased to Paise 22/kWh and Paise 104/kWh respectively during 1996-97. The overall tariff during the year increased to Paise 158/kWh[37]

The agricultural sector accounted for one-third of total energy sales, but contributed only 4-5% of total revenue. Similarly the domestic sector accounted for nearly 18% of total energy sales, but contributed only 10-11% of the total revenue. The major sector that brings higher percentage of revenue is the industrial sector. But its percentage share of energy consumption has declined from above 50% to around 35%[38], thus causing heavy loss of revenue to the Indian Power System. The political inability to raise the price of power for domestic and agricultural sectors has contributed to the structural weakness of the power system[39]. Suggestion to introduce marginal cost pricing principles have been virtually disregarded. Apart from these facts, there has been heavy backlog of revenue collection due to the administrative inefficiency and political apathy. Thus the poor financial status of SEBs prevented them from investing in additional installed capacity and system improvement. Power investment is in effect decided by the States and the Centre, through budgetary allocations and World Bank loans[40].

Conclusion and Recent Policy Changes

The above analysis of the Indian power sector has shown that there existed several issues of concern. These issues are – (1) the impacts of fuel shift away from hydro source in favour of thermal source. (2) decline in the rate of growth of energy generation in the post 1978 period, (3) near stagnancy of energy productivity in hydel stations, (4) relatively low plant load factor of thermal stations (5) increasing share of energy consumption by the agricultural sector, (6) declining share of energy consumption by the industrial sector, (7) widening energy demand supply deficit, (8) rising commercial loss faced by all SEBs (9) increasing energy intensity, and (10) uneconomic pricing of power.

As these issues were chronic and persistent in Indian power system, Government of India, as part of liberalization launched several policies and programs to make the power system efficient and economical. The CEA admitted that the present tariff policy needs a thorough change, in favour of marginal cost pricing principle. In order to overcome the financial crunch, the Central government announced the policy of privatisation in the power sector. To smoothen the restructuring of SEBs, the Central government amended the Indian Electricity Act of 1948, thus allowing for privatisation in power generation, transmission, and distribution fields. The power policy has comprehensively covered the legal administrative and financial environment to make private investment attractive.

As SEBs are unpopular due to inefficiency and progressive commercial loss, Private Power Producers (IPPs) demand guaranteed return on investment. IPPs are basically power contractors, and therefore they are eligible to get a minimum rate of return. This implies that SEBs are obliged to pay for a negotiated minimum level whether they accept delivery of power or not. IPPs are willing to follow the tariff structure, which is essentially a cost plus return on equity (ROE) formula. All the costs of producing power, fixed and variable, along with the return on equity for the achieved plant load factor will be charged to the SEBs.

In order to co-ordinate the activities of both SEBs and IPPs the Expert Group on Power[41] presented a model for Indian power sector, in line with the Federal Energy Regulatory Commission (FERC) of the USA. The recommendations of the expert group are:-

- Restructuring of the power sector facilitating the inflow of domestic and international investment.
- Dismantling of SEBs in favour of private corporations in generation, transmission anddistribution areas.
- Tariff restructuring both at the Central and State level.
- Establishment of Central Electricity Regulatory Commission (CERC) a compact technical and co-ordinating Central authority, and Regional authorities for five regions.
- State governments should form State Electricity Regulatory Commission (SERC) on line with CERC.

As CERC and SERC will act as a semi judicial authority, all matters relating to electricity like tariff policy, licensing environmental issues etc will be heard and final decision will be taken.

All the recommendations of the EG have been implemented in the country. CERC has been formed with Mr. S.L. Rao as its founder Chairman. Three state governments have already formed SERC and many are in the processes of its formation. In state like Orissa and Andhra Pradesh SEBs have been restructured into independent corporations for generation, transmission and distribution.

It is too early to critically assess the impact of liberalization on the power sector of India. It is a fact that the existing tariff will be drastically changed. But the state governments may not be possible to enhance the power tariff to agricultural consumers, due to their strong political influence. As power sector grows, so also will grow the balance of payment issues due to the international fuel linkage and the hefty increase in investment by international power developers.

Notes and References

1. Handerson P.D., (1980) *"Energy Resources, Consumption and Supply in India"* in Sanil, V Know Land W.H, (ed.) "Energy in the Developing World" Oxford University Press. New York. p. 186.
2. CEA (1993) *"Public Electricity Supply – All India Statistics, General Review —1992-93"*. New Delhi. p. 2.
3. Ibid. p. 3.
4. According to the latest assessment, the total forest area in the economy is some 75 million hectors or 2/3 of the total land area. However in view of the over-riding importance of the firewood in the rural areas, this sector should receive topmost priority in formulating energy policy.
5. GSI Report *"Geological Survey of India" – 1992"*. New Delhi. Quoted in TERI's ECOMILES – 1995. New Delhi. p. 9.
6. TERI (1995) *"Environmental Considerations and Options and Options in Managing India's Long-term Energy Strategy"* (ECOMILES). p. 10.
7. Ibid. p. 10.
8. Ibid. p. 11.
9. Government of India, (1997) *"India Infrastructure Report—1997"*. Ministry of Finance, New Delhi.

10. Ibid. p. 81.
11. Ministry of Power (1997) *"Annual Report"* – 1995-96" New Delhi. p. 1.
12. Ibid. p. 1.
13. Ibid. p. 27.
14. Ibid. p. 27.
15. Ibid. p. 33 and 37.
16. Gujarati, N. Damodar (1995) *"Basic Econometrics"* Mc. Graw Hill Book Co., Singapore—1995. p. 166.
17. Gujarati, N. Damodar (1995) *"Basic Econometrics"* Mc. Graw Hill Co., Singapore p. 171.
18. Plant Load Factor (PLF)=kWh/kW×100÷8760. The maximum units that can be generated per kW[1]per year is 8760 kWh, at 100% PLF. For hydel stations, the maximum units to be generated is 5256 kWh/kW at 60% PLF.
19. Abbi. Y.P. and Ghosh A.K. (1997) "Clean Coal Technologies for Power Generation". In "Sustainable Energy Supply in Asia—Vol-I", Chaturvedi Pradeep (Ed) (1997) Concept Publishing Co., p. 61.
20. Power Line—August 1997. p. 27.
21. Power Line—July 1997. p. 26.
22. Plant Availability Factor (PAF)= The ratio of the days the power stations are in operation with the total days in a year.
23. Power Line- February 1997, p. 24.
24. Raikhy P.S. (1990) "Energy Consumption in India—Pattern and Determinants". Deep and Deep Publishing Co., New Delhi. p. 187.
25. Reddy B. Sudhakara (1992) *"Consumption Patter of the Metropolis of Bangalore"* –Ph.D. Thesis Indian Institute of Science –Bangalore.
26. Lefevre Thierry *"Evolution of Energy Efficiency Indicators in Asian Countries—A Comparative Study"* in Pradeep Chaturvedi (Ed) (1997) "Sustainable Energy Supply in Asia" World Energy Council. Concept Pub. Co., New Delhi, p. 45.
27. Joshi, M.D. and Vaja Daksha, *"Meeting energy needs through renewable: Can it meet the Socio-economic needs*

of 930 million Indians" in Chaudari Pradeep (Ed) "Sustainable energy supply in Asia", World Energy Council. Concept publishing Co. New Delhi. 1997. p. 192.

28. Power Line—December 1996. New Delhi. p. 55.
29. Tata Energy Research Institute. *"TEDDY—1994-95"*. New Delhi. 1995. p. 118.
30. Power Line. New Delhi. February, 1997. p. 10.
31. CEA: *"Electric Supply Industry, Salient Data"*. New Delhi. 1997. p. 73. (Annexure- 3.33).
32. Nadal Steven et. Al. *"Opportunities for Improving End Use Electricity Efficiency in India"*. EPPDP, 936-5228. International Development and Energy Associates. Inc. D.H.R. November 1991.
33. Xiang Zhang Zhong (1995). *"Energy Conservation in China —At International perspective"*—Energy Policy, Vol. 23, No. 22. pp. 159-166. Butter Worth Heinnemann. U.K.
34. CMIE *"Current Energy Scene in India"*—Mumbai. 1993. p. 114.
35. Power Line, July 1997, New Delhi. p. 26.
36. Planning Commission – *"Annual Report of the Working of State Electricity Boards and Electricity Departments"*— New Delhi. 1992
37. Godbole Mahadeve. *"Private Sector Generation—Unresolved Issues"* in EPW 2 – 1998. Mumbai p. 255.
38. Ibid. p. 225.
39. Morris Sebastian—*"Political Economy of Electric Power in India"* EPW. May 18th 1996. Mumbai. p. 1201.
40. Ranganathan. V. *"Electricity Privatisation Revisited—A Commentary on the Case of New Initiatives in India"* – energy Policy, Vol. 27. No. 29, ELSEVIER, U.K. 1996. p. 821.
41. Ministry of Finance *"India Infrastructure Report—1995-96"*, Government of India, New Delhi. p. 78.

4

The Power System of Kerala: Evolution and Growth

Introduction

Kerala, the Southern most tip of India, is situated between Arabian Sea and the Western Ghats. It is located in the North latitude between 8°12' and 12°48' and East longitude between 74°52' and 72°22'. The coastline is about 580 kilometers in length, while breadth of the state varies from 11 kilometers to 121 kilometers. The total area of the state is 38,864 square kilometers, which comes about 1.3% of the total area of the Indian Union. The region presently known as Kerala, prior to independence in 1947, consisted of three distinct entities- Travancore, Cochin, and Malabar, the first two being under the native kings of Travancore and Cochin respectively, and the latter under the direct British administration.

The genesis of power development in Kerala dates back to the first decade of the 20th century when a private business firm, Kannan Devan Hill Produce Company, installed a hydroelectric power plant with capacity of 200 kW in their tea estate at Munnar in the erstwhile Trvancore state[1]. Governmental efforts for power generation came for the first time when a small thermal station of 5 MW was opened in Trivandrum in 1929[2]. During the thirties small diesel generating stations were setup in the towns of Kottayam, Kollam, Kalamassery, Aluva and Nagarciol. In the Cochin State the Government of Cochin gave permission to the Cochin Power and Light Corporation to supply electricity to the towns of Ernakulam in 1935-36[3]. In the Malabar region the West Coast Electrical Power Company started diesel power stations at Calicut and Cannanore with a view to supply power to the British led Industrial units in these two localities.[4] The power generated till 1940s were mainly to cater to the requirements of Royal families and urban elites and only to a very limited extent to meet the requirements of street lighting and industrial use.

Growth of Power Projects

The commissioning of the Pallivasal Project in the district of Idukki in 1940 marked a new era in the development history of Kerala Power System. It was the first hydro electrical power project started on a commercial basis under state initiative in the year 1933[5]. Its first stage became operational in 1940 when the Swiss made Pelton Prime Mover generated 5 MW electricity from the project constructed in the reservoirs of Kundala and Mattupetty[6]. The commissioning of Pallivasal Project was a significant development. In its wake a number of large industrial units like Aluminum, Plywood and Fertilizers and Chemicals came to be established in various parts of the former Travancore State. The capacity of the project was subsequently raised to 15 MW by 1942 and further to 37.5 MW by 1951[7].

The second power station (Sengulam) started functioning in 1954 at Anayirinkal reservoir. Initially its capacity was fixed at 12 MW, which was later increased, to 48 MW in 1995. Sengulam was the first hydro electrical power project sanctioned and commissioned during the post independence period in Kerala as per the stipulations of Indian Electricity (supply) Act of 1948. Table 4.1 provides a bird's eye view of all hydel power projects taken up by the Government of Kerala during the post independence period. The table shows that till 1995-96, there existed 13 power generating stations, of which 11 were power stations, under Kerala State Electricity Board, one, a privately owned small hydro power station of 12 MW owned by M/s. Universal Carborandum Ltd. And a wind farm of 2 MW owned by K.S.E.B[8].

These stations varied widely in respect of installed capacity with the highest in Idukki Hydel Project (780 MW) and the lowest (2 MW) in the wind farm at Kanjikode. Among the power projects with a capacity of over 300 MW are the projects of Idukki and Sabarigiri. During the sixties 4 hydel projects with a capacity of 429 MW were commissioned. During the Seventies two hydel stations with a total capacity of 855 MW were completed.

During 1980s, however, only one project of 75MW could be commissioned. During a span of 11 years, between 1976 and 1987, not a single project was set up in the State. It may also be noted that after 1976, no major hydel power project (above 250 MW) could be set up in the State. Knowledgeable sources ascribe present power famine largely to the tardy growth in installed capacity since 1976.

The Table also indicates that Idukki project alone accounts for 51.8% of the total installed capacity and

Table 4.1: Growth of Power Stations in Kerala (1940-95)

Name of Power Station	Reservoirs	Year of Commissioning	Number of Generators and Capacity	Installed Capacity (MW)	Firm Power (MW)	Design Value of Generation (MU)
1	2	3	4	5	6	7
Pallivasal (Idukki)	Kundala and Matupetty	1940	3×5 3×7.5	37.5	32.5	284
Sengulam (Idukki)	Anayarinkal	1954	4×12	48	20.8	182
Poringalkuthu (Trichur)	Poringalkuthu	1957	4×8	32	19.6	170
Neriamangalam (Idukki)	Neriamangalam	1961	3×15	45	27.0	237
Panniar (Idukki)	Ponmudi	1963	2×15	30	17.0	158
Sabarigiri (Pathanamthitta)	Pamba and Kakki	1966	6×50	300	138.5	1338

Table 4.1: Contd...

1	*2*	*3*	*4*	*5*	*6*	*7*
Sholayar (Trichur)	Sholayar	1966	3×18	54	26.6	233
Kuttiadi (Wynad)	Kuttiadi	1972	3×25	75	28.0	268
Idukki (Idukki)	Idukki	1976	6×130	780	230	2398
Edamalayar (Ernakulam)	Edamalayar	1987	2×37.5	75	36.5	380
Kallada (Kollam)	Kallada	1994	2×7.5	15	6.05	65
Maniyar (Private) (Pathanamthitta)	Maniyar	1994	3×4	12	4.1	36
Kanjikode (Wind Farm) (Palakkad)	Kanjikode	1995	9×0.225	2.0	-	NA
Total				1505.5	586.65	5749

N.A= Not Available.
Source: KSEB (1997) "Power System Statistics 1995-96" p. 10.

41.7% of the design value of generation and 39.45% of total firm power. The firm power in this project is relatively low, as the hours of planned maintenance shut down and reserves shut down are relatively higher for this project[9].

At the time of the formulation of the State the firm power was of the order of 73 MW, which rose to 540 MW in 1976 and further to 587 MW in 1995. In the hydroelectric power generation it is the firm power, which is more relevant than the installed capacity in explaining the energy productivity of a generating system. Firm power capacity depends on factors like inflow of water into reservoir, efficiency of turbines and generators and evacuation of power from generating stations.

The design value, i.e. the maximum technically sustainable units of generation, remained at 636 MU at the time of formation of the state in 1957 (Refer Table 4.1). It increased to 5749 MU in 1995-96. However actual generation in 1995-96 exceeded the design value by 912 MU. The reason for the difference in actual generation and the design value of generation is that while designing the maximum units of generation, a 25% allowance (Margin) is considered. The maximum units that can be generated, given 60% plant load factor is 7913 MU[10], which has never been achieved in the state so far. Any increase in the generation higher than 5749 MU shows that the conditions for generation during that year are relatively favourable.

Analysis of Power System Variables (Supply side)

Growth of power system can be examined in terms of the changes in power system variables. Power system variables like installed capacity, generation, maximum system demand, maximum internal demand, energy sales, transmission loss, distribution lines, distribution of transformers, total number of consumers, connected load, average tariff revenue and expenditure and other variables are mutually interactive and inter-dependent. Therefore the study of Kerala Power System means the study of the trends in the growth of all these variables, which constitutes the supply side and demand side of the state power system. An attempt is thus made to study the trends in the rate of growth of these variables, with out which it is near impossible to analyze the key issues which the power system has been witnessing. The trends in the growth of power system variables on the supply side like the installed capacity, generation, internal maximum demand, the system maximum demand,** the magnitude of energy sales by the system, the T&D loss, length of distribution lines, and distribution transformers have been examined in the Table 4.2.

Installed Capacity

Installed capacity, which was 38 MW in 1951 steadily, rose to 1508.5 MW in 1996-97, i.e. an increase of 3970 points. During the first four five-year plans perceptible increases were recorded in the installed capacity, as could be learnt from the Table 4.1. During the fifth and sixth plan periods there was no increase in installed capacity (refer Table 4.2). During the eighth plan the system was able to add only 83-point increase in total installed capacity. Though installed capacity is the basic determinant of power generation; its rate of growth is not

** To work out the gap between IMD and SMD, the IMD is considered on the supply side. IMD is equal to maximum power supplied by the system from its own projects and power borrowed externally. Usually power supplied is equal to its demand, since power cannot be stored.

Table 4.2: Trends in the growth of installed capacity, demand, generation T&D loss, distribution lines, transformers and sales during the plan periods.

Plan Period*	Installed Capacity (MW)	Maximum Demand (Internal) (MW)	Maximum Demand (System) (MW)	Generation (MU)	Energy Sales (MU)	Total Energy Sales in the State (MU)	T&D Loss (MU)	Distribution Lines (CKtm)		Distribution Transformer (MVA) (Numbers)
								HT	LT	
1	*2*	*3*	*4*	*5*	*6*	*7*	*8*	*9*	*10*	*11*
1950	38 (100)	25 (100)	25 (100)	151 (100)	140 (100)	140 (100)	90 (100)	1067 (100)	992 (100)	324 (100)
First Plan	86 (226)	63 (252)	63 (252)	350 (232)	274 (196)	274 (196)	98 (109)	2802 (263)	3783 (381)	845 (261)
Second Plan	133 (350)	116 (464)	116 (464)	591 (391)	518 (370)	506 (361)	113.1 (126)	5549 (520)	8899 (897)	2998 (894)
Third Plan	193 (508)	174 (694)	174 (696)	842 (558)	750 (536)	750 (536)	190.3 (211)	6570 (616)	14189 (1430)	3930 (1213)
Annual Plans	547 (1439)	278 (1112)	353 (1412)	1923 (1274)	1336 (954)	1338 (956)	258.8 (288)	7241 (679)	16952 (1709)	4907 (1515)

Table 4.2: Contd...

1	*2*	*3*	*4*	*5*	*6*	*7*	*8*	*9*	*10*	*11*
Fourth Plan	622 (1637)	434 (1736)	500 (2000)	2510 (1662)	2121 (1515)	1806 (1290)	367.7 (409)	9645 (904)	25968 (2619)	8285 (2557)
Fifth Plan	622 (1637)	609	852 (3408)	2659 (1761)	4516 (2991)	2419 (1728)	649.7 (722)	12645 (1185)	42507 (4285)	10330 (3188)
Annual Plan	1012 (2663)	620 (2436)	854 (3416)	5119 (3990)	4318 (3084)	2384 (1703)	816.3 (907)	13348 (1251)	47606 (4799)	10821 (3340)
Sixth Plan	1012 (2663)	911 (3644)	939 (3756)	4885 (3235)	3705 (2646)	4940 (3529)	1233.92 (1371)	16317 (1529)	71259 (7183)	12597 (3888)
Seventh Plan	1477 (3887)	1270 (5080)	1171 (4684)	5071 (3361)	4794 (3424)	6144 (4389)	1349.68 (1500)	19127 (1793)	95938 (9671)	16394 (5060)
Annual Plan	1477 (3887)	1308 (5232)	1265 (5060)	5326 (3527)	5596 (3997)	7153 (5109)	1557.0 (1730)	25151.0 (2020)	108420 (10929)	18843 (5816)
Eighth Plan	1508.9 (3970)	1652 (6608)	1235 (4940)	5503 (3644)	7021 (5015)	9275 (6625)	1959.0 (2167)(P)	26000 (2437)(P)	140000 (14113)(P)	25100 (7747)(P)

Note: *The entries correspond to the terminal year of each plan period.
(i) Figures in brackets show the change in indices.
(ii) Energy sales = Sale of energy generated within the state.
(iii) Total energy sales = Sale of energy generated within the state plus energy imported from the central grid and from neighboring states.

Source: (i) KSEB "Power System Statistics" Various Issues.
(ii) Government of Kerala (1998) "Economic Review" 1997-98, Thiruvananthapuram.

in proportion to the changes in other variables, as it appears to be based mainly on governmental decision, which are influenced by non-economic factors.

Maximum Demand*

Energy literature distinguishes between two types of maximum demand, namely maximum demand (internal) and maximum demand (system)[11]. The former refers to the MD taking into consideration the peak load demand of the consumers. The latter refers to the MD that the power system in the state can meet during the peak hours (6.30 p.m. to 10 p.m.). From the table 4.2, it could be found that upto sixth plan, the system maximum demand exceeded the internal maximum demand. Thereafter the internal maximum demand tended to exceed the system MD. Power engineering principle explains that the system (Power system within the state) shall able to meet the internal maximum demand. In the context of Kerala, the system has been unable to meet the internal maximum demand from mid 1980s and therefore load management techniques like load shedding and power cut have been implemented to overcome persistent power shortages. The gap between system demand and internal maximum demand is made up through power imports.

Internal maximum demand in the state is based on the connected load and the time factor. Given the time factor, as connected load increases; the internal maximum demand also increases. To meet the increase in internal maximum demand, the installed capacity of the system should be increased at least 30% above the maximum

* Conventionally Maximum Demand (Peak Load Capacity) is considered as supply side variables in energy literature. We have also followed the same convention. The MD is the maximum capacity that can be supplied by the power system. However MD is determined by the demand side variables.

internal demand[12]. From the sixth five-year plan onwards the rise in capacity addition tend to lag behind the increase in internal maximum demand (Refer Table 4.2). Based on the official statistics, the desired level of installed capacity was to be 1184 MW, 1651 MW and 2146 MW respectively for the 6th, 7th and 8th five-year plan periods. An earlier important economic study[13] on the Kerala power system did not consider this point, since during the period under study the internal maximum demand was much less than the system maximum demand. Therefore internal maximum demand can be considered as one of the best determinants of the total installed capacity of the power system.

Some individual researchers have pointed out that the internal maximum demand would not be a true reflection of the power demand, since it does not reckon the choked demand due to low voltage and load shedding. Considering this point, the researchers have pointed out that the actual power demand would be 30% higher than the official figures.* So that the desired installed capacity figures would be 1539MW, 2146MW and 2790MW respectively during the corresponding plan periods[14]. Thus we find that the installed capacity remained well below the desired level for several years.

The quantitative relationship between installed capacity and maximum demand (System as well as internal) is verified by fitting linear regression of the form:

$$Y_T = \beta_2 + \beta_2 X_t + U_t$$

Where:

Y_t = Installed capacity

β_1 and β_2 = Parameters

X_t = Maximum demand (system as well as Internal)

1. Installed capacity =	40.645	+	1.1777 (System M.D)	R^2=0.97.
Standard Error	(28.119)		(0.03576)	
Student's T	(1.45)		(32.93)	
P= 0.000.	Case = 39 Years.			Significant at 5% level

The result shows that more than 90% of the variation in installed capacity is explained by maximum demand. It can be said that maximum demand (system) in Kerala Power system is a highly significant determinant of installed capacity. As per the results of regression, the installed power capacity has increased only 1.18 times the maximum system demand (System Peak Load).

The rate of increase of system maximum demand and internal maximum demand was equal upto 1967-68. After then, the system maximum demand was relatively higher than the internal maximum demand. This trend continued upto 1981-82. From 1982 onwards upto 1988, the trend in the rate of increase was almost equal for both system demand and internal maximum demand. It means that from 1982 onwards the power system was experiencing peak load power deficit. The power shortage was acute from 1988 onwards due to the fact that the internal maximum demands became higher than the system maximum demand. Internal maximum demand tended to exceed the total installed capacity of the State since 1994. In this context, we observed that the power system should have installed power capacity at least 30% higher than the maximum internal demand. The quantitative relationship between installed capacity and internal maximum demand worked out here reveals that the internal maximum demand shall be considered as a substitute for the installed capacity in the economy. The result of the quantitative relation (linear regression) is as under:

2. Installed capacity = 172.91 + 1.0024 (Internal Maximum Demand)

   Standard Error (42.324) (0.05250) R^2=0.91

   Student's T (4.09) (19.09)

   P= 0.000, Case = 39 Years Significant at 5% level.

The result shows that more than 90% of variation in installed capacity is explained by internal maximum demand. The value of B coefficient is 1.00, which explains that the internal maximum demand can reasonably be considered as a substitute for installed capacity.* The power shortage that has been experiencing in the state is due to the inability of the power system to and installed capacity at least 30% higher than the internal maximum demand, particularly from fifth five-year plan onwards.

Generation

Power generation depends on several variables like installed capacity, internal maximum demand, the load factor, availability of sufficient quantities of water, evacuation of power from the generating end. However, of all the factors affecting generation, installed capacity is the most crucial factor. It is true that as the internal maximum demand increases, the power system may try to enhance the volume of generation beyond the desired level of generation capacity. However for supplying adequate and qualitative power on a sustained basis, installed capacity has to increase paripassu with energy requirement.

Total energy generated by the Kerala Power system was 151 MU in 1950-51. The rates of increase in

---

* The coefficient is statistically significant at 5% level. The result further explains that if internal maximum demand increases by one unit, installed capacity should also increase by one unit.

generation during the first three 5 year plans and the annual plan (1966-69) were considerably higher than the succeeding Five-Year Plans. In the year 1979-80, there was a sudden increase of 3990 point of energy generation in the state, due to the increase in system demand and generating capacity was available due to the commissioning of Idukki hydel project. During the fifth, sixth, seventh and eighth five year plans, there was little or nominal increase in energy generation. During the fourth year of eighth five-year plan, (1995-96) energy generation registered an increase of 177 points over the previous annual plan (1990-92) due to the commissioning of Kallada power project in 1994. From the inception of the State of Kerala in 1957 to the present, energy generation increased from 441MU to 6662 MU in 1995-96, showing an increase of 3644 points (Refer Table 4.2). In the year 1996-97, energy generation has declined to 5503 MU.

Given the installed capacity, generation depends upon maximum system demand (Peak Load). When the maximum system demand increased, generation also increased correspondingly, taking into account, both technical and non-technical limitations. From 1987 onwards the internal maximum demand exceeded the system maximum demand and thus in recent years the influence of internal maximum demand (peak load demand) became dominant. The relationship between generation and maximum demand (system and internal) is examined by running linear regression equation and the result is as under.

1. Generation =	116.74	+	3.8254 (installed capacity)	R^2= 0.88
Standard Error	(219.03)		(0.22695)	
Student's T	(0.53)		(16.86).	
P = 0.0000,		Case = 39 Years.		Significant at 5% level.

2.	Generation =	740.06	+	3.9091 (Internal MD)	R^2= 0.85,
	Standard Error	(219.83)		(0.27272)	
	Student's T	(3.37)		(14.33).	
	P = 0.0000,	Case = 39 Years.			Significant at 5% level.
3.	Generation =	149.22	+	4.7056 (system MD)	R^2= 0.95,
	Standard Error	(143.13)		(0.18203)	
	Student's T	(1.04)		(25.85).	
	P = 0.0000,	Case = 39 Years.			Significant at 5% level.

The installed capacity, the system maximum demand and the internal maximum demand are significant determinants of power generation. But the system maximum demand is more significant determinant than the installed capacity and internal maximum demand as could be seen from the regression results (High R^2 value). Generation has by and large increased at the rate of 4.71 times the system maximum demand. But in relation to internal maximum demand, the generation increase has been 3.91 times only. Generation has increased at the rate of 3.83 times the installed capacity. The decline in the β coefficient value of maximum demand (internal) is due to relatively higher levels of internal maximum demand; but corresponding increase in generation could not be affected due to non-availability of adequate power capacity.* Therefore we may argue that the difference in the magnitude of the β coefficient is an indicator of energy shortage in the state's power system. The quantitative relationship between generation and its other determinants will be examined at length in chapter IV.

* Internal maximum demand is the true reflection of power demand, whereas system maximum demand is the ability of the system to meet the maximum demand. When the internal maximum demand exceeds system maximum demand, there will be import of energy as well, which normally is independent of internal energy generation.

Energy Sales

All the units generated by the system will not come for distribution. The power stations themselves consume energy for various purposes. This is known as auxiliary consumption. Thus energy sales in the economy is total generation minus auxiliary consumption minus energy loss. [Energy Sales = Generated energy – (Energy lost due to T&D loss) – (Auxiliary consumption)] Energy loss occurs during transmission and distribution of power from the generation point to the end consumers in various electrical equipment, conductors and components.

As internal maximum demand exceeds the system maximum demand, the power system is constrained to import energy from the central grid and from neighboring states. The total energy sales within the economy consist of energy available for sale plus the units of energy imported. The absolute value of energy imports has increased from 1000 MU in 1987-88 to 2400 MU in 1995-96. It shows the degree of dependency of Kerala Power System to deliver energy demanded by various categories of consumers.

Total energy sales in the state was 140 Million Units in 1950-51. It rose to 506 MU during the end of the second plan and further to 2380 MU during the end of the fifth plan. Energy sales within the state have increased to 9275 MU by the end of the 8th five-year plan period. During the first plan period the energy sales registered a very high increase (95.7%) but during the subsequent plan period's sales steadily declined recording an absolute decline of 1.45% during the seventh plan. Net imports began to influence Power sales markedly from the 6th five-year plan onwards, when the state began to experience acute power famine. The total imports of energy during the terminal years of sixth, seventh and eighth five year plans were respectively 79 MU, 1160 MU and 2642 MU. It means that imports[15] accounts for 2.13%, 24.19% and 35.62% of total sales during the 3 five year plan periods respectively.

T&D Loss

We have explained elsewhere that all units of energy generated are not available for consumption. There is energy loss when power is transmitted from generating station to the end user, which is known as T&D losses. There are technical and non-technical reasons for higher T&D loss in the State. The internationally acceptable level of T&D loss is roughly 8%, whereas in Kerala it is more than 20%. The absolute value of T&D loss has steadily increased overtime from 90 MU in 1950 to 1950 MU in 1996-97. (For plan –wise increases in T&D loss refer Table 4.4). The T&D loss in the state is segregated as[16],

1. Loss from generation voltage to main transmission voltage
2. From main transmission voltage to sub transmission voltage, and from
3. Sub transmission voltage to distribution voltage.

The poor status of the T&D network is mainly due to insufficient distribution lines and inadequate transformers[17]. Power generated has to be evacuated through proper lines. There is line loss in the form of overheated wires, due to insufficient capacity of wires to transmit current. The technical losses are due to the energy dissipation in the conductors and equipment's used for the transmission and distribution of power due to their inherent characteristics[18].

Distribution Lines

Transmission loss has been on the increase due to insufficient HT and LT lines. The circuit kilometer of HT lines in 1950 was 1067, which increased to 26000 circuit kilometers in 1967-97, i.e. an increase of 2430 percentage. The rate of increase of HT lines during the plan period has become relatively lower in fourth and fifth five-year plan periods.

Low voltage distribution lines are also equally important to deliver power properly. Between 1950 and 1996-97, the circuit kilometers of LT lines increased to 14113 points. The indices of the rate of increase of LT lines show that during the second, third, fifth and sixth plan periods, the rate of increase were relatively higher. The distribution efficiency of power system depends to a great extend on LT lines as they are mainly distribution lines. In Kerala, power is distributed through lengthy distribution lines, which are in many cases far away from transformer[19]. Power experts[20] point out that the ideal ratio between HT and LT is 1:1[21]. Not only that the ideal ratio was never maintained in Kerala, but in recent years this ratio also has been becoming increasingly diverting from the ideal. The ratio of HT and LT lines in Kerala context is even higher than the all India average of 1:3[22] (See Table 4.3).

Table 4.3: Ratio of HT and LT Lines During the Plan Periods

1950	51-56	56-61	61-66	66-69	69-74	74-79	80-85	85-90	92-97
1:0.93	1:1.35	1:1.6	1:2.2	1:2.3	1:2.7	1:3.7	1:4.4	1:50	1:51.5

*Author's calculation.
Source: KSEB "Power System Statistics" Various Issues.

Kerala Power System has some how managed to maintain the all India ratio of 1:3 during the fourth plan period. However since then the ratio has been widening in the state. The implication of this feature is that the power system of the state is unable to maintain voltage level at the technically acceptable rate. The HT andLT lines are insufficient to deliver current ampere to the HT and LT distribution end. Studies conducted on practical distribution network reveals the effectiveness of HVDS (High Voltage Distribution System) where the HT line is taken nearer to the consumer end and small capacity transformers are installed which minimizes the length of LT lines[23]. Therefore to reduce peak power losses by 80% and energy losses by 70% from the existing level the circuit kilometers of HT lines are to be increased and the length of L.T. lines are to be reduced.

Transformers

Transmission and distribution lines are connected to transformers of varying capacities. The transformer capacities are different in substations and in HT and LT distribution centers. If the transformer capacity of substation is below the expected rate, there will be higher levels of energy loss and low voltage at the consumer end. Similarly if the transformers capacity is insufficient in the distribution centers, there will be higher levels of transformer loss and energy loss. Therefore a reliable power system should install sufficient quantities of transformers to maintain load balance. Electric engineering principles explain that there is a standard normal range of distance between substations, so also with transformers. This range is to be maintained to reduce power loss and to provide desired level of voltage at the tail end of distribution lines. However in the context of Kerala, the peak hours voltage level is about 20% of the rated voltage of 230 in the regions of Malabar.

There is steady increase of distribution transformers of million-volt ampere (MVA) in the state power system. The indices of distribution transformers have increased from 100 points in 1950 to 7747 points in 1996-97. However it is necessary to verify whether this much number of distribution transformers are sufficient to meet state's power distribution system. A general view in this regard is that even such a high number of distribution transformers are quite insufficient to dispatch better quality power due to the fact that there exists abysmally low level of voltage in the state. To examine this point further, the transformers per 1000 consumers and the number of transformers per Mega Watt of connected load are worked out as shown in Table 4.4.

Per capita transformer (Per 1000 consumers) was 11.57 in the year 1950-51. This declined to 5.10 transformer in 1996-97. It could be observed from the Table that since the fourth five year plan (1969-74), the number of transformer per '000 consumers has been declining. In the Eighth five-year plan, the value is relatively higher due to the special drive taken by the board to boost up voltage level in the regions of Malabar. Thus we may point out that the reason for higher levels of power loss and abysmally low level of voltage profile in the state of Kerala is due to insufficient quantities of transformers.

When there is an increase in connected load, the power system shall be ready to deliver reliable and qualitative power to the end users. This is possible when sufficient transformers are installed. The analysis of number of transformers per connected load (MW) show that during the third plan onwards there is steady decline in this ratio (see Table 4.4). In the seventh five-year plan, three was only 2.49 transformers per megawatt of power

Table 4.4: Number of Transformers per '000 Consumers and per MW of Connected Load

Plan Periods	1950	51-56	56-61	61-66	66-69	69-74	74-79	80-85	85-90	92-97
Number of Transformers per' 000 Consumer	11.57	10.59	16.56	12.02	11.15	10.66	8.81	5.68	3.23	5.10
Number of Transformers per MW of Connected Load	4.63	5.95	9.32	7.71	6.10	6.73	5.94	4.49	2.49	4.72

*Author's calculation.

Source: KSEB "Power System Statistics" Thiruvanandapuram (Various Issues).

demand. There is slight improvement in this ratio during the eighth plan. It is also observed from several writings on Kerala that, the transformers are unevenly distributed in the state#, which is another direct factor for low voltage in the regions of Malabar[24]. Therefore we observe that the reasons for heavy power loss and energy loss in the state include insufficient quantities of transformers per MW of connected load as well.

Growth Rate of Power System Variables on the Supply Side

The rates of growth of the power system variables shown in table 4.2 are worked out using semi log linear regression equation of the form:

$\ln Y_t = \beta_1 + \beta_2 X_t + U_t$ where

β_1 and β_2 = Parameters to be estimated

X_t = Year (1957 to 1995)

U_t = Disturbance term

The results of the regression are given in Table 4.5. The Table shows that the installed capacity increased by 7.62% per annum while that of internal maximum demand increased to 8.33%. Power experts maintain that the rate of growth of installed capacity should comfortably exceed the rate of maximum internal demand, if the system is to perform efficiently. The rate of growth of generation is 0.82% less than that of internal maximum demand which is the result of relatively low rate of growth of installed capacity. The rate of growth of energy sales (from internal production which also includes exports) in the state (7.84%) is marginally higher than that of the total energy sales (including imports) within the state, (7.74%) while imports have been increasing at the rate of 0.1% during

Table 4.5: Growth Rate of Power System Variables on the Supply Side 1957-1995

Variables	Constant	Co-efficient	R^2	P. Value	Case (Years)	Growth Rate
1	*2*	*3*	*4*	*5*	*6*	*7*
Installed Capacity	4.9532 (0.10319)* (48.0)+	0.07344 (0.004496)* (16.33)+	0.88	0.0000	39	7.62%
Maximum Demand (Internal)	4.5208 (0.43531)* (103.85)+	0.080053 (0.001897)* (42.20)+	0.98	0.0000	39	8.33%
Maximum Demand (System)	4.6702 (0.08664)* (53.90)+	0.075957 (0.003775)* (20.12)+	0.92	0.0000	39	7.89%
Generation	6.3538 (0.10169)* (62.48)+	0.072438 (0.004431)* (16.35)+	0.88	0.0000	39	7.51%

(Table Conte...)

Table 4.5: Contd...

1	2	3	4	5	6	7
Energy Sales (Including Exports)	6.1644 (0.89170)* (69.13)+	0.075485 (0.003886)* (19.43)+	0.91	0.0000	39	7.84%
Total Energy Sales (including Imports)	6.0635 (0.44661)* (135.77)+	0.074507 (0.001946)* (38.29)+	0.96	0.0000	39	7.74%
T&D Loss	4.4949 (0.049667)+ (90.48)*	0.084791 (0.0021642)+ (39.18)*	0.98	0.0000	39	8.85%
HT Lines**	9.3826 (0.10626)+ (882.99)*	0.039730 (0.000931)+ (42.63)*	0.99	0.0000	19	4.05%
LT Lines**	10.630 (0.031094)+ (341.87)*	0.064035 (0.0027271)+ (23.48)*	0.97	0.0000	19	6.65%
Distribution Transformers**	9.1352 (0.031153)+ (290.42)*	0.047046 (0.0027588)+ (17.05)*	0.95	0.0000	25	4.82%

© Author's calculation. *= Standard Error. += Student's T

**Continuous data for the entire period ranging from 1957 to 1995 are not readily available. Data for some years are found missing. Therefore data from 1978 to 1995-96 has been used to determine the growth rate.

Source: Kerala State Electricity Board "Power system Statistics" Various Issues.

the entire period of 39 years. It may however be noted that imports tended to become sizable since the mid eighties. The growth rate of T&D loss, Ht lines, LT lines, and the distribution transformers are 8.85%, 4.05%, 6.65% and 4.82% respectively. Considering all the above variables together, one is led to believe that it is the relatively lower rate of growth of installed capacity, which has been responsible for inadequate energy geneation[25].

The forgoing trend analysis helps us to admit that there is insufficient capacity addition of installed capacity of power in the state of Kerala. The deficit in capacity is well pronounced from the sixth five-year plan onwards. As capacity was limited, generation too was insufficient. This led Kerala to depend upon other States for energy. Though the gap between power capacity and energy availability has been widening over the past 3 five-year plan periods (1979-95), the system was able to add only 494 MW of installed capacity. It is worth analyzing the reasons for such low capacity addition in the state grid. Such an attempt will be made in the next chapter.

Demand Side Analyses

The power system variables examined so far are supply side factors. Factors like number of consumers connected loads and per capita consumption influence the demand side. There fore an analysis of these factors will be in order.

Power Consumers

Power consumers in the state remained at 0.28 Lakhs in 1950-51, which rose to 49.23 Lakhs in the year 1995-96, showing an increase of 17582 points. (In 1998, it rose to 52 Lakhs.) The indices of total consumers have risen at a faster rate. The rate of changes of indices were relatively higher during the sixth, seventh and eighth five year plan periods. The trend analysis of total power consumers in the state power system shows that from fourth five year plan (1969-74) onwards, there has been considerable increase in the number of consumers. (See Table 4.6.) It further means that the demand for electricity has started increasing at a faster rate since 1969. A detailed analysis of sector wise consumers is attempted in next chapter VI. The trends in the rate of growth of power system variables on the demand side are analyzed. (Refer Table 4.6).

Table 4.6: Trends in the Growth of demand side variables during the Plan Periods

Plan Periods	Total Consumers (Lakhs)	Total Connected Load (MU)	Per capita Consumption (kWh)*	Consumption Per capita (kWh)**
1950	0.28 (100)	70 (100)	13 (100)	5000 (100)
First Plan (1951-56)	0.79 (282)	142 (203)	18.5 (142)	3468 (69)
Second Plan (1956-61)	1.75 (625)	311 (444)	30 (231)	2891 (58)
Third Plan (1961-66)	3.25 (1161)	510 (729)	40 (308)	2308 (46)
Annual Plans (1966-69)	4.40 (1571)	805 (1150)	66 (508)	3044 (61)
Fourth Plan (1969-74)	7.77 (2775)	1231 (1759)	79 (608)	2320 (46)
Fifth Plan	11.72	1738	96	2064

(Table Conte...)

(1974-79)	(4186)	(2483)	(738)	(41)

Table 4.6: Contd...

Annual Plan (1979-80)	13.37 (4775)	1887 (2696)	96 (738)	1783 (36)
Sixth Plan (1980-85)	22.17 (7918)	2803 (4004)	124 (954)	1523 (31)
Seventh Plan (1985-90)	31.90 (11393)	4166 (5951)	164 (1262)	1926 (39)
Annual Plans (1990-92)	36.98 (13207)	5526 (7894)	192 (1477)	1513 (30)
Eighth Plan (1992-97)	4923 (17582)	6089 (8699)	240 (1846)(P)	1582 (32)(P)

P = Provisional.

Note: Figures in brackets show the change in indices.

Source: *(i)* KSEB "Power System Statistics" Thiruvanandapuram. Various issues.

(ii) Government of Kerala "Economic Review" Thiruvanandapuram. Various issues.

Connected Load

Demand for electricity is expressed in terms of the connected loads i.e. the power capacity (kW) requirements of consumers. When the power capacity requirements of all consumers are added together, we get the total connected load of the power system. Connected load in the state has been steadily increasing and in the fourth, sixth and eighth five year plan, the rate of increase is relatively faster as this is evidenced from the changes in its rate of changes of the indices (See Table 4.6). It is also observed that the rate of changes of the indices of total connected load is relatively slower than that of total consumers. That is due to the fact that there is no one to one correspondence between consumers and connected load. Energy demand by a consuming unit is not only the function of connected load, but also the duration of power consumption by these units. There may be higher levels of connected load, but all this entire loads necessarily do not demand corresponding levels of power. Instead, even without an additional increase in connected load, there will be higher levels of energy consumption, if the duration (hours) of power consumption increases. The total connected load of the Kerala Power system was 70 MW in 1950, which rose to 6089 MW in 1996-97 showing an increase of 8599 points.

The number of consumers mainly determines the connected load. The ratio of connected load to the number of consumers presented in the table 4.7. shows that the connected load per consumer generally declined over the years. Per capita consumption per actual consumers also declined during the same period, from 5000 units in 1950 to 1884 units in 1996-97. The consumption per connected load declined from 2 units/ Watt to 1.52 units/Watt. However from the fifth five-year plan onwards the units of consumption per connected load has shown a slight increase. During these periods the connected load per consumer (kW) shows a declining trend. The implication is that the existing consumers with given connected load are using more power for long hours. The explanation for higher demand for power in the face of sluggish growth in connected load can be explained in terms of changes in living standards, increase in members of households, changes in favour of nuclear families liberal use of power driven household appliances, relatively lower tariff and improvement in educational standard.[26]

The quantitative relationship between connected load and consumers is examined by fitting the linear regression model and the result is as under:

Table 4.7: Consumption and Connected Load Per Consumer During Plan Periods

Plan Period	1950	51-56	56-61	61-66	66-69	69-74	74-79	80-85	85-90	92-97
Consumption per Connected Load (kWh)	2	1.93	1.63	1.47	1.66	1.47	1.39	1.76	1.47	1.52
Consumption per Consumer (kWh)	5000	3468	2891	2308	3044	2320	2064	1523	1926	1846
Connected Load per consumer (kW)	2.5	1.80	1.78	1.57	1.83	1.58	1.50	1.26	1.31	1.24

*Authors calculation.

Source: Kerala State Electricity Board "Power System Statistics" Various Issues.

Connected Load =	14875	+	1.2840 (Consumers)	R^2=0.97
Standard Error	(7095)		(0.034254)	
Student's T	(2.10)		(37.49)	
P=0.0000	Case=39 Years			Significant at 5% level.

Connected load has by and large increased at the rate of 1.28 times power consumers in the state power system. Likewise the quantitative relationship between consumption and connected load is verified by fitting the linear regression equations and the result is as under:

Consumption =	770.09	+	0.001027 (Connected Load)	R^2=0.85
Standard Error	(198.90)		(0.00007136)	
Student's T	(3.87)		(14.38).	
P=0.0000	Case=39 Years			Significant at 5% level

Consumption increases 0.001 times the increase in connected load. It also implies that according to the changes in connected load, the system is generating energy to meet the consumption demand[27].

Per Capita Consumption and Actual Consumption Per Capita

We have already examined the trends in the rate of growth of energy consumption and the number of power consumers. The per capita energy consumption, one of the key variables of economic growth has been on the increase in the state. Per capita energy consumption, one of the key variables of economic growth has been on the increase in the state. Here per capita energy consumption means the total energy consumption divided by the total population in the state. The per capita energy consumption was 13 units in 1950, which rose to 240 units in the year 1995-96, showing an increase of 1846 points (Refer Table 4.6).

Per capita energy consumption has been steadily increasing overtime and the rates of increase were relatively better in fourth, sixth, seventh and eighth five year plan periods. It is to be observed in this context that the State's per capita energy consumption is one of the lowest in India[28]. Per capita energy consumption would have increased if a sufficient quantity of power were available in the state. This is well reflected from the fact that the actual energy consumption per power consumers has (consumption per consumer) continually declined over the years. There is a relatively higher level of changes in the values of denominator, but the value of numerator (energy consumption) has increased at a relatively lower level. Therefore the consumption per capita has declined (Refer Table 4.6). The indices of consumption per capita have declined from 100 points in 1950 to 32 points in 1995-96.

Growth of Variables on the Demand Side

Trends in the rates of growth of total number of consumers, total connected load, per capita consumption and actual consumption per capita have been worked out using the semi log linear model and the results are given below.

The growth rates of consumers, connected load, per capita consumption and actual consumption per capita are 10.38%, 9.26%, 5.81%, and –2.29% respectively. Among the variables examined the growth rate of total consumers is the highest one. The growth rate of per capita consumption is 5.81%, which is slightly lower than the growth rate of total energy consumption of 7.14%. We may observe that since the growth rate of energy consumption is higher than the average growth rate of population of 2.68% per annum the per capita energy consumption in the state has been increasing, inspite of a tardy rate of growth of actual energy consumption (-2.29%). The rate of growth of connected load is also

Table 4.8: Rate of Growth of Power System Variables (Demand Side)

Variables	Constant	Co-efficient	R^2	P. Value	Cases	Growth Rate
Consumers	11.759 (0.039448)+ (298.09)*	0.098783 (0.0017189)+ (57.47)*	0.99	0.0000	39 Years	10.38%
Connected Load	12.373 (0.041373)+ (299.06)*	0.088578 (0.0018028)+ (49.13)*	0.98	0.0000	39 Years	9.26%
Percapita Consumption	3.2830 (0.038612)+ (85.03)*	0.056442 (0.0016825)+ (33.55)*	0.97	0.0000	39 Years	5.81
Consumption Percapita	8.2193 (0.070954)+ (115.81)*	-1.023179 (0.0030918)+ (-7.50)*	0.60	0.0000	39 Years	-2.29%

+ = Standard Error * = Student's T.

much higher than the power system variables appeared on the supply side. Chronic power shortage experienced in the state is partly due to the differences in the rate of growth of demand and supply side variables.

Trends in Revenue, Expenditure, and Agricultural Connection

Total revenue of the Kerala Power System was Rs. 5.84 million in 1950, which rose to 7113 million units in 1995-96, showing an increase of 121798 points. The system gets revenue by way of sale of energy to various categories of consumers[#]. Revenue includes the amount of subsidy extended by State Government. The trend analysis of revenue collection shows that the indices of revenue have considerably increased during the third, fourth, sixth, seventh and eighth five- year plan periods. Energy metered is normally subject to revenue realization. But there are large quantities of energy, which cannot be metered due to faulty energy meters, and errors in meter connections. For these units, revenue cannot be realised and thus revenue loss to the state power system.

On the other hand revenue expenditure of the power system continued to increase steadily during the second five-year plan[*]. The total expenditure of KSEB stood at Rs. 20 million, which rose to Rs. 587 million during the fifth plan and jumped to 7447 million in 1995-96. Revenue expenditure began to increase very steeply after the fifth five-year plan, as can be seen from the Table 4.9. After the seventh five-year plan revenue expenditure began to exceed revenue receipts in absolute terms. (Refer table 4.9)

Average revenue per unit of energy was just Paise 4 in 1950. It rose to Paise 93 in 1995-96, showing an increase of 2325 points. There has been steady increase

Table 4.9: Trends in the Growth of Revenue, Expenditure and Agricultural Connections during the Plan Periods (1950-95)

Plan Periods	Total Expenditure (Rs. Million)	Total Revenue (Rs. Million)	Revenue per Unit (Paise)	Agricultural Connection (Numbers)
1	*2*	*3*	*4*	*5*
1950	NA	5.84 (100)	4 (100)	191 (100)
First Plan (1951-56)	NA	14.07 (241)	5 (125)	893 (468)
Second Plan (1956-61)	20 (100)	31.17 (534)	6 (150)	4616 (2417)
Third Plan (1961-66)	40.6 (203)	70.68 (1210)	9 (225)	7007 (3669)
Annual Plans (1966-69)	82.6 (413)	116.51 (1995)	9 (225)	13909 (7282)
Fourth Plan (1969-74)	203.1 (1016)	237.91 (4074)	11 (275)	37611 (19692)

Table 4.9: Contd...

1	2	3	4	5
Fifth Plan (1974-79)	479.7 (2399)	842.18 (14420)	19 (475)	66240 (34681)
Annual Plan (1979-80)	587.1 (2936)	912.5 (15625)	21 (525)	77863 (40766)
Sixth Plan (1980-85)	894.0 (4470)	1363.3 (23344)	37 (925)	131991 (69105)
Seventh Plan (1985-90)	2598.3 (12992)	2699.78 (46229)	43 (1075)	199504 (104452)
Annual Plans (1990-92)	3760.0 (18800)	3432.70 (58779)	61 (1525)	238206 (124715)
Eighth Plan (1992-96) (4 Years)	7447.1 (37236)	7113.0 (121798)	93 (2325)	300113 (157127)

Note: Figures in brackets show the changes in indices. NA= Not Available.

Source: (i) KSEB "Power System Statistics". Thiruvanandapuram- Various issues.

(ii) Government of Kerala. (1997) "Economic Review 1995-96" Thiruvanandapuram.

in the average revenue of Kerala Power System during the entire plan periods. Relatively higher levels of increase in average revenue were noticed during the sixth and eighth five-year periods. Average revenue is considered as average tariff as well, since revenue of the power system is by way of the sale of energy units. Average tariff (Total revenue ÷ total units sold) of State Power system is one of the lowest in India[29] due to its exclusive reliance on hydro generation up to 1996-97. Secondly it is observed that the state government heavily subsidize tariff particularly to domestic and agriculture consumers. Thirdly, as pointed out by knowledgeable sources the method of tariff fixation is unscientific and irrational. Till now the pricing procedures followed were based upon historical pricing as well as cost plus pricing principles[30]. Though experts recommended marginal cost pricing[31] procedure which is adopted in Utilities abroad, Indian utilities including Kerala State Electricity Board are yet to experiment this method.

Due to the factors mentioned above the cost revenue differences tended to increase significantly in recent years. The aim of the tariff should be to price the consumers of utility according to the cost imposed by the consumer on the utility for consuming energy. The cost revenue differences have been on the increase in the state. The average cost and average revenue difference was Paise 11 per unit in 1990-91, which rose to Paise 18 in 1995-96[32]. This calls for a revamping of tariff policy as warranted by the economic considerations. Though researchers had pointed out the need for involving power economists in designing the tariff policy the Kerala State Electricity Board till now seems to have kept them at bay[33].

Agricultural Connections

Energy used for agricultural purpose has been on

the increase in the state. In the agricultural sector energy is used for irrigation pump sets. Therefore irrigated pump sets can be considered as an index of growth of power consumption in the agricultural sector. In the year 1950 there were 191 agricultural connection. It rose to 300113 in 1995-96, showing an increase of 157127 points. (See Table 4.8). There was steady increase in the rate of growth of irrigated pump sets in the state. The rate of increase was much faster in the post 1970 periods. Agricultural consumers are 6.04% of total power consumers in the state (1995-96) and consume 4.34% of energy sold in the market. The trends in the rate of growth of irrigated pump sets show that dependency of rural and urban flocks on power has been on the increase.

However the increasing trends in energy consumption by the agricultural consumers are subjected to severe criticism from many quarters. This point of criticism is that the Board as well as the state government has joined together in granting agriculture connections even for non-agriculturists. Having considered agricultural connection as the easiest way to get power connections, many people have utilised this facility. The net result is that the genuine agriculturists are denied of power connections under the pretext of non-availability of posts, wires and other accessories.

Growth Rates of Revenue, Expenditure and Agricultural Connections

The growth rates of power system variables mentioned in the Table 4.8 are worked out using the semi log linear model and the results are given in Table 4.9. Total revenue as well as average revenue of the state power system has been increasing at the rate of 16.79% and 7.8% respectively per annum. The growth rate of

Table 4.10: Growth rates of revenue, tariff, expenditure, and agricultural connection during the pan periods (1957-95)

Total Revenue	5.1148 (0.047867)+ (106.85)*	0.15522 (0.002086)+ (74.42)*	0.99	0.0000	39 Years	16.79%
Average Tariff (Revenue)	-3.1761 (0.17146)+ (106.85)*	0.075118 (0.0074713)+ (10.5)*	0.73	0.0000	39 Years	7.80%
Agricultural Connections	8.4057 (0.23061)+ (153.97)*	0.12936 (0.00370)+ (43.38)*	0.97	0.0000	36 Years (1960 to 1995.96)	13.81%
Expenditure	4.3617 (0.20425)+ (21.35)*	0.17877 (0.0089001)+ (20.09)*	0.92	0.0000	39 Years	19.58%

*Author's calculation. + = Standard Error *= Student's

total expenditure has been increasing at much higher rate (19.57%). The point elasticity of revenue per expenditure works out to 0.86. It means that one percentage increase in expenditure leads to only 0.86 percentage increase in revenue. This trend throws light on the poor financial performance of the state power system.

Conclusion

The forgoing trend analysis of the power system has thrown up several issues of serious concern in the context of power system restructuring. The main findings of this chapter were (1) the key supply side variables viz. installed capacity and power generation grew much slower than demand variables like connected load and consumers. This led to widening gap between power supply and power demand, in turn, leading to very fast increase in power imports. (2) The per capita power consumption increased steadily but the units of consumption per actual consumer has been declining, a phenomenon reflecting shortage of adequate and reliable power supply. (3) The rate of growth of T&D loss has not only been very high but also even exceeded the rate of growth of generation. The inordinate T&D loss is due to insufficient transmission and distribution network. (4) The rate of growth of revenue expenditure not only exceeded the rate of growth of revenue receipts, but also from 7th plans onwards the absolute amount of expenditure tended to exceed that of revenue leading ultimately to severe commercial loss.

Notes and Reference

1. Pillai P.P. (1981) *"Dynamics of Electricity Supply and Demand – A Macro Econometric Analysis of Kerala"*. Agricole Publishing Academy. New Delhi. p. 7.

2. Ibid. p. 7.
3. Ibid. p. 8.
4. Kutty, Kader, A.K.- *The Industrial Pioneer of Malabar*. Interview held at his residence at Thalassery on 25-4-96.
5. Pavithran, G. (1995) *"The Possibilities of Achieving a Reliable Power Supply in Kerala"* in IEEE- a journal of Institute of Electrical and Electronic Engineers, Thiruvananthapuram. KSEB (1993) "System Operation – 1992-93", Thiruvananthapuram. p. 8.
6. KSEB (1993) *"System Operation – 1992-93"*, Thiruvananthapuram. p. 8. Ibid. p. 8.
7. Ibid. p. 8.
8. Kerala State Electricity Board (1996) *"Power System Statistics 1995-96"*. Thiruvananthapuram. p. 12.
9. Kerala State Electricity Board (1996) *"Power System Statistics 1994-95"*. Thiruvananthapuram. p. 47.
10. Maximum units that can be generated assuming 60% PLF=1505.5×0.6×8.760=7913MU.
11. There is daily maximum demand. The highest peak shown in a daily load curve is taken as the system maximum demand. Similar to this, yearly Maximum demand can be calculated based on monthly maximum demand.
12. Pavithran, G. (1995) 'o.p.c.i.t.' (Refer 5.) p. 17.
13. Pillai, P.P. (1986) "o.p.c.i.t." (Refer 1). p. 98.

* The peak demand shortage in Kerala in 1998-99 was 24%, as was recorded by the Southern Regional Electricity Board, Bangalore.

14. This estimate is nearer to the peak demand (MW) envisaged in the 12th Power Survey Report of Central Electricity Authority. The expected installed capacity in the state is 3221 MW in 2002 AD.
15. Energy is imported from Southern Central grid according to Gadgil formula. The State of Kerala gets 12% (2400MU) as Power Allocation from the Central grid which generate around 20,000MU (1995-96). It is expected to get more units of energy from the unallocated quota of the central grid. However to avail this, the present Gadgil formulae

to be altered. This is why even with Central allocation; the state has been facing severe energy deficit.

16. The existing transmission system cannot carry more than 1450 MW of power capacity and there fore would trip off the supply leading to undeclared power cut. For details see 'Hydel' Vol. 42. No. 3. Sept. 1996.
17. Pavithran G. (1994) *"Transmission and Distribution Losses – Problems and Remedies"* in Hydel – The Journal of KSEB Engineers Association, Vol. 40. No. 3. p. 3.
18. IRTC (1996) *"Exercises for Integrated Resource Planning for Kerala end use Analysis-an Empirical Study"* Technical Report-1 Electricity, p. 9.
19. Pavithran G. (1994) *"Transmission and Distribution Losses – Problems and Remedies"* in Hydel – The Journal of KSEB Engineers Association, Vol. 40. No. 3. p. 3.
20. Power Line (1997) February, New Delhi. p. 11.
21. Ibid. p. 11.
22. IRTC (1996) 'o.p.c.i.t.' (Refer 18) p. 9.
23. "Hydel" Various issues and "Hi tech" Various issues.

\# Writings appeared in journals like "Hydel", "Hi tech Voice", and various "Seminar Proceedings".

24. IRTC (1996) 'o.p.c.i.t' (Ref. 18) p. 9.
25. The point elasticities of generation and installed capacity are 0.99, generation and installed maximum demand is 0.90: and generation and system maximum demand is 0.95.

* Per Capita Consumption = Total Consumption ÷ Total Population

** Consumption Per Capita = Total consumption ÷ Actual power consumers.

26. Raiky. P.S. and Singh Paraminder (1990) *"Energy Consumption in India – Pattern and Determinants"* – Deep and Deep Publication. New Delhi. p. 28 and
27. Integrated rural Technologies Centre (IRTC) (1996) *"Exercises for Integrated Resources Planning for Kerala and Use Analysis—An Empirical Study"* Technical Report –1. Electricity p. 9.

28. Ministry of Power, Government of India *"Power Sector Reforms"* – Power Finance Corporation Ltd. Annexure-9. 1997. p. 36.

.. During the years between 1951-1991, the average rate of growth of population was 2.68% per annum.

Above 98% of total revenue comes from the sale of power and the balance as grants and subsidies.

* Data relating to revenue expenditure of the state power system is not available till 1956 as power system expenditure was treated as part of total expenditure on power PWD and telephones.

29. Ministry of power Government of India (1996) *"Annual Report"* 1995/96, New Delhi (All India average: 319 kWh in 1994-95).

30. Reddy Sudhakara B, *"Electricity Pricing and Load Management for Maharashtra"* Energy Sources Vol. 17, July 1995, p. 337-357.

31. Munasingh, M., Sudhakara Reddy and others have recommended for Long Run Marginal Cost Pricing Principle in the Electric Power Industry.

32. Ministry of Power, Government of India (1997) *"Power Sector Reforms"* – Power Finance Corporation Ltd. Annexure-9. p. 36.

33. Pillai P.P. (1981) *"Dynamics of Electricity Supply and Demand in Kerala –A Macro Econometric Analysis"*. Agricole Publishing Academy, New Delhi. 1981.

5

Techno Economic Analysis of the Kerala State Electricity Board

Several Issues follow from the trend analysis attempted in the previous chapter. In this chapter we shall examine these issues.

Installed Capacity

Till recently Kerala enjoyed the reputation of being an electricity surplus state. During the period 1974-1985, the state used to export bulk quantities of electricity to the neighbouring states, largely because the internal demand then remained at a low level presumably due to the industrial backwardness of the state and sluggish domestic demand. This scenario rapidly changed after 1985, when net import of power into the state began to increase significantly. In 1996 the imports accounted for 30% of the total internal power generation. Table 5.1 shows the trends in the power system variables during the post energy surplus period (1989-1995). In the year 1969 (first year of the third five- year plan period) installed capacity stood at 547 MW and generation at 1923 MU. Maximum System Demand was lower than the installed capacity and hence made the export possible. However, during the third plan export remained quite marginal in quantity. Things began to change drastically by the end of the fourth five-year plan, when exports of power markedly increased and imports sharply declined.

Between 4th and 5th five-year plan exports increased from 318 MU to 2097 MU, the largest ever recorded. The hefty increase in the exports was partly due to the commissioning of the first phase of Idukki Hydel Project in 1976, with an installed capacity of 390 MW (present capacity 780 MW), and relatively lower internal system demand (see Table 5.1). During the sixth five-year plan period, exports declined to 329 MU, partly due to the decline in energy generation of 305 MU and increase in internal demand of 302 MW. During the seventh plan period, inspite of the increase in installed capacity (due to the commissioning of II phase of Idukki hydel project) and the resultant increase in power generation, exports declined sharply to 104 MU, due to the increase in the maximum internal demand to 359 MW. Bulk import of power began to emerge from the seventh plan onwards as is obvious from the Table 5.1. During the eighth plan there was an increase of 31.5 MW of installed capacity. But generation increased to 176.86 MU. Maximum internal demand exceeded the system demand during this plan period, leading to sharp decline in exports and further growth in imports. The volume of imports has increased to 3298.38 MU in 1996-97 (59.94% of internal energy generation) the largest ever import. During the 92-97 period, both installed capacity and generation increased but during the same period, maximum internal demand overtook installed capacity, a very unusual phenomenon occurred as a result of persistent increase in power demand leading to unprecedented power

Table 5.1: Post energy surplus period (1969-1996)

Period	Installed Capacity (MW)	Maximum Demand (System) (MW)	Maximum Demand (Internal) (MW)	Generation (MU)	Export (MU)	Import (MU)
End of the 3rd Plan (31-3-69)	547	353	278	1923	28	119
End of the 4th Plan (31-3-74)	622	500	434	2510	318	1
End of the 5th Plan (31-3-79)	1012	852	609	5190	2097	14
End of the 6th Plan (31-3-85)	1012	939	911	4885	329	79
End of the 7th Plan (31-3-69)	1477	1171	1270	5075	104	1160
End of the Annual Plan (31-3-1992)	1477	1265	1308	5326	2.2	1856
End of the 8th Plan (31-3-97)	1508.5	1235	1652	5502.86	1.97	3298.38

Source: *(i)* KSEB (1997) "Power System Statistics 1995-96" Thiruvananthapuram, p. 7.
(ii) Government of Kerala (1998) "Economic Review-1997" Thiruvananthapuram. p. 60 and 61.

shortage. Taking the entire period 1979-97, we find that installed capacity increased only 49.06%, while internal maximum demand increased 171.26% and maximum system demand 44.95%. The tardy growth in installed capacity in relation to internal maximum demand appears to be the major reason for energy shortage. In this context a look into the possible reasons for the slow growth in installed capacity is justified. As was pointed out earlier the power development in Kerala is exclusively hydro based. Power Pundits[1] had warned several years ago that the state's power requirements could not be met fully from hydro stations alone.

Experts like Menon[2], pointed out that at least 200 MW of non hydel generating capacity had to be added every year from 1982, if the State was to avert an energy crisis in the imminent future. The exclusive reliance on hydel station made the Kerala grid highly susceptible to the vagaries of monsoon. However there was inordinate delay in completing several ongoing projects that were started years ago, resulting in inadequate installed capacity and heavy loss to the exchequer (Refer Table 5.2).

The table indicates that certain projects started in the seventies and early eighties still remain un-commissioned. Had all the ongoing projects been completed by 1996-97, it would have resulted in an additional generation of 997.8 MU [1642.8-645=997.8] of energy*. Out of the 10 projects shown in the Table only one project, lower Periyar was commissioned in 1997. Pooyankutty (Stage-I) which had evoked a lot of interest and controversy in recent years is yet to receive Central clearance, although Rs. 53 million has already been

---

* Values in column 8 are added together, except the value of 645MU.

Table 5.2: Cost Overrun and Time Overrun of Hydel Projects

Name of the projects	Year of Starting	Original Estimated Cost (Rs. Million)	Latest revised estimate cost (Rs Million)	Expenditure till the end of 3/94. (Rs. Million)	Expected year of Commissioning	Percentage increase of revised estimate	Energy potential (MU)
Kakkad	1976	186	1093.5	818.5	95-96	488	262
Kallada	1981	118	180.2	156.7	93-94	53	53
Lower Periyar	1983	884.3	2730.0	1516.7	95-96	208	493
Malampuzha	1987	29.5	48.6	35.2	94-95	64	5.6
Malamkara	1987	78.0	166.5	9.0	96-97	113	36
Pooyamkutty (Stage-I)	1985	2500	5900	53.3	2003-03	136	645
Azhutha Diversion	1983	37	78.4	47.9	95-96	208	36.6
Kuttiadi Tail race	1988	21.4	66.0	59.1	95-96	208	36.6
Kuttiadi Diversion	1992	21.4	49.6	17.1	96-97	131	37
Kuttiadi Extension	1994	307.3	307.3	NA	96-97	NA	38

NA= Not Available

Source: Government of Kerala (1996) "Economic Review 1995" Thiruvanandapuram 1996, p. 69.

spent on this scheme. A combination of factors like delayed extension of various hydel projects, slow initiation of new projects and obstinate insistence on a totally hydro based system seems to have contributed to the sluggish growth of installed capacity in the state[3]. Both the central and State governments are responsible for this slow growth in capacity. In all the southern states, except Kerala, there is at least one centrally sponsored project. Till 1997, there was no central investment in the power sector of Kerala. (In 1998 the central government gave clearance to set-up 360 MW thermal project at Kayamkulam under NTPC, the first phase of 110 MW of which was commissioned in November 1998). Apart from the centre's total neglect of the state power sector, the state's own share in power investment has been going down as is clear from the Table 5.3. The percentage share of investment has been falling right from the first five-year plan. During the fifth plan, there was a 33% fall in the magnitude of investment. Though the quantum of investment tended to increase from sixth plan, the actual magnitude remains quite small in relation to the requirement. According to a calculation of Kerala State Electricity Board, the State Power System would requires Rs. 151200 Million by 2000AD for providing additional generation, transmission and distribution facilities[4]. But the total investment in the eighth five-year plan was only a fraction of this (Rs. 13000 Million). Thus insufficient financial allocation was one important factors responsible for insufficient growth of power capacity and the resultant power shortage.

The total dependence on major hydro projects to a virtual exclusion of other options also can be one of the possible reasons for the tardy growth of capacity. The sate has, for instance, enormous potential of mini and

Table 5.3: Plan wise investment and Expenditure on Power Sector

Plan	Power Sector Investment (Rs. Million)	Total Plan Investment (Rs. Million)	Percentage share on Power Sector
First Plan (1951-56)	118.5	300.0	39.5
Second Plan (1956-61)	234.5 (97.89)	857.7 (190.57)	26.9
Third Plan (1961-66)	438.6 (87.04)	1701.6 (95.2)	25.6
Fourth Plan (1969-74)	762.5 (73.85)	7262.0 (326.8)	10.5
Fifth Plan (1974-79)	1068.4 (40.12)	4845.4 (-33.3)	
Sixth Plan (1980-85)	2800.7 (162.14)	14897.3 (207.5)	18.8
Seventh Plan (1985-90)	4413.1 (57.57)	22176.4 (48.86)	19.9
Eighth Plan (1992-97)	13000 (194.58)	54621.8 (146.31)	23.8

Note: Figures in brackets show the percentage increase.
Source: Government of Kerala "Economic Review 1995" Thiruvananthapuram, 1996. p. 5 and 68.

micro hydel projects. A conservative estimate of this potential is of the order of 510 MW that is roughly one third of the installed capacity of the power system at present. Experts maintain that mini-micro hydel projects are environmentally benign and sustainable and without time and cost over run[5]. Had the relatively cheaper potential been tapped, it would have made a significant contribution to the existing power capacity of the State.

It has already been pointed that, several projects taken up in the past remain to be completed. Even if all the ongoing projects are completed, the resulting installed capacity (supply) will fall short of demand. The total installed capacity from already completed power projects amounts to 1491.5 MW. The ongoing projects are expected to add another 314.25 MW by 2000AD (Refer Table 5.4).

Table 5.4: Details of hydro power potential of Kerala

Category	Installed Capacity (MW)	Firm Power at 100% PLF (MW)	Annual Generation Potential (MU)
Schemes Completed	1491.50	650.8	5701.00
Schemes Under Execution	314.25	128.02	1121.50
Schemes Pending Sanction	408.00	119.00	1043.00
Schemes Requiring Inter-state agreement	700.00	119.00	1726.00
Schemes Dropped/ Sanction rejected	1025.00	374.00	3276.00
Remaining Exploitable Schemes	1181.00	314.85	2758.50
Total	5119.75	1783.75	15626.00

Source: IRTC (1996) "Technical Report on Electricity" Integrated Rural Technology Centre, Palakkad"- p. 2.25.

The hydro schemes awaiting sanction from the environmental ministry are capable of contributing 408 MW. Projects held up in inter state disputes are worth 700 MW. Potential capacity of the exploitable schemes, apart from those dropped due to environmental consideration will be of the order of 1181MW. The total installed capacity in 2000 A.D would be 2214 MW (1492 + 314 + 408 MW), if the schemes under execution and those pending sanction were taken into consideration. As per KSEB study, Kerala Power System would require an installed capacity of 3880 MW[6] in 2000A.D. The 15th electric Power Survey* has revealed that the peak demand in the State of Kerala would be 3226 MW in 2001-02 (disregarding unmet demand). To meet this demand, the installed capacity has to be enhanced to 419.8 MW, i.e. 30% higher than the projected value of 3226 MU by the CEA**. It implies that even if all the available hydel schemes are fully utilised, the state may not be able to meet the present demand in the immediate future. The installed capacity in 1996-97 was 1508.5 MW, whereas the maximum internal demand was 1652 MW. If internal maximum demand is considered as the basis of installed capacity the latter should have been raised to 2793# MW in 1996-97. In other words the present installed capacity is 46% short of the desired capacity level (1508.5¸ 2793 = 54%) in 1996-97.

We shall now attempt to forecast the future energy capacity on the basis of internal maximum demand. It may be noted here that prediction of power capacity or energy requirements with accuracy is nearer impossible

---

* CEA prepares the Power Survey Report. 15th Power Report is published recently.

** While projecting for different terminal years, existing demand was considered, which was nearly 30% below the expected demand, since unmet demand is not properly treated in the projection estimation. For further details see "The Economics of Electricity Supply in India" by Govinda Rao et. al. Macmillan. 1998.

\# 1652+1652 × 0.30 (unmet demand) = 2148MW × 0.30 (marginal increase) = 2793 MW. 2148 + 2148 MW × 0.30 = 2793MW.

as several uncertainties and stochastic factors are involved. For forecasting purposes three regression models namely simple linear, semi log, and Gompertz relation[7] were tried for the years 1957-95 (The unmet demand is not considered in the model). Since Gompertz relation was found a better fit, prediction was made on its basis, by adding 30%*** to the estimated figures of internal maximum demand. The projected values are given in Table 5.5.

Table 5.5: Projections of Installed Power Capacity (MW)

Year	1995	2000AD	2005	2010	2015	2020
Installed Capacity (MW)	1652 (Actual internal maximum demand)	2774	3345	4006	4694	5394

*Authors Calculation

The installed capacity of the state power system in 1996-97 was 1508.5MW. An import of nearly 627 MW of power to the state was made. Thus as on 31-3-97, the total installed capacity made available to the consumers was 2136 MW. This was quite insufficient as being reflected in the form of load shedding power cut and low voltage during the peak and even in off peak hours, in several regions of the state. Therefore, for providing dependable and qualitative power the installed capacity has to be increased to a minimum of 2777 MW in 2000A.D (2136 + 2136 × .30 = 2777 MW). To meet the power requirements for 2010, an installed capacity of 4006 MW would be essential. For an additional capacity of 1 MW of power generation an average of Rs. 40 Million

*** Based on the Power technologists view that for a comfortable supply of power, the capacity system shall be at least 30% higher than the internal maximum demand (1652 + 1652 × .30 = 2148 (Unmet demand).

is being estimated as the installation cost by power experts***. An additional capacity of 2498 MW (4006-1508) is to be installed in the Kerala Power System to meet the power requirement for the terminal year 2010A.D, for which an investment worth Rs. 1,00,000 Million is expected.

Performance Analysis of Generating Stations

In Kerala, electricity is generated from 12 hydroelectric power projects of varying capacities and from one small wind farm. Out of 12 hydro projects, one is in private sector (Maniyar-12 MW). Internal Power Generation is through these above mentioned power projects. All the generating stations are not operating simultaneously. Reservoir capacity and water inflow vary from project to project. Generation, design value and capacity utilisation of the 12 projects are shown in table 5.6. The total design value of the 12 projects amounts to 5749 MU. Of this Idukki accounts for 41.71% (2398 MU), Sabarigiri 23.27% (1338 MU), Idamalayar 6.661% (380 MU) and all the remaining 8 power projects together having less than 28.41% (1633 MU) of total design value of generation (See table 5.6). The design value of generation of a station is determined on the basis of installed capacity and Plant Load Factor.

Kuttiadi hydel station on an average generated 265 MU during the period 1980-81 to 1995-96. (See Table 5.6). The average capacity utilisation factor (CUF*) was 99% for the period. In several years the actual generation

*** CEA and other independent power producers consider Rs. 40 Million as the average installation cost per Megawatt of installed capacity.

* CUF = Capacity Utilisation Factor = Actual Generation in MU ÷ Design Value in MU.

Table 5.6: Generation, Design value and capacity utilisation of Hydro stations – 1980-81 to 1995-96

Power Stations	Design value (MU)	80-81	81-82	82-83	83-84	84-85	85-86	86-87	87-88
1	*2*	*3*	*4*	*5*	*6*	*7*	*8*	*9*	*10*
Kuttiadi	268 (4.66)	257 (96)	294 (110)	210 (78)	251 (94)	273 (102)	239 (89)	244 (91)	214 (80)
Sholayar	233 (4.05)	185 (79)	258 (110)	177 (76)	221 (95)	282 (121)	236 (101)	203 (87)	212 (91)
Poringalkuthu	170 (2.96)	178 (105)	224 (111)	173 (102)	215 (126)	237 (139)	212 (1250)	212 (125)	159 (94)
Pallivasal	284 (4.94)	234 (82)	241 (132)	209 (74)	209 (74)	236 (63)	217 (76)	206 (73)	196 (69)
Sengulam	182 (3.17)	156 (86)	161 (88)	114 (63)	131 (80)	150 (82)	119 (65)	128 (70)	123 (68)
Panniar	158 (2.74)	107 (68)	120 (76)	24 (15)	76 (48)	109 (69)	129 (82)	77 (49)	86 (54)

Table 5.6: Contd...

1	*2*	*3*	*4*	*5*	*6*	*7*	*8*	*9*	*10*
Neriamangalam	237 (4.22)	244 (103)	289 (130)	189 (80)	255 (108)	289 (122)	292 (123)	245 (103)	269 (114)
Idukki	2398 (41.71)	2613 (109)	2413 (101)	2321 (97)	1434 (60)	1968 (82)	2512 (105)	2314 (97)	1143 (48)
Sabarigiri	1338 (23.27)	1268 (95)	1542 (115)	1071 (80)	851 (64)	1375 (103)	1402 (105)	958 (72)	837 (63)
Idamalayar	380 (6.60)	-	-	-	-	-	-	50 (13)	237 (62)
Kallada	65 (1.13)	-	-	-	-	-	-	-	-
Maniar	36 (0.63)	-	-	-	-	-	-	-	-
Kanjikode [Wind Farm]	-	-	-	-	-	-	-	-	-
Total	5749	5242 (91.2)	5541 (96)	4488 (78)	3643 (63)	4885 (85)	5357 (93)	4637 (81)	3776 (66)

(Table Conte...)

Table 5.6: Contd...

Power Stations	88-89	89-90	90-91	91-92	92-93	93-94	94-95	95-96	Average
	11	*12*	*13*	*14*	*15*	*16*	*17*	*18*	*19*
Kuttiadi	282 (105)	285 (106)	288 (107)	370 (138)	261 (97)	253 (94)	259 (97)	260 (97)	265 (99)
Sholayar	208 (89)	246 (106)	314 (135)	241 (103)	265 (114)	269 (115)	273 (117)	173 (74)	235 (101)
Poringalkuthu	222 (131)	265 (156)	225 (133)	304 (179)	216 (127)	193 (114)	222 (131)	191 (112)	216 (127)
Pallivasal	238 (84)	225 (79)	200 (70)	316 (111)	246 (87)	237 (83)	203 (71)	226 (80)	227 (80)
Sengulam	149 (82)	141 (77)	125 (69)	135 (74)	154 (85)	149 (82)	127 (70)	136 (75)	137 (75)
Panniar	86 (54)	323 (204)	71 (45)	117 (74)	146 (92)	96 (61)	154 (97)	81 (51)	113 (72)
Neriamangalam	250 (105)	408 (172)	464 (196)	164 (69)	290 (122)	257 (108)	292 (123)	262 (111)	279 (118)
Idukki	1687 (70)	2884 (120)	2116 (88)	2336 (97)	3271 (136)	2216 (92)	2866 (120)	2576 (107)	2292 (96)

Table 5.6: Contd...

Power Stations	88-89	89-90	90-91	91-92	92-93	93-94	94-95	95-96	Average
	11	*12*	*13*	*14*	*15*	*16*	*17*	*18*	*19*
Sabarigiri	1068 (80)	1625 (121)	1207 (90)	1228 (92)	1728 (129)	1369 (102)	1514 (13)	1280 (96)	1270 (95)
Idamalayar	20 (0.5)	344 (91)	271 (71)	344 (91_)	432 (114)_	346 (91)	483 (127)	310 (82)	177 (47)
Kallada	-	-	-	-	-	4.27 (6.6)	50.4 (77)	63.06 (97)	39.23 (60)
Maniar	-	-	-	-	-	-	1.24 (3.4)	34 (94)	17.62 (.50)
Kanjikode [Wind Farm]	-	-	-	-	-	-	-	2.04	2.04
Total	4507 (73)	6747 (117)	4980 (87)	5755 (100)	7009 (122)	5390 (94)	6455 (121)	5588 (97)	5299 (92)

*Authors Calculation. Source: KSEB "Power System Statistics" and "Power System Operations" Thiruvanandapuram, Various Issues

Note: *(i)* Bracketed values in the second column is the percentage share of design value of generation by each power project.

(ii) Bracketed values in other columns are the capacity utilisation factor of each year. (CUF= Generation ÷ Design value of generation × 100)

(iii) The figures in brackets in the last column are the average capacity utilisation factor.

went above the design value. During the years 1088-89 to 1991-92, the capacity utilisation factor exceeded 100%**.

The generation figures for Sholayar project does not exhibit any definite trend. The average actual generation for the year 80-81 to 95-96 comes to 235 MU. The average CUF in this case is 101%. The CUF figures however exceeded the design value during the years 1989-90 to 1994-95.

Peringalkuthu station has exhibited a relatively high CUF for a longer time span, compared to all other projects. In the case of this station, generation exceeded design value for the entire period 1980-81 to 1995-96, the only exception being 1987-88. With an average generation of 216 MU, this project recorded an utilisation factor of 127%, the highest among all projects.

In the case of Pallivasal, actual generation remained well behind the design value for the last sixteen years. The average generation was 227 MU, giving a CUF of 80%. Being the oldest (Installed in 1940) hydel project in the State of Kerala it is presumed that technical reasons are mainly responsible for the comparatively poor capacity utilisation.

The performance of Sengulam in terms of capacity utilisation is also comparatively very poor. Power generation from this project was considerably below the design value. With an average generation of 137 MU, its CUF is only 75%. Sengulam is the second oldest station, (established in 1954) and like Pallivasal, technical factors may be the major reasons for the poor utilisation rate. Recently the authorities have introduced

---

** Generation can go upto 125% of the design value.

certain measures with the technical support of international bodies to enhance generation capacity of these stations.

Power generation from Panniar Station shows violent fluctuations from year to year. In 1982-83, generation stood at an abysmally low level of 24 MU, roughly 15% of the design value. But in 1989-90, the generation jumped to 323 MU, i.e. 204% of the design value, an unusually high figure. Surprisingly the very next year the generation plummeted to 71MU. The average generation from the station for the period under review was 113 MU, giving a CUF of 72%. Even when state is beset with energy crises, power generation from this generation station did not record any significant increase. This station which was built up relatively early (established in 1963) is now under renovation and modernisation.

Neriamangalam Project has been able to generate power more than the design value during the period under review, except for 2 years – 1982-83 and 1991-92. The average generation from this station was 279 MU and the average capacity utilisation factor 118%. In the year 1990-91, generation from this station was as high as 464 MU, yielding an utilisation factor of 196%.

Idukki is the premier generating station of Kerala accounting for 42% of total energy produced in the state. Capacity utilisation factor varied from 48% in 1987-88 to 136% in 1992-93. In all years under review, capacity utilisation rate remained well above 80%, except for three years 1983-84, 1987-88 and 1989-90. When three units (generators) worth 390 MW was commissioned, the capacity utilisation factor was relatively high (above 80%). But after commissioning of the remaining 3 generators in 1986, capacity utilisation did not proportionately increase. During the period 1980-95, the average generation from this station was 3217 MW or 96% of the design value. From available data one is led to infer that during the years when generation from Idukki projects fell below by 10% of the design value, the power system of Kerala imposed power cut and load shedding. Such a pattern became discernible particularly after early 1980s.

Sabarigiri station with a design value of 1338 MU is the second largest and accounts for 23% of total energy generated by all stations. During 1980-81 to 1995-96 1270 million units of average energy were generated annually resulting in an utilisation rate of 95%. In the year 1992-93, generation was 29%, higher than the design value. In that year when generation from Idukki and Sabarigiri increased to 36% and 29% of the design value of each respectively, the state recorded a generation of 7009 MU, the highest figure ever recorded in the power history of Kerala. Idukki and Sabarigir together, at present, account for 65% of the total design value of 5749 MU and a little more than 68% of total generation in the state.

Idamalayar, the third largest in terms of capacity (6.7% of total design value) and generation (3.4% of the total generation) was commissioned in 1986.

Since its commissioning, generation exceeded its design value only in 2 years 1992-93, and 1994-95. The average generation was 177 MU and the average capacity utilisation factor was 47%. The unimpressive performance of this project merits a deeper probe, in view of the fact that Idamalayar is one of the latest entrants among the hydel stations of the state.

The first phase of the Kallada project (First small hydropower project in the state) was commissioned in

1994 with an installed capacity of 7.5 MW (Project upto ratings of 15 MW are classified as Small Hydro Projects). Later in 1995 the second unit worth 7.5 MW was commissioned. The design value of the project at present is 65 MU, with a firm power of 6.05 MW. In 1995-96, 63 MU of energy was generated. The CUF is nearly 100%.

Maniyar is the second small hydropower project owned by a private. Three units (generators) of 4 MW each have started generating electricity from 1995 onwards. The design value of this project is 36 MU and the CUF in 1995-96 was 100%.

The Kanjikode wind farm (Under Kerala State Electricity Board) was commissioned in 1995 with 12 generators of 0.225 MU capacity each (Total capacity of 2 MW). From this station 2.0409 million units were generated in 1995-96. This is the first project undertaken in Kerala with a view to harnessing non-conventional sources of energy. It is too early to examine the technical efficiency of this project.

Performance analysis of yearly generation shows that during the period 1989-95, power generation has been generally higher, as compared to the earlier phase (1980-81 to 1987-88), the plausible explanation being higher demand for energy during the second phase (1989-99). During the 16 years from 1980-81, generation exceeded the design value in four years- 1989-90, 1991-92, 1992-93 and 1994-95. The increase in generation over the design value during these years were respectively 20%, 2%, 24% and 13%. On an average, generation is found to have exceeded the design value by 15% during the years from 1989-95. But if we take the average for 16 years, (1980-81 to 1995-96) generations remained 7% below the design value.

It would be worthwhile to examine the technical and non-technical factors responsible for keeping generation below the design value in certain years. Design value is determined on the basis of firm power after giving due allowance for maintenance shut down and reserve shut down. During the period 1988-89 to 1995-96, the actual generation exceeded the design value in all the years (Design value upto 1994 was 5648 MU), an indication that water availability was not a constraint for power generation and more significantly the operation performance of the power stations were reasonably good.

The power system authorities have a tendency to inflate the capacity utilisation rate beyond the design value. When water availability is not sufficient, they boost up the utilisation factor, by keeping down the reserve margin of water below its desired level. The energy technologists have warned the system authorities on several occasions that increasing capacity utilisation beyond 100% would adversely affect the operational efficiency of the stations in the long run. There fore what is required is to examine whether it is possible to increase the magnitude of the design value of generation, by augmentation schemes, etc., rather than increasing the capacity utilisation rate. There are several technological constraints to be over come before thinking of enhancing design value of power stations. Thus what is desirable is to construct new power stations to increase the installed capacity of the power system so as to meet the peak load demand. In 1995-96, the peak load demand was of the order of 1652 MW (this too is the choked demand). To meet at least this much demand, supply should have increased to 11288 MU.[#] The actual generation on the other hand was 5491MU, i.e. a deficit of 5797 MU, 94 51%. In other words the state is producing only half of its total energy requirement.

Analysis of Plant Load Factor (PLF) of Power Stations

From the earlier analysis we have seen that generation depends on installed capacity. Generation volume from a given installed capacity is determined by the technical parameter called the load factor of hydel stations. Higher the load factors, higher the units of energy generation. The plant load factor depends on the power demand (both average and peak demand) of the consumers, besides the technical factors. The PLF is found to vary over time. The trends in the PLF of hydel stations are given in Table 5.7. This is worked out from the data given in "power System operation" of Kerala State Electricity Board.

It is an indicator of the performance efficiency of hydel stations. Considering PLF as a measure of efficiency of power stations we found that Peringalkuthu stands out as the first. The economic advantage of higher load factor is that generation will be maximum when PLF is the highest. More generation means lesser unit cost and higher revenue collection and better energy availability and thus minimum loss of value addition. Though Idukki is the biggest power project in terms of installed capacity and generation, in terms of PLF, it comes only in the 9th position. Similarly Sabarigiri, the second largest is ranked only fifth in terms of efficiency. (PLF) On the basis of PLF, Power stations in the state can be classified into 3 groups[8].

Group-I- Average PLF above 60%

Group-II- Average PLF above 40% but less than 60%

Group-III- Average PLF below 60%

As per this grouping, Peringalkuttu, Pallivasal and Neriamangalam power stations belong to the 1st group.

Table 5.7: Trends in the PLF of hydel stations- 1985-86 to 1994-95

	85-86	86-87	87-88	88-89	89-90	90-91	91-92	92-93	93-94	94-95	Avg.	Rank
Peringalkuthu	85	75	76	77	79	73	68	70	71	69	74	1
Pallivasal	72	66	63	67	68	73	68	85	83	88	73	2
Neriamangalam	74	74	62	62	64	67	66	67	72	67	68	3
Idamalayar	-	-	-	-	56	44	52	47	45	60	52	4
Sabarigiri	52	53	37	37	41	52	49	49	59	55	48	5
Sholayar	59	50	43	32	58	45	26	50	47	56	47	6
Periyar	42	49	29	31	37	46	31	39	55	38	40	7
Kuttiadi	42	36	37	31	44	39	39	35	38	41	38	8
Idukki	57	55	34	22	25	28	38	34	40	38	37	9
Sengulam	36	28	31	29	32	40	32	37	41	52	36	10

*Author's calculation.

Source: Kerala State Electricity Board "Power System Operations". Various Issues.

Chart 5.3. PLF of Hydel Stations

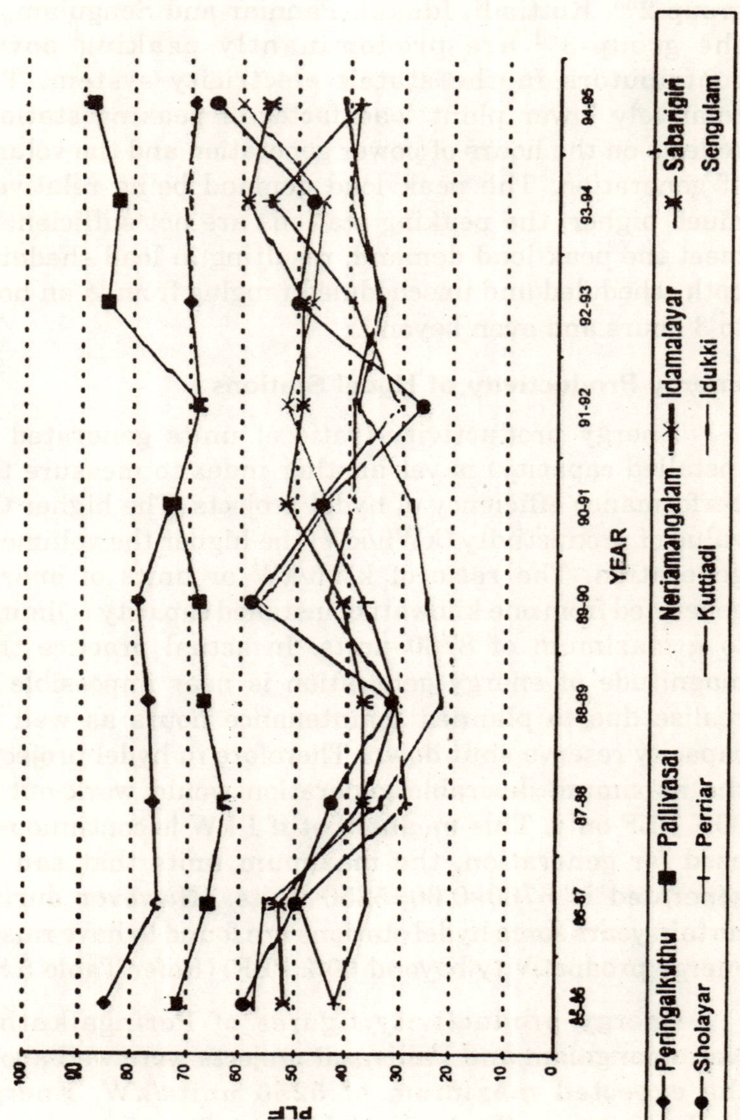

Idamalayar, Sabarigiri and Sholayar stations fall under group 2nd. Kuttiadi, Idukki, Panniar and Sengulam, in the group-3rd are predominantly peaking power contributors in the state's electricity system. The relatively lower plant load factor of peaking stations reflects on the hours of power generation and the volume of generation. The peak load demand being relatively much higher, the peaking stations are not sufficient to meet the peak load demand, resulting in load shedding both scheduled and unscheduled ranging from ½ an hour to 3 hours and even beyond.

Energy Productivity of Hydel Stations

Energy productivity (ratio of units generated to installed capacity) is yet another index to measure the performance efficiency of hydel projects. The higher the value of productivity (kWh/kW) the higher the volume of generation. The ratio of kWh/kW or units of energy generated from one kilowatt of installed capacity is limited to a maximum of 8760 units. In actual practice this magnitude of energy generation is near impossible to realise due to planned maintenance hours as well as capacity reserve shut down. Therefore in hydel projects, the maximum desirable generation would work out to 60% PLF only. This means that if I kW is continuously used for generation, the maximum units that can be generated is $8760 \times 0.60 = 5256$ units. (However during certain years some hydel stations are found to have raised energy productivity beyond 60% PLF) (Refer Table 5.8).

Energy productivity figures of Peringalkuthu, Neriamangalam and Pallivasal projects were well above the expected maximum of 5256 units/kW. Energy productivity, on the basis of design value of generation exceeded the maximum limit in the case of 4-power projects-Peringalkuthu, Neriamangalam, Pallivasal and

Chart 5.3. PLF of Hydel Stations

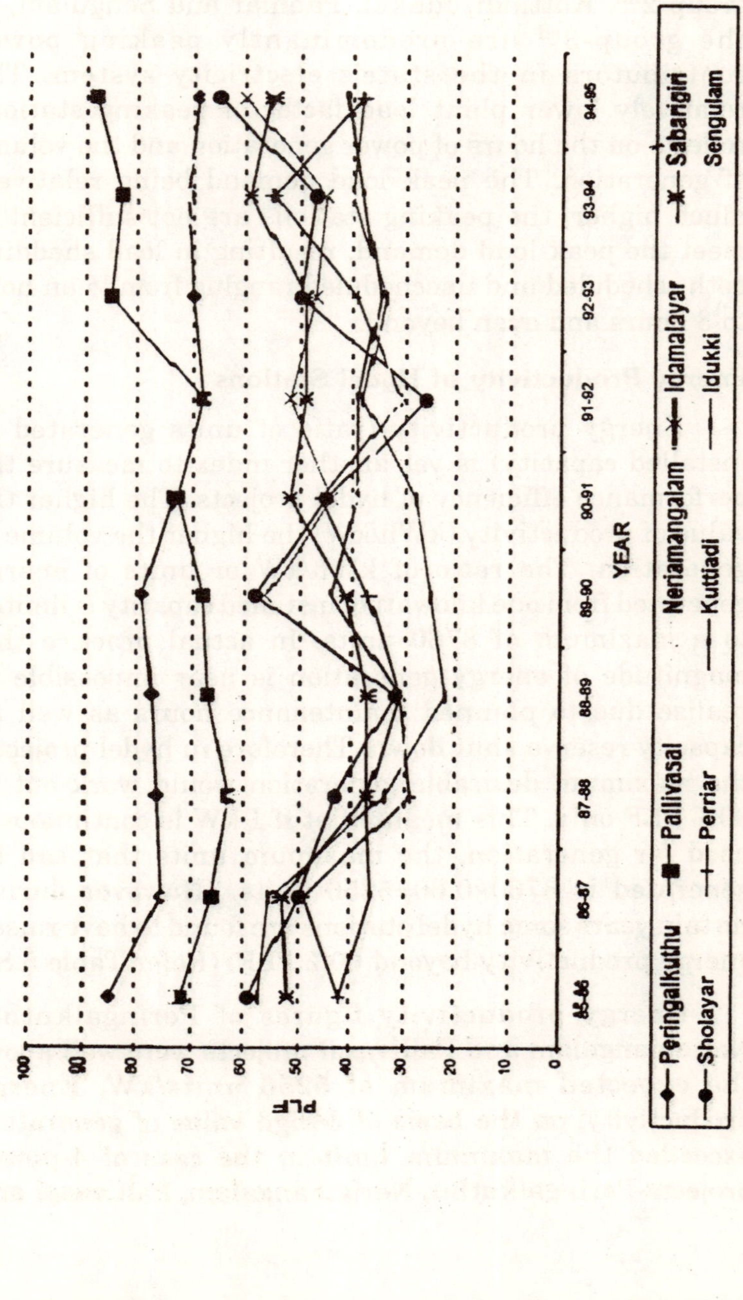

Idamalayar, Sabarigiri and Sholayar stations fall under group 2nd. Kuttiadi, Idukki, Panniar and Sengulam, in the group-3rd are predominantly peaking power contributors in the state's electricity system. The relatively lower plant load factor of peaking stations reflects on the hours of power generation and the volume of generation. The peak load demand being relatively much higher, the peaking stations are not sufficient to meet the peak load demand, resulting in load shedding both scheduled and unscheduled ranging from ½ an hour to 3 hours and even beyond.

Energy Productivity of Hydel Stations

Energy productivity (ratio of units generated to installed capacity) is yet another index to measure the performance efficiency of hydel projects. The higher the value of productivity (kWh/kW) the higher the volume of generation. The ratio of kWh/kW or units of energy generated from one kilowatt of installed capacity is limited to a maximum of 8760 units. In actual practice this magnitude of energy generation is near impossible to realise due to planned maintenance hours as well as capacity reserve shut down. Therefore in hydel projects, the maximum desirable generation would work out to 60% PLF only. This means that if I kW is continuously used for generation, the maximum units that can be generated is $8760 \times 0.60 = 5256$ units. (However during certain years some hydel stations are found to have raised energy productivity beyond 60% PLF) (Refer Table 5.8).

Energy productivity figures of Peringalkuthu, Neriamangalam and Pallivasal projects were well above the expected maximum of 5256 units/kW. Energy productivity, on the basis of design value of generation exceeded the maximum limit in the case of 4-power projects-Peringalkuthu, Neriamangalam, Pallivasal and

Table 5.8: Energy Productivity of Hydel Stations (1980-95)

Power Projects	Installed Capacity (MW)	Generation (Design Value) (MU)	Average Actual Generation n (MU)	Designed Energy Productivity (kWh/kW) (3÷2)	Actual Energy Productivity (kWh/kW) (4÷2)	Ranking
Peringalkuthu	32	170	216	5313	6750	1
Neriamangalam	45	237	229	5267	6200	2
Pallivasal	37.5	284	277	7573	6053	3
Sholayar	54	233	235	4315	4352	4
Sabarigiri	300	1338	1270	4460	4233	5
Panniar	30	158	113	5267	3767	6
Kuttiadi	75	268	265	3573	3533	7
Idukki	780	2398	2292	3074	2939	8
Sengulam	48	182	137	3792	2854	9
Idamalayar	75	380	177	5067	2360	10
Total	1476.5	5648	5211	3825	3529	

Note: Average actual generation is the average annual generation of 16 years from 1980-81 to 1995-96.
*Authors Calculation. Source: KSEB "Power System Statistics" Various Issues.

Panniar. Energy productivity of Idukki, in-terms of both actual generation and design value of generation is considerably lower. With respect to energy productivity, Idukki goes down to the 9th position. We had earlier noted that even after the second phase of Idukki project was commissioned in 1986, no proportionate increase in energy generation was recorded. Had the productivity level of Idukki gone upto the 60% PLF, additional energy productivity would have been 2182 units per kW (5256-3074). So the excess energy that would have been available with 60% PLF at Idukki=2182×780 MW×1000kWh=1701.96 MU. To obtain additionally this much power in the system an additional generating station having a capacity of 324 MW* would be required.

The reason for the under utilisation of capacity needs deeper inquiry. Considering all the ten projects we found that the average productivity for the period 1980-1995 in terms of actual generation was 3529 units and in terms of design value 3825 units, a difference of 296 units (See Table 5.8). This being a difference between what is actually achievable and what is potentially achievable, it can be considered as an index of system inefficiency. The reason for this inefficiency may include variation in the inflow and storage, outages, planned maintenance shut down and reserves shutdown.

The Reliability Analysis

A power system is said to be reliable if it is able to supply good quality power without interruption and voltage surges and dips at an economically affordable tariff. System unreliability is generally manifested in the forms of low voltage, load shedding, power cut, frequent

---

* MU = MW × PLF × 8760 ÷ 1000. MW = MU × 1000 ÷ PLF × 8760 = 1701.96 × 1000/0.6 × 8760 = 323.81 MW.

line interruptions, low power factor and poor attendance to energy problems*. Cent per cent reliability cannot be expected from any power system. In advanced countries reliability is found to be nearer to 100%. The Loss of Load Probability (LOLP) in these countries is also very low, even less than 0.01.

System efficiency consists of technical efficiency and economic efficiency. Technical efficiency is reflected in better transmission and distribution network, high plant load factor, better reactive compensation (Power factor near to one) sufficient lines of various voltage levels (HTandLT) to evacuate power from the generating point to the consumer end, required number of transformers which help to deliver power at stipulated voltage levels.

Economic efficiency is characterised by optimum level of tariff based on long run marginal cost principle, optimum level of cost per kWh of generation, consideration of kVA or kVAR in the tariff policies, financial self dependency, undependability of Government subsidy and zero backlog of revenue collection. In the ensuing section an attempt has been made to examine both the technical efficiency and economic efficiency of the power system of Kerala. The important parameters used to list the technical efficiency are (i) the load factor, (ii) the diversity factor (iii) the demand factor and (iv) the transmission and distribution factor. Though technical in nature, we shall also look at these efficiency parameters from economic angle also.

---

* Personals at the bottom level are relatively meagre, therefore whenever an energy problem (technical or otherwise) arises it would take several hours and even days to attend to these problems. This is an index of poor quality of system performance.

The Load Factor

Load factor is the ratio of average load to the maximum load to the system in a given year. Technically it is the ratio of units (kWh) supplied by the system in a year divided by the product of peak load and the total number of hours in a year (8760 hours)[9]. The value of the result will be less than one or equal to one. Since energy is generated at par with demand, and not usually stored, the quantity of power generated is treated as equal to demand. Thus the load factor of a power is the load factor of demand. The more is the value of load factor, the more is the demand for energy during a given year. Higher energy demand leads the system to generate higher volumes of energy (within the limits) and thus more energy consumption and more revenue to the power system. Higher load factor is therefore an instrument to generate more units of energy, which in turn would help to bring down the average cost per unit of generation.

Normally, load factor is determined by the ratio of average demand to maximum demand. [(AD÷MD)×100] Average demand is the ratio of energy consumed to the duration of hours (AD = (kWh per hours)). Maximum demand is the peak load demand for power in a given year. Thus when the average demand changes or the maximum demand changes, load factor varies. There is no one to one relationships between maximum demand and load factor. The trends in maximum demand average demand and load factor of the power system during 1950-95 is listed in Table 5.9.

While average demand and maximum demand (system) increased to 245.3MW and 433.4MW respectively in 1970, the load factor declined to 56.6. Similarly when AD and MD further increased in 1990-

Table 5.9: The Trends in Maximum Demand and Load factor

Year	System Maximum Demand (MW)	System Average Demand (MW)	Load Factor
1950-51	24.8	16.99	68.5
1955-56	62.9	39.9	63.5
1960-61	116.3	73.97	63.6
1965-66	173.7	109.4	63.0
1970-71	433.4	245.3	56.6
1975-76	547	317.8	58.1
1980-81	843.1	602.2	71.6
1985-86	1033.8	637.9	61.7
1990-91	1147.8	776.0	67.7
1991-92	1264.6	816.9	64.6
1992-93	1302.0	843.7	64.8
1993-94	1235.4	817.8	66.2
1994-95	1329.8	750.0	56.4
1995-96	1372.6	760.4	55.4

*Authors Calculation. Source: KSEB "Power System Statistics" Various Issues.

Note:

1. Maximum Demand is the System Maximum Demand.
2. Average Demand is worked out as Maximum Demand LF. (Average Demand) for the system as whole cannot be worked out using equation AD= kWh/Hours, since the hours of energy consumption is not given.
3. Internal Maximum Demand is influenced by the import of energy as well, and hence excluded from the analysis.

91, the load factor again declined to 67.7. But when AD declined and MD increased in 1994 and 95, the load factor again declined to 56.4 and 55.4 respectively. The abnormal behaviour of the load factor can be explained in terms of the failure of the system to meet the peak hour demand and the escapism resorted to in the form of load shedding and power cut. This behaviour would keep the load factor at low level than that it would otherwise be. The average load factor for the entire period 1950 to 1995 worked out in Table 5.10 is found to be 63% in the case of Kerala. This is significantly higher than the corresponding Indian average[10] of less than 40%. Though Kerala's efficiency parameter is better than India's, on comparison with other countries, Kerala's figure is on the low side#. More over load factor of the Kerala Power System appears to have declined during 1970, 1994 and 1995. Knowledgeable sources maintained that the load factor of the state's system could be significantly improved if the following conditions are satisfied. (i) Availability of adequate water in the reservoir, (ii) limited hours of maintenance shut down (iii) averting forced outages and (iv) minimum reserve shut down. Available data on system operation, indicate that the hours of planned maintenance shut down and forced outages are on the increase, in some of the dominant power projects like Idukki and Sabarigiri[11].

Diversity Factor and Demand Factor

Diversity factor and Demand factor are other indices of power system efficiency. Diversity factor is the ratio of the sum of the individual maximum demands of various subdivisions of a system to the maximum demand of the whole system.[12] Demand factor is the

At the global level, in several countries PLF is>70%.

Table 5.10: The demand factor of the state power system (1950-95)

Year	Connected Load (MW)	Maximum Demand (MW)	Demand Factor	Diversity Factor TCL × DF ÷ MD
1950-51	70	25	0.36	1.0
1955-56	135	63	0.47	1.0
1960-61	311	116	0.37	1.0
1965-66	510	174	0.34	1.0
1970-71	880	318	0.36	1.0
1975-76	1405	482	0.34	1.0
1980-81	2045	735	0.36	1.0
1985-86	3145	1002	0.32	1.0
1990-91	4643	1272	0.27	1.0
1995-96	5776	1652	0.29	1.0

*Authors Calculation. Source: KSEB "Power System Statistics" Various Issues.

ratio of maximum demand to the total connected load of the system. The value of the demand factor is always less than one. It is an indicator of the simultaneous operation of the total connected load. When the maximum demand and connected load became closer, the value of the demand factor tends nearer to one. For a power system low value of demand factor is a boon.

The relationship between diversity factor and demand factor could be observed like this.

Diversity factor (DFr) = Sum of the Individual Maximum Demand ÷ Maximum Demand. (IMD ÷ Maximum Demand)...............(i)

Or = Total Connected Load × Demand factor ÷ Maxim Demand.[13]
(TCL × DF ÷ MD).................(ii)

Demand factor (DF) = maximum Demand ÷ Total Connected Load.
(MD ÷ TCL).......................(iii)

Because of the diverse nature of demand by various groups of consumers and that all of them will not demand energy for all the time throughout the hours, it is possible for the power system to generate energy as per demand.

The diversity factor of each consumer and each category of consumers can be worked out. However, such an attempt would require primary data, the collections of which require engineering skill. The System Diversity Factor is worked out using the equation (ii) and the values are given in table 5.10.

Demand factor of the state power system is worked out using secondary date. The demand factor in 1950 was 0.36. This has declined to 0.24 in the year 1995-96.

The overall trend analysis of the demand factor shows that during the post eighties, the demand factor has shown a declining trend. It means that the maximum demand per total connected load had declined over the years. This was due to the fact that the rate of increase in connected load was higher than that of increase in maximum demand*. As the simultaneous maximum demand declined, it seems to be a boon to the power system. Otherwise even greater stringent measures would have to be applied to control the peak load demand of the consumers.

The economic loss of relatively lower demand factor is to be verified. As the demand factor declines, the annual average energy generation declines. As average energy generation declines, there will be higher cost per unit generated.** Thus the existing suppressed demand (unmet demand) is a bane from the economic angle too. It even weakens the financial position of the State Power System.

Transmission and Distribution Loss

The technical and economic performance of a power system can be measured in terms of the transmission and distribution net work developed and maintained by it. The loss of energy due to poor T&D network has had its ultimate impact on the economic efficiency of that power system. The T&D facilities available in the State power system are analysed to examine its performance in the state power system#.

---

* Another plausible reason for the declining values of demand factor may be that the maximum demand was suppressed due to meagre power availability. This tactics brought the power system to level down the Maximum Demand, at a lower position.

An analysis of flow-chart –1 of energy loss given below reveals that there are technical and non-technical (commercial) ways of loss of energy during transmission and distribution. About 70% of total energy loss are due to technical reasons and 30% due to non-technical[14]. Transmission loss is different from distribution loss, in the sense that the former is through the delivery of power at high voltage (220kV, 110kV, and 66kV) and the latter, is through the delivery of low voltage (11kV, 230V) to the consumer end. Substations are of various voltage levels. (220kV, 110kV and 66kV). When the line length is beyond the stipulated circuit kilometres there is voltage drop at the tail end of the line. This is due to the fact that sufficient number of transformers is not installed to curb the energy loss. We shall attempt to verify the available transmission facilities in terms of number of substations, number of transformers and

Chart-5.4. Flow Chart of Energy Loss

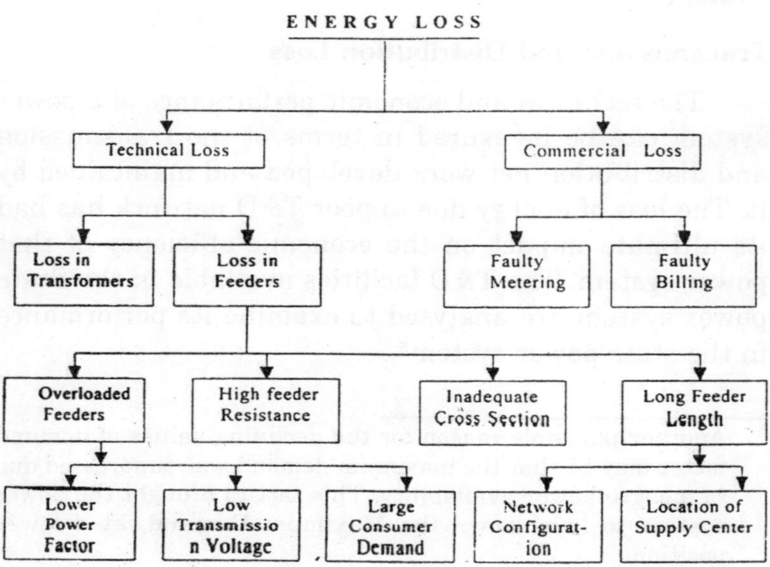

circuit kilometers of various lines. The circuit kilometres of lines of various capacities are quite insufficient in the context of state power system*.

As mentioned earlier, energy loss** is a part of the Power system and thus the aim of the system shall be to bring down the T&D loss*** to the minimum extent possible. Modern and efficient technologies and equipments used by the developed countries are rarely used in Kerala in curbing T&D loss[15]. It is a matter of concern that the T&D in Kerala is above the national average of 21%[16]. At the same time the maximum level of T&D suggested by World Bank Report is 15.5%* and

---

* Only 25% of 647CKm of 220kV lines and 50% of 910 CKm 110kV lines planned to be added during 1980-95 has materialised. For details see "Present Power Scenario in Kerala – Solutions for Tomorrow" Kerala State Electricity Board 1996.

** Causes of T&D losses are (1) Low power factor loads and inadequate compensation (2) Lengthy distribution lines (3) Inadequate size of conductors (4) Improper location of distribution transformers (5) Overloading of transformers (6) Poor quality and maintenance of equipment (7) Loose connection in joints (8) Theft including unmetered energy (9) Faulty energy meters (10) Errors in meter and (11) Loopholes in the rules and regulations.

*** Remedial measures to bring down high T&D loss are (1) Optimisation in the length of conductors (2) Modification and reconfiguration of the existing feeders (3) Conductor size modification (4) Transformer reallocation (5) Increase in the number of transformers of lesser capacity (6) Power factor improvement scheme (7) Strengthening administrative measures effectively (8) Proper energy auditing among all groups of consumers (9) Decentralised materials, purchase (10) Decentralised power planning (11) Under loading of distribution transformers and (12) Shut compensation to bring down heavy inductive load.

* T&D loss of countries are:- India 21%, China 7%, Thailand 10%, Argentine 12% and Chile 11%, Philippines 15%, Indonesia 17% (1991 data).

the target-level being 8.25%[17]. Energy loss is the state over the entire plan periods has been worked out in the previous chapter. The annual compounded rate of growth of T&D loss in the state is worked out as 8.85%, whereas, the rate of growth of energy generation is 7.51. The point elasticity of loss per generation in the state, is 1.18. It means that for 1% increase in energy generation in the state, there is 1.18% change in the energy loss.

Several literatures in T&D network reported that the ideal ratio of investment on generation and T&D facilities are 1:1[18]. Any investment on T&D reduction can be considered as an investment on energy generation,[19] since any reduction in the T&D loss means bringing additional units of energy to the grid. The ecological and environmental damage so created when energy is generated doesn't apply in this case. If the power system of Kerala can reduce the energy loss at least by one percentage, there will be an additional availability of 19 million units of energy to the system; (Energy loss 1994-95 is 1859.5 million units). The economic cost of generating this much energy is about Rs. 150 Million {(19 ÷ 5.25 (@ 60% PLF) = 3.61 MW} × 4 Million = 145 Million.) Thus any investment less than 145 Million for bringing down 1% of the existing level of T&D will be cost effective to the Power System.

Investment data on T&D improvement activities are not properly recorded in the power system statistics due to the reason that investment is not normally segregated into generation and distribution. However it could be observed that investment on T&D has declined over the years as evidenced from an analysis of the growth pattern of transformers per million units of consumption, consumers per transformer, transformer per connected load (MW) and consumers per circuit kilometres (110 kv) (See Table 5.11).

From the Table 5.11, it could be observed that during the first five-year plan period, there were no 110kV lines. In the second plan period, there were 332 consumers per circuit kilometres of 110kV line. The trend analysis of this variable (consumer per circuit kilometres) shows that in all the successive five year plan periods, consumer per circuit kilometre increased, which seems to be an indication that efforts, including investments, to enhance the circuit kilometres, corresponding to the increase in the number of consumers in the State Power System was relatively lower.

In the year 1950, the number of consumers per transformer was 86. In the first plan, the number of consumers per transformer increased to 94. However in the succeeding 2 five year plan periods, the number of consumers per transformer was relatively lower. From forth plan onwards, the number of consumers per transformer has increased to above 190. The rising trend of consumers per transformer can be considered as an index of insufficient T&D facilities within the power system. Investment on T&D network should have been increased proportionate to the growth in consumers.

Another index of T&D efficiency is the number of transformers per MW of connected load. In the year 1950 there was five transformers per megawatt of connected load. In the next five-year plan transformers per connected load increased to 9. Fluctuations in the number of transformer per connected load have a direct bearing on the energy loss. From the annual plan period onwards, the number of distribution transformers per megawatt of connected load declined. The number of transformers per megawatt of connected load remained

Table 5.11: Ratio of Transformers per Consumption, Consumer, Connected Load and Consumer/ Circuit Kilometers. (1950-95)

Year	Circuit KiloMeters (110 kV)	Consumers (Lakhs)	Consumption (MU)	Connected Load (MW)	Number of Transformers	Consumer/ C.K.M. (110kV)	Consumer/ Transformer	Transformer/ Connected Load (MW)	Transformer/ Consumption (MU)
1	*2*	*3*	*4*	*5*	*6*	*7*	*8*	*9*	*10*
1950	0	0.28	140	70	324	-	86	5	2
1951-56	0	0.79	274	142	845	-	94	6	3
1956-61	527	1.75	518	311	2398	332	60	9	6
1961-66	617	3.25	750	510	3930	527	83	8	5
1966-69	1106	4.40	1138	805	4907	398	90	6	4
1969-74	1350	7.77	1803	1231	8285	576	94	7	5
1974-79	1545	11.72	2419	1738	10330	759	114	6	4

Table 5.11: Contd...

1	*2*	*3*	*4*	*5*	*6*	*7*	*8*	*9*	*10*
1980-85	1896	22.17	4940	2803	12597	1169	176	5	3
1985-90	2297	31.90	6144	4166	16394	1389	195	4	3
1990-91	2329	34.50	6798	4643	17839	1481	193	4	3
1991-92	2329	36.98	7153	5526	18843	1588	196	3	3
1992-93	2345	39.30	7391	6576	19885	1676	198	3	3
1993-94	2390	41.54	7391	4933	21141	1738	197	4	3
1994-95	2444	44.17	8794	5397	22478	1807	197	4	3
1995-96	2425	46.86	9274	5776	24711	1932	190	4	3

Note: Figures in column No. 7, 8, 9, 10 are rounded of to the next digit.

*Authors Calculation. Source: KSEB "Power System Statistics" Various Issues.

4 from 1985 onwards. It is an indication that investment on sufficient quantities of transformers, in accordance with the changes in the power system variable like consumers and connected load, has been relatively lower.

An equally important index of distribution efficiency is the ratio of transformers (distribution) per MU of energy consumed. In the year 1950, there were 2 transformers per MU of energy consumed. In the second plan the ratio improved to 6 members. The declining trend continued during the third and fourth five-year plans periods. The number of transformers per consumption (MU) remained static from 1980 onwards (See Table 5.11). A tardy growth in transformers in relation of the energy consumption implies high levels of energy loss and poor quality of power supply. The indices of T&D network in Kerala are below the rates approved by the power system engineering. Thus we hypothesise that the heavy T&D loss in the state is due to inadequate investment in this area.

Inadequate Lines and Substations

Besides adequate number of distribution transformers, installation of adequate conductors in various voltage levels of transmission and distribution is yet another pre-condition for system performance. Many studies both at the micro and macro level revealed that the resistance of conductors (mainly distribution) is above the desired level. This is another area where huge investment is required. But the state power system was not capable of attending to issues like this, due to its poor financial status. The line loss in Kerala is comparatively higher among South Indian states due to the fact that hydro projects are location specific. All the ten-hydel projects are located in the eastern part of

Kerala, but bulk consumers are concentrated (mainly EHT Industrial Units) in the West Coast of Kerala. Thus to enable the transfer of power at the stipulated ratings throughout the state, a number of substations of various capacities are essential. But the rate of growth of substations and conductors are relatively lower than compared with other variables like the growth of consumers, consumption and connected load. For the evacuation of high voltage power from the generating point to the various substations located in different parts 440/220 kV substations are required*. It was only in the year 1992, a substation of 440 kV was commissioned. As per the proposal** at least three 440 kV substations are required in the state. It is also to be noted that there is no 440 feeder to deliver power various substations, whereas in other South Indian states it does exist#. It shows the poor level of T&D system in the state.

In the late 80s there was greater demand for energy. However the distribution network was not developed corresponding to the changes in the power system variables. In the year 1981-82, there were four 220/110kV substations in the state. 15 years later, the number of 220/110kV substations increased to five only (See Table 5.12). There is severe disparity of distribution of substations within the state. The region of Malabar comprising of five districts in the northern side of Kerala had only one 220/110kV-substation upto 1997. Recently two more 220/110kV substations were commissioned. The severe voltage crisis and the intolerable level of power

---

* In advanced countries power is transmitted through 750kV lines, in order to bring down power loss to the minimum extent possible.

** KSEB "Present Power Scenario in Kerala and Solutions for Tomorrow" Memeo-1996.

\# For details see "All India Statistics- General Review" by CEA.

outages in this region are partly due to this factor. The load distribution is highly skewed in the region of Malabar. There are eighteen, 110/66kV substations, and forty-five, 100/11kV substations and hundred and one, 66/11kV substations in the state power system (Refer Table 5.12). The trend in the pattern of increase of these substations became almost static (with some increase in the latter two types of substations) towards the end of 1980s. However in the post 1990s, low voltage transmission substations have increased comparatively faster. The trend shows that till the close of 1980s, the investment in T&D network seems to be very low. The number of substations began to increase after the turn of the nineties.

Energy loss is undesirable, but it does exist due to technical and non-technical reasons. In recent years the system authorities have showed an increasing inclination to use T&D looses as iron shield to cover up the loss, since all types of energy loss irrespective of their nature and origin are dumped under the category T&D loss. Non technical energy loss arises due to system inefficiency to identify the sources of energy loss. Computer softwares are used in advanced countries to identify technical and non-technical losses. But in the context of state power system, even the investment on T&D improvement itself is far from satisfactory. It implies that there are solutions to energy loss, but it would require huge investment by way of modernisation, renovation and computerisation. Energy loss during transmission and distribution entails financial loss too. The financial loss of unavailable energy (Generated, but not available for end-use) is on the increase. There are two types of financial losses – (1) Loss to the Power System (2) Loss to the society. Loss to the Power System worked out for the last 25 years is shown in Table 5.13.

Table 5.12: Number of Substations (1981-1995)

Capacity	'81-82	'82-83	'83-84	'84-85	'85-86	'86-87	'87-88	'88-89	'89-90	'90-91	'91-92	'92-93	'93-94	'94-95	'95-96
440/220kV	0	0	0	0	0	0	0	0	0	0	0	0	1	1	1
220/110kV	4	4	4	4	4	4	4	4	5	5	5	5	5	5	5
110/66kV	12	12	13	15	15	15	15	15	15	15	15	15	15	17	18
110/11kV	6	6	6	8	10	10	10	10	13	17	21	21	23	21	45
66/11kV	74	74	78	79	79	80	87	91	92	93	99	102	103	99	101

Source: KSEB "Power System operations", Thiruvanandapuram. Various Issues.

Chart 5.5. Growth of Substations

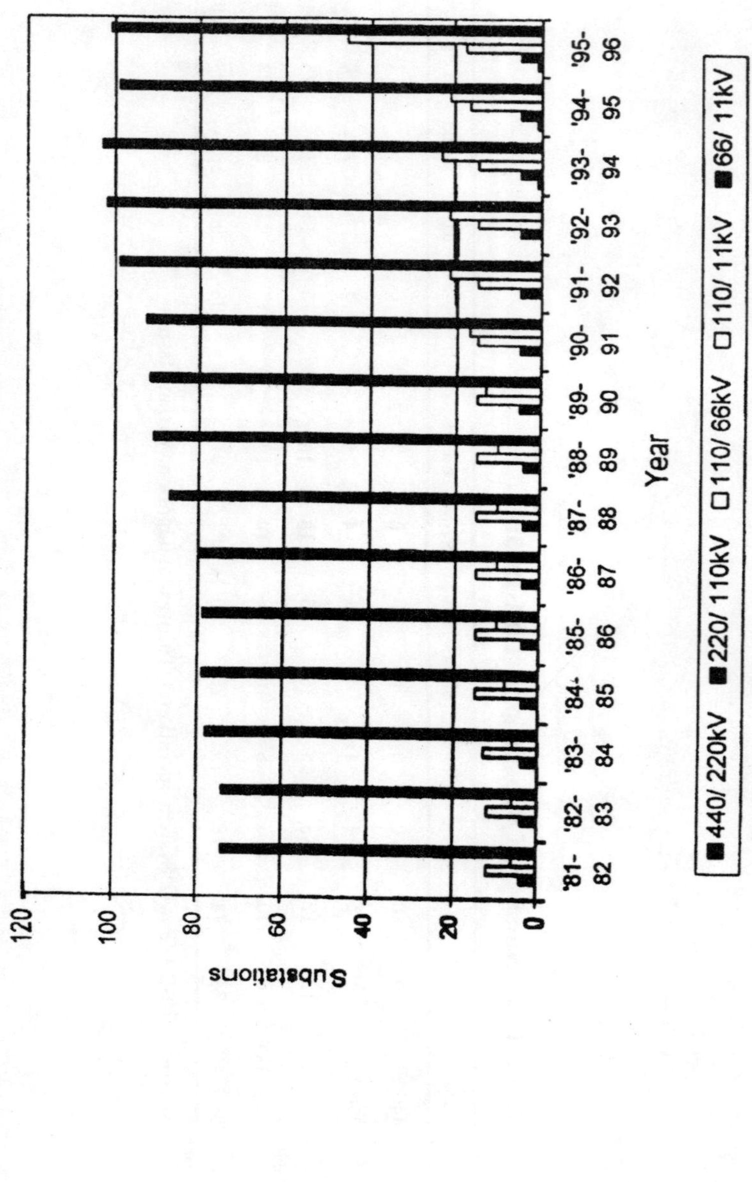

Table 5.13: Unit Loss and Revenue Loss (1970-95)

Year	Energy Sales (MU)	Energy Loss (MU)	Paise/Unit (Average)	Revenue Loss (Rs. Lakhs)	Total Revenue Collected (Rs. Lakhs)	% of Energy Loss	% Revenue Loss
1970-71	1858.7	272.3	8.64	235.3	1606.0	14.65	14.65
1975-76	2317.8	445.8	12.04	537.6	2795.5	19.23	19.23
1980-81	4499.9	747.1	21.20	1583.9	9539.2	16.60	16.60
1985-86	4172.0	1385.9	30.8	4264.3	12837.6	33.22	33.22
1990-91	5332.0	1466.4	53.0	7771.8	28046.9	27.50	27.50
1991-92	5596.0	1557.0	60.0	9342.0	33068.8	27.82	27.82
1992-93	5838.5	1552.0	73.95	11477.1	43176.9	26.58	26.58
1993-94	6234.2	1575.2	82.06	12925.7	54064.8	25.26	25.26
1994-95	7027.7	1766.7	86.68	15313.8	60915.1	25.14	25.14
1995-96	7414.2	1859.5	92.92	1727.8	68900.4	25.08	25.08

*Author's Calculation.

Source: KSEB "Power System Statistics" Various Issues.

During the decade 1970-71 to 1980-81, the percentage of energy loss (% of revenue loss also) varied between 15 to 19%. By the mid-nineties it increased to 25%. The above discussion shows that energy loss continued to increase together with the increase in consumption. In order to get a rough idea about the extent of energy loss in relation to the energy sales, a log linear regression model was fitted considering energy loss as dependent variable.

In Energy loss =	-1.7732	+	1.0376 (Energy sales)	R^2=0.91
Standard Error	(0.40187)		(0.052019)	
Student's T	(-4.41)		(19.95)	
Case=39 Years	P=0.0000		(Significant at 5% level)	

The regression coefficient shows that 1-% increase in energy sales results in 1.04-% increase in energy loss. This is indicative of the serious nature of the problem of energy loss in the Kerala power system.

Besides the revenue loss to the power system due to heavy T&D loss, there is an element of social cost as well. There are indirect evidences to the effect that the social costs involved in maintaining the rated voltage at the consumer end has been on the increase. Consumers depend upon self-generation and captive power generation and also on step ups and inverters to meet the low voltage and power interruptions particularly during the peak hours. The consumer dependence on such devices appears to have enormously increased. A recent investigation carried out by the author in the Kannur district[20] noted that about 90% of the urban consumers depend on such devices, either on individual units or simultaneously, although they are not legally permitted to do so. Power experts are of the opinion that use of inverters would adversely affect the quality of the power system due to harmonics. Besides these, social costs caused by burning out of distribution transformers and substation transformers due to overloading and short circuit are also reported to be on the increase.

Thus considering the major parameters of system reliability and performance, the state has been experiencing severe problems. In order to get rid of these problems in this regard, a recent study carried out by KSEB argues for transmission and distribution facilities as given in the following table 5.14.

Table 5.14: Additional transmission facilities required

Voltage	Substations	Lines-CKM	Total Cost (Rs. Million)
440kV	3	600	3300
220kV	18	900	5400
110kV	50	3000	9500
33kV	120	3000	1800
Total	191	7500	20000

Source: Kerala State Electricity Board (1996), "Present Scenario in Kerala and Solutions for Tomorrow" Memeo.

The financial investment required for this purpose would be of the order of 20000 million according to this organisation.

Economic Efficiency: The Role of Pricing

Given the technical efficiency, economic efficiency is determined essentially by revenue and cost factors. Revenue in turn is determined by the level of tariff, extent of subsidies allowed and the degree of buoyancy in the collection of sales revenue.

Revenue receipts of electricity boards depends mainly on tariff policy. Pricing policy has a very important bearing on production and consumption of electricity, as well as investment in this sector. Power tariff policy generally aimed at the following objectives:[21]

- Earning financial returns to sustain the growth of the utility, without excessive dependence on external finance,
- Prescribing tariffs related to costs, as well as the consumers capacity to pay,
- Designing tariffs to discourage waste, promote justified use of power and increase capacity utilisation by flattening the load curve, and
- Achieve the socio- economic objectives set by the states by granting explicit subsidies to special categories of consumers and levy duties on others.

Section 49 and 59 of Indian Electricity (Supply) Act, 1948 empower the state electricity boards to fix tariffs. According to section 63 of the Act, the Board "should adjust its tariffs so as to ensure that the total revenue in any year of account shall, after meeting all expenses properly chargeable revenues, including operating, maintenance, and management expenses, taxes (if any) on income and profits, depreciation and interest payable on debentures, bonds, and loans, leave such surpluses, the state government may from time to time specify".[22] An amendment to the Act in 1978 stipulated that the SEBs should earn at least 3% net return (after interest and depreciation) on a historic cost-asset base.

The Venkataraman Committee constituted in 1964, and the Rajadhyaksha Committee in 1980, examined at length the tariff policy of the SEBs and affirmed that all the SEBs should make more than 3% net rate of return on the capital invested. The various Finance Commissions constituted from time to time, which examined the performance of SEBs from the viewpoint of the state finances, have lamented their poor financial performance.

The recommendations mentioned above seem to have remained largely on paper, and in reality, SEBs continued to drain the resources of the state governments. The SEBs have been continuously incurring heavy losses in the range of 10 to 15% on capital invested, and in the last four years, the situation has worsened with losses ranging from less than 12% in 1992-93 to 13.5% in 1995-96, at the all India level. The commercial losses of SEBs without subsidy amounted to Rs. 71.3 billion and with subsidy Rs. 54.4 billion.[23] None of the SEBs excepts that of Orissa showed a positive rate of return. In Jammu and Kashmir, the losses were as high as 46% on capital used. Losses were higher in agriculturally advanced states of Punjab (29%), Haryana (22%) and were more than 20% in West Bengal and Gujarat. In the context of Kerala the cumulative profit up to 1985-86 was Rs. 7.6 million, whereas in the year 1992-93, the cumulative loss went up to Rs. 139.5 million. The net commercial loss of Kerala State Electricity Board started in the year 1985-86 with Rs. 3.3 million which went up to Rs. 51.8 million in 1991-92.[24]

The Main reason for this state of affairs appears to be lack of economic pricing. The average tariff has remained below the average cost of energy since mid 1980s and the cost – revenue differences, if anything, have widened over the years.

Economists have different perspectives regarding pricing of electricity.[25] The welfare maximising approach indicates that the prices of electricity should equal the marginal cost. However in a decreasing cost industry, fixation of tariff equal to the marginal cost would not enable the utility to cover the total costs, which makes the departure from marginal cost pricing rule necessary.

The second best solution considers electricity as a multi-product firm, (Product differentiation may be in terms of the time of use, or the category of consumers) and according to this, optimal prices ought to vary inversely with own price elasticity of the product. The demand pattern varies not only with respect to different consumer categories, but also between different time periods. The hydel plants are both peaking and off peaking stations. Even there have been differences in marginal cost generation of electricity in peak and off peak periods. But generally these differences have been over looked due to lack of strict economic pricing. Recently thermal stations started generating power during the peak hours, which increases marginal cost of supplying electricity during the peak hours. Implementation of peak load pricing requires installation of time of day meters at user's premises, which increases administrative cost. Kerala State Electricity Board has implemented TOD meter in the state from 1st April 1999 onwards to EHT and HT consumes on an experimental basis, with the aim of limiting the peak load demand, by imposing higher rate of tariff per unit of consumption during the hours between 6.30 PM to 10. PM. (30% higher than the normal tariff).

Another method suggested is to apply two-part tariff to EHT and HT consumers. The two components of this kind of pricing are (i) the KVA charges (Capacity charges) and (ii) the energy charges. The KVA charges are the fixed charges for the maximum demand of power drawn by the consumers and the energy charges are the tariff for the total units of energy consumed by such consumers. (Even if there are no energy consumption, the EHT&HT consumers are expected to pay the fixed demand charges to the Board.) The Pricing system followed in Kerala, is not according to the marginal cost pricing principle, inspite of the fact that this could be introduced. The fixed charge is a lum-sum charge to cover the fixed expenses like installation, meter reading, and billing. The capacity charge depends on the power factor, which the consumers maintain in the system. If the power factor is less than 0.85, in some states, a penalty charge is imposed. In Kerala such a system is not introduced, inspite of the fact that, it would help the consumers to avoid energy wastage, and the Board to earn maximum revenue.

Practical application of optimal pricing of electricity, as pointed out by Rao[26] is impossible, as it requires the measurement of marginal costs at all points, and the administrative and information costs of designing these prices can be prohibitive. Besides the problem of complexity, the approach can also lead to inequity. However in contrast to the average cost pricing, evaluated historically, usually used in accounting sense, the marginal cost pricing is more rational.

Thus in actual practice most countries use the principle of relating prices of marginal costs, but indirectly. Many countries including the USA adopt a cost based price regulation, called the "fair rate of return regulation". This method estimates a total cost of supplying electricity, which includes a fair rate of return at a normatively determined capacity utilisation.

Significant differences in determining the structure of prices for different consumer categories exist among countries, depending upon the extent of regulation, policy constraint, and social objectives. The traditional and the most easy approach has been to average the cost elements across different classes of consumes, which reflects in cross subsidisation among different categories of consumes. The state electricity board in Kerala has been following this practice since long.

Pricing Method in Kerala—An Over View

By convention tariff determination by Kerala State Electricity Board is done in three stages. In the first stage, the generating cost involved in meeting a given level of demand is estimated. The operating cost item considered for estimation in this stage include operating costs like the cost of duel, power purchase, operation and maintenance, establishment and administration and miscellaneous costs. Capital costs include, depreciation, interest on debt and return on equity (introduced very recently) are also considered.

In the second stage, the costs at different voltage levels like EHTandHT and LT ends are estimated. For this purpose the cost of power per unit is estimated. The costs at various transmission ends are computed using information on T&D costs, after considering these losses. A weighted average of these costs is estimated for arriving at units of power supply at these voltage ends.

The final stage is the fixation of tariff. At this stage socio, economic and political considerations play an important role. Although cost at LT ends are higher than that of HT end, electricity board charge lower rate for domestic and agricultural consumers (LT consumers) and higher rate for HT and EHT consumers. The determination of unit cost of energy at distribution low voltage, and high voltage ends and the weighted average of these costs in Kerala Power System are shown in Table 5.17.

Cost per unit at distribution high voltage end is available only upto 1985-86, as Kerala State Electricity Board discontinued publication of this information there after. This caused serious constraints in computing the average cost per unit sold. We have therefore resorted to an indirect method. Between 1978 to 79 and 1985-86, (the phase during which separate data are available for high voltage and low voltage distribution ends) the unit costs at distribution ends increased at an almost uniform rate of 5% per annum both for low voltage and high voltage ends. We assumed that during the post 85-86 phase also the unit cost at distribution ends moved at identical rates. During these periods the average annual increase in the cost at low voltage end was 6.16%. Applying this rate to the high voltage end, the unit cost at the high voltage end was worked out for the different years from 1986-87 (See table 5.15). Average cost per unit of energy sold in the State has been calculated by computing the weighted average of the cost at distribution low voltage end as well as at distribution high voltage end. The weights assigned being the relative percentage sales to HT; EHT and LT consumers.

The cost at the generation end has increased from 5.29 Paise per unit in 1978-79 to 10.62 Paise in 1995-96 (An increase of 101%) However the cost at the transmission end was 7.62 Paise per unit in 1978-79, which rcse to 49.32 Paise in 1995-96, registering an increase of 547%. The cost at the distribution high voltage end has increased from 14.03 Paise per unit in 1978-79 to 35.61 Paise in 1995-96, showing an increase

Table 5.15: Cost per Unit Sent Out at Different Voltage Ends (Paise/kWh) 1978-95

Year	Cost at Generation End	Cost at Transmission End	Cost at Distribution High Voltage End	Cost at Distribution Low Voltage End	Weighted Average Cost**
1	*2*	*3*	*4*	*5*	*6*
1978-79	5.29	7.62	14.03	42.99	33.72
1979-80	5.58	8.67	15.22	55.89	42.47
1980-81	5.98	9.50	17.00	59.31	42.89
1981-82	5.95	10.61	19.65	69.16	51.34
1982-83	6.96	12.03	20.10	68.66	47.78
1983-84	8.15	14.58	22.38	67.81	46.00
1984-85	6.26	11.35	19.03	66.58	42.81
1985-86	4.96	10.74	19.51	60.51	41.24

Table 5.15: Contd...

1	2	3	4	5	6
1986-87	6.15	15.88	20.71*	71.31	48.03
1987-88	3.32	18.73	22.00*	84.18	58.06
1988-89	6.46	20.83	23.37*	69.56	49.27
1989-90	6.47	23.50	24.82*	70.14	50.65
1990-91	6.61	24.05	26.36*	70.34	50.99
1991-92	7.80	32.25	27.99*	76.93	55.89
1992-93	8.11	27.89	29.73*	75.95	58.85
1993-94	8.83	41.43	31.57*	93.05	70.92
1994-95	9.55	44.65	33.53*	96.91	73.46
1995-96	10.62	49.32	35.61*	115.22	86.12

Note: *(i)* Cost per unit sent out including interest charges.
(ii) *Author's calculation based on an average of 6.2% growth rate per annum
(iii) **Worked out by the author applying weighted average

Source: KSEB, "Power System Statistics", Thiruvanandapuram, (Various Issues)

of 154%, and that of low voltage end from 42.99 Paise per unit to 115.22 Paise during the same period. (An increase of 155%) From the Table 5.15, it is seen that the average cost per unit sold was 35 Paise in 1978-79, which doubled in 1995-96. (There may be some discrepancy between the average cost per unit of energy sold by the Kerala State Electricity Board, and the weighted average cost worked out by us.)

Though there is case for setting power tariff on an economic basis, there are considerable difficulties in evolving such a rational policy. As generation, pooling, transmission and distribution involve joint costs, maintenance of frequency, reactive compensation, etc. besides common cost of administration, differing plant load factors in different generating stations, and T&D losses, there is no unique way of rationally distributing these costs between different categories of consumers. It is also not possible to calculate accurately, the cost to each individual consumer or group of consumers (though it is essential) as unit costs vary continuously during the course of a day. Further energy policy objectives such as rural electrification, the use of renewable sources of energy, or simple equity often dictate a departure from strict cost related pricing.[27]

Tariff Structure of Kerala Power System

Actual tariff levied by the SEBs are at variance with the broad principles of rational pricing policy, which must be incentive compatible, and resources generating for investment. Economic considerations do not seen to have dictated the determination tariffs, as tariff on different category bears no relationship to marginal cost of supplying power to them. A comparison of growth rate in average revenue (which is equivalent to tariff) of different categories of consumers is given in Table 5.16.

Table 5.16: Growth in average tariff- category wise (Paise/unit) 1985-86 to 1995-96

Year	Domestic	Commercial	Industrial (LT)	Industrial (EHTandHT)	Agriculture	Overall
1985-86	29.00	60.52	23.15	24.48	14.83	30.77
1986-87	41.37	78.66	55.74	45.05	24.88	48.25
1987-88	41.28	96.76	69.09	54.87	26.44	55.66
1988-89	44.87	92.88	71.27	57.55	20.70	56.69
1989-90	46.00	94.00	75.00	54.00	21.00	55.00
1990-91	43.00	76.00	67.00	54.00	25.00	53.00
1991-92	53.00	89.00	73.00	57.00	25.00	60.00
1992-93	54.45	105.50	93.34	80.95	25.10	73.95
1993-94	574.53	117.84	101.54	90.82	29.35	82.06
1994-95	58.67	120.64	111.55	98.91	23.94	86.68
1995-96	60.98	195.08	116.80	101.75	23.94	92.92
Average Increase (%)	110	222.3	404.5	315.6	60	202

Source: KSEB "Power System Statistics" Thiruvanandapuram (various issues).

The average tariff was 29 Paise per unit for the domestic sector in the year 1985-86, which rose to 61 Paise in 1995-96, registering an increase of 110%. Commercial tariff per unit was 60.5 Paise in '85-86, and it has increased to 195.08 Paise in 1995-96. (Refer Table 5.18). There was 223% increase in tariff for this sector during the period under review. The average tariff of industrial (LT) sector was 23.15 Paise per unit and that of industrial (EHTandHT) 24.48 Paise in 1985-86. These tariffs have increased to 116.8 Paise, and 101.75 Paise respectively for these two sectors. The highest percentage increase in tariff was noted for the industrial (LT) sector with 404.5% and those of Industrial (EHT&HT) sector 315.6%. There was 60% increase in the tariff of agriculture sector in the state, during the years between 1985 and 95. It was observed that since 1986, the agriculture tariff hovered around 25 Paise per unit in the state, while the tariff of other categories have shown considerable change. The overall tariff in the state changed from 31 Paise per unit in 1985-86 to 92 Paise in 1995-96, registering an increase of 202%. The average percentage changes in the prices of domestic and agricultural consumers are less than that of the percentage changes in overall tariff. Differential pricing of electricity to various consumer categories results in subsidies to some sectors and taxes on others due to the policy of cross subsidisation. The energy prices per units in commercial, industrial (LT) and industrial (EHT&HT) sectors are well above that of the overall prices, and hence these three sectors are said to be the subsidising sectors in the state.

Based on the available data on the average cost per unit sent out at the distribution low voltage end, (for domestic, commercial, industrial (LT) and agricultural sectors) and high voltage end, (for industrial EHTandHT consumers) and the tariff per unit of energy sold to these various categories of consumers, the cost-revenue differences of these sectors are worked out in the Table 5.17. This kind of analysis would be helpful in getting an idea of net revenue contributed by each category of consumers to the board, given the number of million units of energy consumed by these sectors. It is also an indication of the extent of subsidy received to the domestic and agricultural sectors, and the extent of cross subsidy contributed by the commercial and industrial consumers. (Refer Table 5.17.)

Table 5.17: Cost-tariff differences of categories of consumers (Paise/unit) 1985-1995

Year	Domestic	Commercial	Industrial (LT)	Industrial (EHTandHT)	Agriculture
1985-86	-31.5	0	-37.25	+4.97	-45.7
1986-87	-29.9	+7.4	-15.69	+24.34	-46.4
1987-88	-42.9	+12.6	-15.10	+32.87	-57.8
1988-89	-24.7	+23.3	+01.70	+34.18	-48.9
1989-90	-24.2	+23.8	+4.80	+29.18	-49.2
1990-91	-27.4	+05.6	-3.4	+27.64	-45.4
1991-92	-24.0	+12.0	-4.0	+29.01	-52.0
1992-93	-22.1	+28.9	+13.7	+51.22	-51.5
1993-94	-35.6	+24.7	+8.4	+59.25	-63.7
1994-95	-38.3	+23.6	+14.6	+65.38	-73.1
1995-96	-54.2	+79.9	+1.6	+66.14	-91.5

*Author's calculation. Source: KSEB "Power System Statistics" Various Issues.

It is patently clear from the table that price of electricity in the domestic and agricultural sectors has been consistently much lower than the average cost, where as it has been consistently higher in the industrial (EHT&HT) and commercial sectors, with a fluctuating trend in the industrial (LT) sector. Needless to say that this situation is a clear reflection of inoptimal pricing procedure followed by the state power system for a long period of time.

The average cost-revenue relation can be taken as a rough indicator of the financial efficiency of the system. Since the data relating to average cost per unit of energy sold by the Board are available only from 1990, we are constrained to relate average revenue with average cost only for a limited period. In Table 5.18 is given the cost-revenue differences. The Table unmistakably shows that the tariff remained well below the average cost during nineties.

More over the differences appears to have increased from 10.59 Paise per unit in 1990-91 to 18.24 Paise in 1995-96, i.e. an increase of 72%. Cost-revenue differences in absolute term are found to be much lower than that of all India average, but the percentage increase at the state level is much higher than the all India level.

Since the average revenue or average tariff is lower than the average cost, one way to rationalise pricing and thus to reduce the losses incurred by the Kerala State Electricity Board is to raise the tariff at least equal to the level of average cost. Alternatively, losses can be brought down by reducing cost per unit. This requires an examination of the cost structure of Kerala State Electricity Board, with a view to exploring the possibilities for reducing cost. The cost structure of KSEB shows certain peculiar features (see table 5.19). The average fuel cost of KSEB is the lowest in India (till 1994-95 it was considered as zero) because the State

Table 5.18: Cost-revenue differences in South Indian SEBs (Paise/unit) 1990-95

SEBs	1990-91	1991-92	1992-93	1993-94	1994-95	1995-96	% changes
APSEB	4.23	5.94	5.80	10.38	15.45	24.67	483
KEB	1.21	9.64	6.77	5.35	14.56	3.32	174
KSEB	10.59	21.3	13.34	15.7	14.23	18.24	72
TNEB	27.79	7.24	17.4	16.36	20.57	31.67	14
All India average	26.79	27.74	28.17	26.04	27.04	29.45	9.9

Source: Planning Commission (1995) "Annual Report of the Working of State Electricity Boards and Electricity Departments" Government of India, New Delhi.

Table 5.19: Comparison of cost structure in South Indian SEBs (Paise/Unit) 1995-96

SEBs	Fuel Cost	Power Purchase	O&M Cost	E&A Cost	Interest Cost	Depreciation	Miscellaneous	Total Cost
APSEB	43.3 (28.7)	37.6 (24.9)	6.3 (4.2)	14.3 (9.5)	31.9 (21.1)	10.0 (6.6)	7.7 (5.0)	151.1
KEB	6.7 (4.6)	86.1 (59.0)	5.5 (2.8)	24.3 (16.6)	12.6 (8.6)	10.7 (7.3)	0.0 (0.0)	145.9
KSEB	2.6 (2.2)	33.7 (28.9)	5.7 (4.90)	36.8 (31.5)	26.8 (23.0)	7.0 (6.0)	4.2 (3.6)	116.7
TNEB	81.3 (45.7)	42.2 (23.7)	4.7 (2.6)	25.2 (14.2)	16.9 (9.5)	7.2 (4.0)	0.5 (0.3)	178.0
All India Average	40 (23.5)	54.1 (31.8)	7.2 (4.2)	24.5 (14.4)	29.3 (17.2)	12.7 (7.5)	2.4 (1.4)	170.1

Note: Figures in brackets show the relative percentage.

Source: Planning Commission (1995) "Annual Report of the Working of State Electricity Boards and Electricity Departments" Government of India, New Delhi.

has been exclusively relying upon hydropower, till quite recently.

The single largest cost component of Kerala State Electricity Board is the establishment and administrative cost. (E&A cost). Both in absolute and relative terms, it is the highest in India. Interest cost of Kerala State Electricity Board is also one of the highest in India. Since E&A cost remains much higher than the rest of the southern states, and all India average, there are chance for bringing down the cost of these two items considerably.

The ratio of employees to energy units sold and the ratio of employees to electricity consumers are lower in Kerala State Electricity Board as compared to the corresponding figures of all India and Southern states. However the establishment and the administrative cost in Kerala State Electricity Board is the highest. This is because the staff pattern in the Kerala State Electricity Board is significantly different from the rest of SEBs. In KSEB the proportion of engineers to the technical staff (lower cadre) is much higher than other southern SEBs.[28] The number of sub-engineers, technicians, and other lower category employees, is much lower compared to other SEBs, in South India. The higher proportion of engineers is one important reason for the high administrative cost. An another peculiar characteristic of Kerala State Electricity board is that larger proportion of labour is employed in administrative sector, rather than in generation, transmission and distribution sectors. This also partly accounts for higher administrative costs. The fact that the service of the so called engineers can as well be rendered by lesser categories of employees and that the volume of employment in the administrative sector can be reduced to some extent without loss of efficiency, there exists scope for reducing administrative expenses. Thus through tariff hike as well as cost reduction losses can be brought down.

Conclusion

Between 1979 and 1997 the installed capacity in the State increased 49% only, whereas internal maximum Demand increased 171% causing severe power shortage. The reason for low capacity addition include (a) total reliance on hydro power stations, (b) inordinate delay in the commissioning of ongoing power projects, (c) slow initiation of alternative power projects, (d) lack of Central investment and (e) drop in State's own investment in the power sector. The performance analysis of ten hydel projects showed that power generation generally exceeded the design value of generation during 1989-95, an indication that water availability was not a constrained for power generation during the period, contrary to the usual official pronouncement. Idukki, the biggest power station in terms of installed capacity and generation goes down to the 9th position in terms of system efficiency parameters like PLF and energy productivity. Average load factor exhibits a declining trend. This abnormal behavior could be explained in terms of the failure of the system to meet peak hour demand and the intermittent power cuts and load shedding. The existing T and D network in Kerala is well below the rates approved by the power system engineering. T and D loss in the state is far higher than international and Indian standards. The severe voltage crisis, heavy T and D loss and frequent power outages in the Malabar region of the State are largely due to insufficient growth of substations of varying capacities.

The economic efficiency of Kerala State Electricity Board has not only been on the low side, but in recent years has further fallen. During the nineties for which relevant cost and revenue data are available, the tariff remained well below the average cost. Cost revenue differences per unit which was 10.5 Paise in 1990 increased to 18 Paise in 1995-96.

Notes and References

1. Parameshwaran M.P. (1990) *"Kerala's Power Predicament: Issues and Solutions"*, Economic and Political Weekly, September, 15th pp. 2089-2092.
2. Menon R.V.G., (1990) *"Electricity and Development"* in Energy Debate, KSSP, Kozhikode.
3. IRTC (1995) *"Exercises for Integrated Resource Planning for Kerala End Use Analysis-An Empirical Study"*, Technical Report-1, Electricity. p. 2.
4. KSEB (1996) *"Present Power Scenario in Kerala, and Solutions for Tomorrow."* Mimeographed p. 22.
5. Devi Ganga. S. *"Energy Perspective of Kerala"* M.Phil. Dissertation, Department of Economics, Pondicherry University, Mahe Centre. p. 100 (Unpublished).
6. Pavithran. G.(1994) *"The Possibilities of Achieving a Reliable Power Supply in Kerala"*, IEEE Annual Journal, Thiruvananthapuram, p. 17.
7. Gompertz Relation: *"The best model searched with the help of software "Curve Expert"* and Statistical software "Regression and Time Series Analysis" (RATS)
8. IRTC (1996) *"Technical Report on Electricity"* p. 7.
9. Sudeesh Uppal (1998) *"Electrical Power"*, Khanna Publishers, New Delhi. p. 224.
10. CEA *"Annual Report of the working of State Electricity Boards and Departments"* October 1995, New Delhi.
11. Kerala State Electricity Board *"System Operation-95/96"* Thiruvananthapuram.
12. Gonen Turan *"Electric Power Distribution System Engineering"* McGraw Hill Book Co; 1986. p. 44.
13. Ibid. p. 44.

14. IRTC "o.p.c.i.t." (Ref. 3) p. 89.

15. Pavithran. G, and Krishnan Ananda. K, *"T&D Loss – Problems and Remedies"*, Hydel September 1994. p. 1.

16. Ibid. p. 2.

17. Ibid. p. 3.

18. Pavithran. G. *"Scope for improving the distribution System of Kerala"* Kerala State Electricity Board Engineers Association Silver Jubilee Souvenir, 1994. p. 41.

19. Sant Girish (1996) *"Least Cost Power Planning in Maharashtra"*, "Prayas" Pune. p. 3.

20. Cross section data of 100 domestic households drawn from the municipal areas of the district revealed that, 90% of the sample has been using step up transformers of various ratings, irrespective of their connected load. Ratings of step up transformers were based on their personal income, and the load requirement. Out of the 100 samples, 18 used generators, 25 used inverters, and 8 used inverters with 0.5kVA and above. Rough calculation based on the Energy Not Served (ENS) and the energy that is being made available through the power electronics appliances refereed above revealed that the cost of energy is Rs. 3.41/kWh and the cost of energy supplied by the grid is 0.89/kWh (in 1995-96). Cost of energy not served (CENS)= The Social Cost of Energy. (SEC) (The cost met on step up transformers, inverters, and generators etc.) Therefore CESN=SEC/Number of units made available, i.e. Rs. 224000 ¸ 65700kWh/year=Rs. 3.41/kWh.

21. *"The Rajadhyaksha Committee Report on Power –1980"* in Govinda Rao, M. el at (ed.) "The Economics of Electricity Supply in India" (1988) Macmillan. p. 87.

22. Sarkar, S.S., and Bhatnakar (1996) *"Law of Electricity in India"* (4th edition) India Law House, New Delhi.

23. Tata Energy Research Institute (1997) *"Tata Energy Data Directory and Year Book-1996-97"*. New Delhi. p. 116.

24. Ibid. p. 116.

25. For details see *"The Economics of Electricity Supply in India"*, Govinda Rao, M. et al (ed.) Macmillan, 1988.

26. Rao, Govinda, M. et al. (1998) *"The Economics of Electricity Supply in India"* Macmillan.

27. Devi Ganga. S. "o.p.c.i.t." (refer-5).

28. CEA (1995) *"All India Statistics- General Review, 1992-93"* Government of India, New Delhi.

6

Demand for Electricity

Introduction

In the preceding two chapters, demand and supply aspects of power system were examined from macro perspectives. In this chapter issues relating to sectoral demand for power are taken up.

Electricity is demanded by various groups-Domestic, Commercial, Industrial, (Low Tension), Industrial (Extra High Tension and High Tension), Agricultural, Public Lighting, Public Water Works and licencees)*. Among these, the share of Energy demand by public lighting, water works and licencees is relatively very small. In the demand analysis attempted here we shall, therefor be examining individually the electricity demand by the first five categories of consumers. The demand by public lighting, water works and licencees will be treated together under the heading "Other Category".

---

* In the publications of KSEB, licencee is a category of consumer who purchases electricity from the KSEB and sells the same to the various groups of consumers within an area. This is now in vogue only in the Municipal area of Trissur.

These consumer groups demand energy for end use purposes, which vary from group to group. The domestic and commercial consumers demand electricity mainly for lighting, fans, refrigerators and drives of smaller capacity. The industrial demand for electricity is mainly as a factor of production for value addition. In the agricultural sector the demand is mainly for irrigation pump-set. In short energy is demanded either as input or for end use purposes.

The demand for electricity by these categories depends on their connected load. Connected load directly varies with the number of consumers and electrical appliances installed. In this context, the correlation worked out by us between consumption and connected load, consumption and consumers, as well as connected load and consumers showed very high coefficient values**. We have already noted that internal maximum demand is mainly determined by connected load and time factor.

Sector wise Analysis of Connected Load

The changes in the growth of connected load of the Kerala Power System with respect to the major categories of consumers are shown in Table 6.1 from the year 1970-71.

During the period 1970-71 to 1995-96, the highest increase in connected load occurred in the domestic sector (10.34%). The domestic sector recorded quinquennial changes of more than 75% during the first fifteen years. The increase in connected load occurred

** Total consumption – Total connected load correlation = 0.87
Total consumption – Total consumers correlation = 0.89 (All worked out for 26 Years)
Total connected load – Total consumers correlation = 0.98

Table 6.1: The trends in the rate of changes of connected load in MW (1970 to 1995)

Year	Domestic	Commercial	Industrial (LT)	Industrial (EHTandHT)	Agricultural	Others	Total (MW)
1970-71	233.21	80.91	172.10	251.11	75.15	14.80	879.71
1975-76	396.38 (77.58)	129.37 (59.9)	264.10 (53.46)	365.11 (45.42)	160.84 (108.48)	24.05 (62.5)	1404.83
1980-81	711.24 (79.43)	187.70 (455.09)	379.07 (43.53)	414.11 (13.42)	261.59 (62.64)	26.53 (10.31)	2045.21
1985-86	1261.79 (77.40)	303.05 (61.45)	545.61 (43.93)	558.64 (34.90)	362.49 (38.57)	47.40 (78.67)	3143.98
1990-91	1748.40 (38.57)	379.61 (25.26)	889.4 (63.01)	1077.21 (92.93)	429.3 (18.43)	71.40 (50.6)	4642.68
1995-96	2601.03 (48.77)	533.21 (40.46)	1099.8 (23.26)	875.91 -18.61	563.85 (31.34)	79.51 (11.36)	5776.09
Growth Rate (%)	10.34	7.8	7.7	5.9	7.8	NA*	8.52

Note: Compound growth rate is worked out using Semi log linear regression.
*Growth rate of connected load of "other category" not worked out.
Source: KSEB "Power System Statistics" – Thiruvanandapuram. Various issues.

in the domestic sector markedly declined thereafter, the reason being the refusal of KSEB to provide new connections to all applicants in view of persisting power shortages and huge back log of applicants.

Commercial connected load has increased at an annual compound rate of growth of 7.8%. It is observed that upto 1985-86, the rate of changes in commercial connected load was higher than that of Industrial (LT, EHT&HT) connected load. However during the 1985-90 period, the rate of changes in commercial connected load fell behind that of domestic and Industrial connected load. In the post nineties, the commercial connected load showed a higher level of percentage changes. This is partly due to the fact that the state's investment was mainly confined to the service sectors.

Connected load in the L.T industrial sector increased faster (7.7%) than the HT&EHT category (5.9). As in the latter the highest increases in the former also occurred during the period between 1985-90. But unlike the EHT&HT category, growth of connected load in the LT sector recorded 23.6% during the ensuing five years. The higher growth of LT as compared to EHT&HT is a reflection of the industrial trend in the state, as Kerala seems to have by and large encouraged growth of small and medium size industrial units.

Connected load in the agricultural sector continued to rise at a faster rate till 1980-81, after which the rate tended to decline perceptibly. However taking entire span of a quarter century, the agricultural sector recorded the highest rate of growth, from 75.15 MW of connected load to 563.85MW of connected load, next to the domestic sector, the proximate reason being priority in connection and the lowest tariff enjoyed by the agricultural sector. The compound rate of growth of connected load in this sector was 7.8%. The rate of growth of commercial sector is also almost the same.

Considering the entire consumer groups, the total connected load increased at the rate of 8.52% per annum. Between 1980-90, there was more than 65% growth in the connected load, but in the post nineties, the rate of percentage change of total connected load in the state has considerably declined. The reason for such a lower rate of percentage changes can be attributed to the negative change in the growth of connected load of H.T and EHT Sector during the same period.

Although the rate of growth of connected load of commercial, Industrial (LT) and agricultural sector remains more or less the same, the percentage share of connected load of these sectors are different. The trends in the sectoral share of connected load are presented in the Table 6.2.

Very clear trends are observable in the case of domestic sector and industry *HT&EHT). The share of the domestic sector steadily increased from 25% in 1970-71 to 45% in 1995-96. Conversely the share of industry (HT) steadily declined from 28.5% in 70-71 to 15% in 95-96. The declining share of industry is reflective of the stagnating industrial sector of the state. The share of the commercial sector appears to have remained unchanged. The peak demand is to a large extent determined by the demand from domestic and commercial sectors. These two sectors together constitute 55% of the total connected load in the state in 95-96. The big increases in the share of the domestic sector and the absence of decline in the share of the commercial sector is a clear indication of the Kerala model of development, characterised by disproportionate growth of the service sector, stunted growth of commodity

Table 6.2: Trends in the Percentage share of connected load

Year	Domestic	Commercial	Industrial (LT)	Industrial (EHTandHT)	Agricultural	Others	Total
1970-71	25.37	9.20	11.56	28.54	8.77	8.56	100
1975-76	28.22	9.21	18.80	25.99	11.45	6.37	100
1980-81	34.78	9.18	18.53	20.25	12.79	4.47	100
1985-86	40.46	9.72	17.49	17.10	11.62	3.60	100
1990-91	41.95	9.11	21.34	15.22	10.30	2.08	100
1995-96	45.03	9.23	19.04	15.16	9.76	1.77	100

*Author's Calculation. Source: KSEB "Power System Statistics" Various Issues.

Chart 6.2. The percentage share of connected load

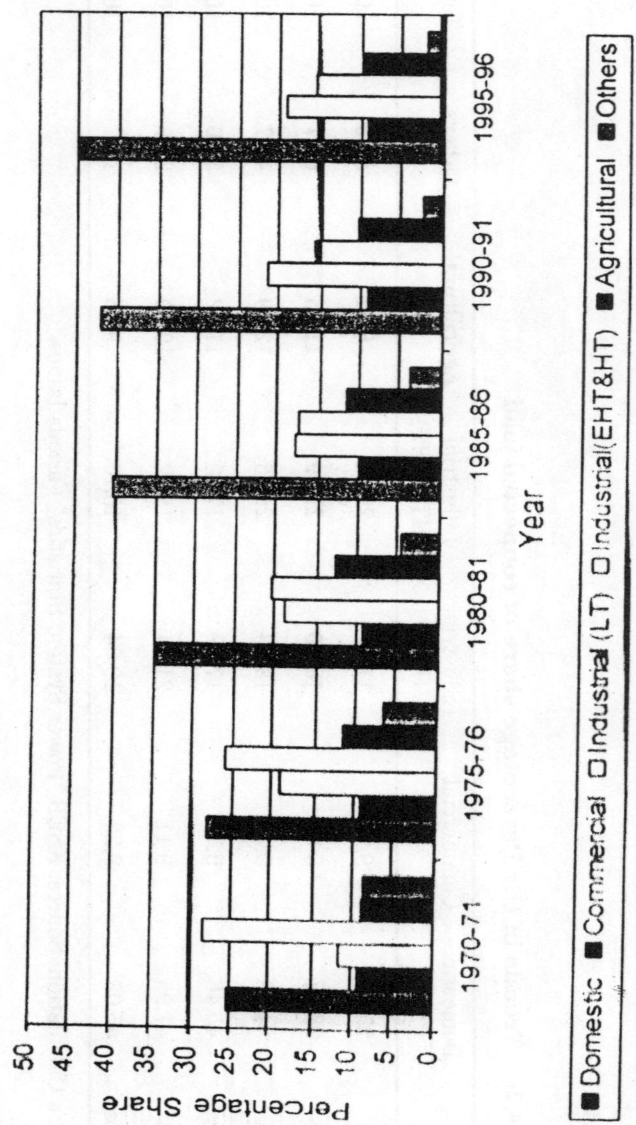

producing sectors and increasing consumerism among people. It also implies that the growing power shortage in the state is not due to increasing demand for power from the agricultural and industrial sectors, but almost exclusively from the domestic and commercial sectors. The peak demand management policy persued at the national level focussing on industrial demand therefore, has very limited applicability in the Kerala context.

Sector wise Analysis of Consumption

The trend in the sectoral consumption of energy will be examined now. In the Table 6.3 is given the sector wise consumption of power in the various Indian states. Kerala accounts for only 2.78% of the total electricity consumed in the country. The highest consuming state is Maharashtra (15.26%) followed by UP, (10.23%) AP (9.4%) and Tamil Nadu (9.18%). At the all India level the share of domestic sector in electricity consumption is 17.12%. This share is even lesser than the national average in such major states like Tamil Nadu, Punjab, Maharashtra, M.P. and Gujarat. Among the states, Kerala account for highest share of domestic consumption (32.7%) (See Table 6.3), after Delhi.

Possible reasons for this highest share include (1) electrification of all villages in the state, (2) high rate of urbanization (3) high density of population (4) high literacy rate, (5) impact of foreign remittance leading to housing boom and (6) increased use of electrical gadgets. In the commercial sector energy consumption also, Kerala holds the leading position (13.5%), while the corresponding all India figures as low as 4.41. By contrast in agricultural sector energy consumption, Kerala has the lowest position (3.91%) as against 30% at the national level. Industrial sector accounts for 35.47% of energy consumption in the country. The

Table 6.3: Customer categories wise consumption of energy (MU) – All India (1995-96)

SEBs	Domestic	Commercial	Agriculture	Industry	Traction	Others	Total
1	*2*	*3*	*4*	*5*	*6*	*7*	*8*
Andhra Pradesh	3750 (15.07)	800 (3.21)	8565 (34.41)	1068 (40.45)	700 (2.81)	1006 (4.04)	24889 (9.47)
Assam	347 (17.49)	159 (8.0)	354 (17.81)	573 (28.82)	0	555 (27.9)	1988 (0.76)
Bihar	757 (11.36)	436 (6.55)	1424 (21.39)	3311 (49.71)	384 (15.76)	349 (5.24)	6661 (2.53)
Delhi (DESU)	4120 (45.78)	0	80 (0.89)	2246 (24.96)	0	2554 (28.4)	9000 (3.42)
Gujarat	2164 (9.03)	602 (2.51)	9416 (39.3)	9197 (38.39)	335 (1.40)	2243 (9.36)	23957 (9.1)
Haryana	1744 (20.17)	276 (3.19)	3577 (41.38)	2121 (24.53)	83 (0.96)	859 (9.94)	8645 (3.29)

(Table Contd...)

Table 6.3: Contd....

1	2	3	4	5	6	7	8
Himachal Pradesh	385 (16.48)	112 (4.80)	14 (0.60)	1044 (44.7)	0	781 (33.4)	2336 (0.89)
Jammu Kashmir	441 (20.9)	105 (4.98)	374 (17.73)	345 (16.35)	0	845 (40.0)	2210 (0.80)
Karnataka	2748 (17.79)	400 (2.59)	7089 (45.89)	4138 (26.79)	24 (0.16)	1049 (6.79)	15448 (5.88)
Kerala	2386 (32.70)	985 (13.5)	285 (3.91)	3268 (44.8)	0	372 (5.1)	7296 (2.78)
Madhya Pradesh	3418 (14.78)	636 (2.75)	7030 (30.4)	8799 (38.1)	1178 (5.09)	2060 (8.91)	23121 (8.79)
Maharashtra	4151 (10.35)	998 (2.49)	12468 (31.0)	14239 (35.5)	821 (2.04)	7447 (18.6)	40124 (15.26)
Meghalay	43 (7.7)	49 (8.7)	2 (0.36)	93 (16.5)	0	375 (66.7)	562 (0.21)

(Table Contd...)

Table 6.3: Contd....

1	*2*	*3*	*4*	*5*	*6*	*7*	*8*
Orissa	1917 (27.05)	338 (4.8)	528 (7.45)	3587 (50.6)	172 (2.43)	490 (6.92)	7086 (2.70)
Punjab	2645 (15.74)	533 (3.2)	6334 (37.7)	6362 (37.87)	0	926 (5.5)	16800 (6.39)
Rajasthan	1816 (13.98)	626 (4.78)	4044 (30.94)	5188 (30.7)	236 (1.8)	1159 (8.83)	13069 (4.97)
Tamil Nadu	3834 (15.6)	1623 (6.72)	6616 (27.4)	9937 (41.2)	360 (1.49)	1771 (7.34)	24141 (9.18)
Uttar Pradesh	6624 (24.7)	2098 (7.8)	9302 (34.6)	6645 (24.7)	784 (2.92)	1405 (5.23)	26858 (10.22)
West Bengal	1650 (18.75)	828 (9.41)	1150 (13.1)	2091 (23.76)	461 (5.24)	2621 (29.8)	8800 (3.35)
Total	44994 (17.12)	11603 (4.41)	78651 (29.9)	93252 (35.47)	5538 (2.11)	28852 (10.9)	262892 (100)

Source: TERI "Tata Energy Data Directory and YearBook (TEDDY) – 1996-97" New Delhi.

Note: *(i)* figures in brackets in column 8 show the percentage share of consumption by the state to the total consumption.

(ii) Figures in brackets in column 2 to 7 show the percentage share of consumption by each category of consumer in different states.

corresponding percentage for Kerala is 44.8%, the highest in India. The explanation for this apparently high figure can be partly sought in the following: (1) Electricity is the major form of energy used by the industrial units in Kerala, while alternative energy sources like coal, and oil are significantly used in the rest of the country and (2) all the 34 EHT units operating in the state are said to be highly power intensive. Typical examples of this are Aluminum, Fertilizers, and Chemicals.

We shall now turn to a discussion on the trends in sectoral consumption of power in Kerala (Refer Table 6.4 given below). Between 1970-71 and 95-96, domestic consumption of power increased by 3340 points i.e. an annual increase of 14.8%. The next highest increase occurred in the commercial sector, 950%, (11.2% per annum) followed by agriculture 687%, (6.26% per annum), LT industry 378% (5.7%), and EHTandHT industry 143.3% (3.4% per annum). Domestic consumption is found to have grown much faster than the rest of categories. The total energy consumption in the state increased by 2995, or an annual compound rate of growth of 4.8% (Refer Table 6.4).

The differential trends in sectoral consumption can be better appreciated. This by looking into what has happened to the sectoral shares of consumption over time. The share of the domestic sector made a quantum jump from 4.34% in 1970-71 to 37.45% in 9596. (Refer Table 6.5). The commercial sector also improved its share from 3.5% to 9.3%. The share of consumption by EHT&HT industrial sector on the other hand declined markedly from 60% to 37%. The share of the agricultural increased from 2.2% to 4.35, during 70-95 period. The observed decline in the share of the industrial sector was cased

Table 6.4: Trends in energy consumption—Sector wise (MU) 1970-95

Year	Domestic	Commercial	Industrial (LT)	Industrial HTandEHT	Agricultural	Others	Total
1970-71	80.71	65.62	111.30	1114.11	40.91	446.7	1858.7
1975-76	200.85 (148.85)	104.48 (59.2)	178.9 (61.1)	1282.8 (15.14)	120.32 194.1	431.1 (-3.5)	2347.8 (26.3)
1980-81	442.98 (120.6)	184.94 (77.0)	208.2 (16.3)	1704.7 (32.9)	79.78 -33.7	1879.4 (335)	4499.9 (92.7)
1985-86	877.0 (98.0)	360.0 (94.7)	258.0 (23.9)	1986 (16.5)	101.0 (26.6)	590.0 (-68.6)	4172 (-7.3)
1990-91	1620.9 (84.83)	499.39 (38.7)	315.9 (22.45)	2344.85 (18.06)	206.4 (104.4)	344.33 (-41.6)	5331.9 (27.8)
1995-96	2777 (71.32)	689 (38.8)	532.0 (68.4)	2711 (15.61)	322.0 (56.0)	384.0 (11.5)	7415 (39.07)
1970-96	3340.7	949.9	377.99	143.3	687.09	-14	298.9
Growth rate	14.8	11.2	5.7	3.4	6.26	NA	4.8

NA: Not worked out.
Note: figures in brackets show the annual growth.
Source: KSEB "Power System statistics" Thiruvanandapuram. Various Issues.

partly by the slow growth of industrial units in the EHT&HT sector, and partly by power cuts imposed on such industrial units from 1982 onwards. (See Table 6.5.)

Even though the relative share of agricultural consumption has increased over time, this share remains one of the lowest in India. The topographical condition and the cropping pattern of the state is largely responsible for this. Paddy which was the most important crop till a few years ago, was cultivated in the low land region for which artificial irrigation is not normally made use of. In the case of the plantation crops raised on the high lands, irrigation was not necessary either. The observed increase in the relative share of agricultural consumption would be explained in terms of the changing cropping pattern. Paddy fields have been increasingly converted into coconut gardens, for which artificial irrigation is essential. This could be understood from the hefty increase in the agricultural connection from 18795 in 1970-71 to 300113 in 1995-96 (an increase of 1497%). Another probable reason could be the priorities and concessions extended to agricultural connection as a part of encouraging food production in the states. As the tariff on agricultural consumption is comparatively lower, there has been large scale misuse of agricultural connections for other purposes. Reportedly many domestic consumers have got agricultural connection to their residential buildings with a view to availing lower tariff per unit. (25 Paise per kWh in 1995-96, as against the average tariff of 93 Paise per kWh).

Now about export demand: The state has been exporting power from 1961 and this was continued up to 1986-87. During 1970-71, the export accounted for 18% of the total demand. During 1978-83 period i.e.

Table 6.5: Percentage share of energy consumption 1970-95

Year	Domestic	Commercial	Industrial (LT)	Industrial (HTandEHT)	Agricultural	Export	Others	Total
1970	4.34	3.53	5.79	59.94	2.20	18.24	4.76	100
75-76	8.55	4.45	7.62	54.64	5.12	12.89	6.73	100
80-81	9.91	4.11	4.63	37.88	1.77	38.50	3.2	100
85-86	21.02	8.63	6.18	47.60	2.42	9.49	4.7	100
90-91	30.40	9.37	5.93	43.98	3.87	0.0000	6.49	100
95-96	37.49	9.29	7.17	36.56	4.34	0.0000	5.20	100

*Author's Calculation. Source: KSEB "Power System Statistics" Various Issues.

Chart 6.3. The percentage share of energy consumption

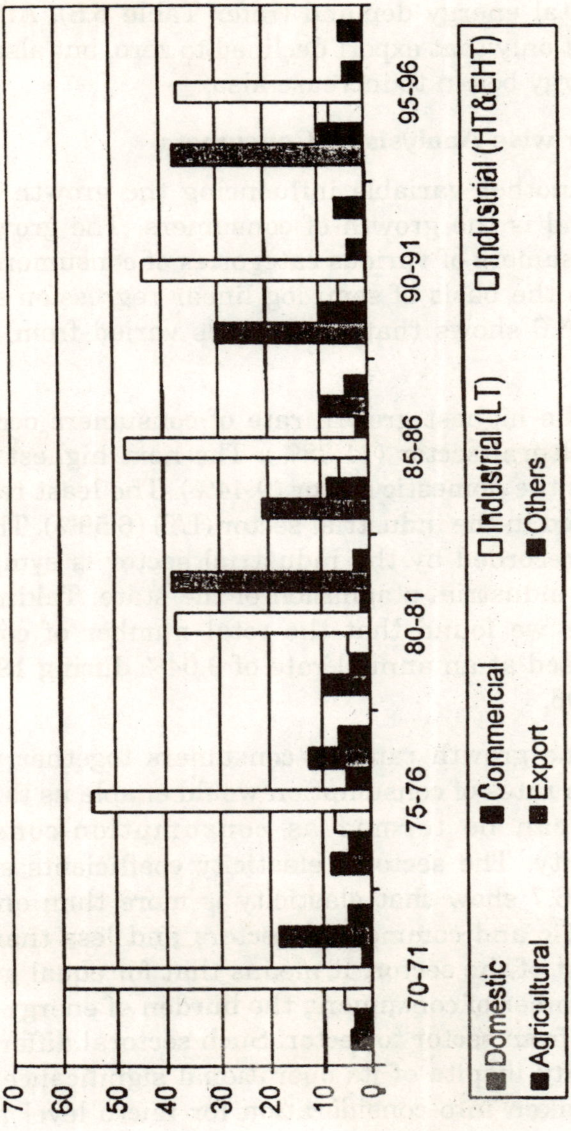

continuously for five years after the commissioning of Idukki Power House, the export continued to increase steadily. In the year 1980-81, export formed 38.50% of the total energy demand (refer Table 6.5). After 1986-87, not only that export declined to zero, but also imports of energy began to increase also.

Sector wise Analysis of Consumers

Another variable influencing the growth of power demand is the growth of consumers. The growth rates of consumers of various categories of consumers worked out on the basis of semi log linear regression shown in table 6.6 shows that these rates varied from sector to sector.

The highest growth rate of consumers occurred in agricultural sector (11.38%). The next highest increase was in the domestic sector (9.44%). The least rates were recorded in the industrial sector (LT) (6.59%). The lowest rates recorded by the industrial sector is symptomatic of the industrial stagnation of the state. Taking all the sectors we found that the total number of consumers increased at an annual rate of 9.04% during 1970-71 to 1995-96.

The growth rates of consumers together with the growth rates of consumption would enable us to workout what can be termed as consumption-consummer elasticity. The sectoral elasticity coefficients shown in Table 6.7 show that elasticity is more than one in the domestic and commercial sectors and less than one in the rest of the sector. It means that for equal growth in the number of consumers, the burden of energy demand varies from sector to sector. Such sectoral differences in elasticity inspite of its operational significance has not been taken into consideration for micro level planning

Table 6.6: Growth rate of consumers (1970-95)

Consumers	Domestic	Commercial	Industrial LT	Industrial HTandEHT	Agricultural	Total
Annual Compound Growth rate (%)	9.44	7.26	6.39	6.59	11.38	9.04

*Author's calculation based on semi log linear regression model.

Table 6.7: Consumption consumer elasticity

Sector wise consumers	Domestic	Commercial	Industrial (LT)	Industrial HTandEHT	Agricultural	Total
Growth rate of consumption	14.84	11.20	5.68	3.31	6.26	4.91
Growth rate of consumers	9.44	7.26	6.39	6.59	11.38	9.04
Elasticity Coefficients	1.57	1.54	0.88	0.50	0.55	0.54

*Author's Calculation.

Source: KSEB "Power System Statistics" – Thiruvanandapuram. Various Issues.

purposes at present. The fact that domestic and commercial sectors whose elasticity coefficients are more than one are also the peak demand sectors further enhances the operational significance of the sectoral elasticity.

Analysis of Consumption Per Actual Power Consumer

The trends in the growth of per capita energy consumption* in the various sectors are given in the Table 6.8. Per capita consumption in the domestic sector went up from 209 units in 1970-71 (i.e. an average monthly consumption of 17.42 units) to 783.25 units (average monthly consumption of 65.3 units) in 1995-96, registering an average increase of 275%. The corresponding increase in the commercial sector was from 544 units (45 units per month) to 909 units (76 units per month), an increase of 67%. The annual compound rate of growth of per capita consumption in domestic and commercial sectors are 4.93% and 3.67% respectively. The per capita consumption in the L.T industrial sector increased only insignificantly, 1.37%. In HT&EHT sector there was a steep fall of 60 percentage. (The growth rate of per capita consumption in EHT&HT sector was –3.02%.) Similarly there occurred a 50% fall in the case of agricultural sector. (Growth rate was –4.59%. See Table 6.8).

The other category consisting of public lighting and public water recorded the highest increase in pre capita consumption, 312%. Per capita consumption considering all the sectors together showed a decline of 116% during the period 1970-71 to 1995-96. This runs counter to the official stand that per capita consumption of power in

* Total consumption in each sector ÷ Total consumers in each sector.

Table 6.8: Per capita consumption (Sector wise and Total) – kWh (1970-95)

Year	Domestic (kWh)	Commercial (kWh)	Industrial (LT) (kWh)	Industrial (MU)	Agricultural (kWh)	Others (kWh)	Total (kWh)
70-71	208.98	543.92	6646.36	4.74 (MU)	2176.6	20218	3416.5
75-76	313.77	541.00	7410.0	3.81 (MU)	2531.6	28810	2578.9
80-81	385.10	632.08	5614.55	2.85 (MU)	918.7	39521	2867.4
85-86	488-71	886.95	5362.04	3.60 (MU)	962.8	87209	1741.05
90-91	628.80	851.50	5507.68	2.26 (MU)	1065.4	140850	1545.5
95-96	783.25	909.21	6737.33	1.89 (MU)	1075.9	83247	1582.4
% Changes	275%	67%	1.37%	-60.13%	-50.57%	311.74%	-115.9%
Growth Rate	4.93%	3.67%	-0.67%	-3.02%	-4.59%	NA	-3.79%

*Author's Calculation.

Note: Growth rate of "others" is not worked out. (Growth rate is the compound growth rate).

Source: KSEB "Power System Statistics" Thiruvanandapuram, Various Issues.

the state has been on the increase during the last several years. For example, according to statistics published by KSEB the per capita consumption of power in the sate jumped up from a low 66 kWh in 1970 to 231 kWh in 1995-96, an increase of 250%. The Board arrived at this figures by comparing the growth rate of power consumption with the growth rate of the population of the state. Our calculation of per capita consumption has considered the actual consumers of electricity belonging to various sectors. Needless to say that the calculation procedure adopted by us is superior to that of the Board as the former considers only the actual consumers and the latter the total population, which includes non-consumers also. The annual compounded rate of growth of per capita consumption of sectoral consumers like Industrial (LT), Industrial (EHTandHT), Agricultural, and the total per capita consumption in the state are - 0.67%, -3.02%, -4.59% and -3.79% respectively.

We shall now account for the reason for the decline in per capita energy consumption. The decline can occur due to three factors - (i) Higher rate of growth of power consumers in relation to power consumption and (ii) Higher rate of growth of connected load in relation to consumption* and (iii) suppressed demand.

Growth Rate of Connected Load, Consumption and Consumer

In the following Table 6.9 the growth rates in connected load and growth rates in consumers are juxtaposed against the growth rates in consumption for the various sectors. In the domestic and commercial sectors, per capita consumption went-up as the rate of growth of consumptions exceeded those of connected load as well as consumers.

---

* The ratio of consumption per connected load has declined.

Table 6.9: Growth rates of Consumption, Consumers and Connected load (1970-95)**

Sectors	Consumption	Consumers	Connected load
Domestic	14.84	9.44	10.34
Commercial	11.20	7.26	7.80
Industrial (LT)	5.68	6.39	7.70
Industrial (EHTandHT)	3.31	6.59	5.90
Agricultural	6.26	11.38	7.77
Total	4.91	9.04	8.52

*Author's Calculation.
**Growth rates are worked out using the semi log linear regression equation.

It may be noted that in the case of these two sectors, per capita consumption increased not only due to a lower growth rate of consumers in relation to consumption, but also due to a higher growth rate of connected load in relation to consumers. In the agricultural sector, on the other hand the per capita consumption declined due to a higher growth rate of consumers (11.38%) as well as connected load (7.77%). A similar decline occurred in the industrial sector also. A word about how per capita consumption is affected by consumption per connected load would be in order at this stage.

Consumption per Connected Load

Consumption per connected load (kWh/kW) is a technical coefficient that explains how much power is drawn or consumed per watt of connected load during a given period, normally a year. Given the connected load, an increase in the duration of power consumption means an increase in the units of energy consumed and vice-versa. In the industrial sector we found that consumption per connected load declined (see Table 6.10). This may be because this sector could draw lesser energy per watt of connected load, due to system unreliability like powercut and low voltage. In the domestic and commercial sector the trend is in contrast to this (see Table 6.10). One plausible reason for the increase in per capita consumption would be the under estimation of connected load in these two sectors. This is why inspite of power system unreliability and inadequacy in the state, consumption per connected load increase. Subsequent additions to the connected load made in the domestic and commercial sectors are normally not brought to the notice of the authorities. Another reason is supposed to be the misuse of the duration of power use by the domestic and commercial sectors.

From the Table 6.10 we can find that consumption per connected load which stood at 2.11 units per watt (per year) in 1970-71 slumped to 1.28 units. The legitimate reason for this decline seems to be non-availability of sufficient quantities of power. If the power system was to maintain the 1970-71 level of energy consumption/watt, energy supply had to be raised to 12187.5 units in the year 1995-96. (5776.09 MW of total connected load × 2.11 = 12187.5 kWh). This estimate comes very nearer to some of the earlier projections made by energy experts and authorities[1]. Actual availability, of power in the year was only 7415 Million units, leaving a deficit of 4772.5 million units, i.e. 39% of the required quantity. It is common knowledge that such a huge magnitude of deficit will have very serious impact on the growth of the economy.

GDP Energy Elasticity

This impact can be examined in terms of energy-

Table 6.10: Consumption per connected load (kWh/W)

Year	Domestic	Commercial	Industrial (LT)	Industrial (EHTandHT)	Agricultural	Others	Total
70-71	0.36	0.81	0.65	4.44	0.53	30.2	2.11
75-76	0.51	0.81	0.68	3.51	0.75	17.93	1.67
80-81	0.63	0.99	0.55	4.12	0.30	70.84	2.20
85-86	0.70	1.19	0.47	3.56	0.28	12.45	1.33
90-91	0.93	1.32	0.36	2.18	0.48	4.82	1.15
95-96	1.07	1.29	0.48	3.10	0.57	4.83	1.28

*Author's Calculation.

GDP- productivity* and output elasticity of energy. By energy productivity is meant the magnitude of the domestic product of the state per one unit of energy consumed. The relevant figures for the major sectors of the economy worked out here are given in Table 6.11. Regarding the overall energy productivity, there is not clear trend. It reached the highest figure of Rs. 13.29 (at constant price) in 1983-84. From 1990, it has been hovering around Rs. 10/-. Industry also does not exhibit a clear tend. During the period 1990-96, the average productivity in industry has been hovering around Rs. 3.30. In the agricultural sector, the energy productivity has been by and large declining over time. It implies that energy intensity has been on the increase. There are reasons to suspect that this increase in energy intensity is due partly to low energy productivity and partly to misuse of energy. The value of energy productivity (overall) has been hovering around Rs. 10/- during the period, 1990-96, at constant prices. It implies at 1 unit loss in energy would be an average, result in a loss of state domestic product worth Rs. 10/-. Assuming that the energy deficit in the state in 1995-96 was of the order of 4772 MU, the resultant decline in output would be to the tune of 47720 million.

Demand Forecast for Sub Sectors

We have been examining the trends in energy demand sector wise. Assuming that the same trend would be continued in future, it may be worth while to forecast energy demand. Various projection models have been made use of for this purpose. Regression models are employed to correlate various socio-economic parameters with energy demand.[2] Econometric and end

* GDP—Energy Productivity = GDP realised per unit of energy consumption

Table 6.11: GDP—Energy Relationship in Kerala – 1980-95 (Constant Price)

Year	Net Domestic Product (Rs. Million)	Agricultural GDP (Rs. Million)	Industrial GDP (Rs. Million)	Total Energy Consumption (MU)	Agricultural Energy Consumption (MU)	Industrial Energy Consumption (MU)	NDP/ kWh (Rs)	Agricultural GDP/kWh (Rs)	Industrial GDP/kWh (Rs)
1	*2*	*3*	*4*	*5*	*6*	*7*	*8*	*9*	*10*
1980-81	38227	12938	5361	4500	80	1913	8.5	162.2	2.8
1981-82	37748	13048	5777	4685	88	1876	8.1	148.0	3.1
1982-83	38685	12864	6267	3518	107	1712	11.0	120.2	3.7
1983-84	37117	11858	5891	2793	110	1531	13.3	107.8	3.9
1984-85	39416	13198	5746	3706	92	2060	10.6	143.5	2.8
1985-86	40864	13792	5898	4172	101	2244	9.8	136.6	2.6
1986-87	39930	13095	5299	3716	131	1962	10.8	99.9	2.7
1987-88	41656	13660	6041	3627	146	1770	11.5	93.5	3.4

(Table Contd...)

Table 6.11: Contd...

1	2	3	4	5	6	7	8	9	10
1988-89	45841	15689	6890	4387	186	2178	10.8	84.4	3.2
1989-90	48924	15473	8217	4794	217	2377	10.2	71.4	3.5
1990-91	52623	17614	8188	5332	206	2661	9.9	85.3	3.1
1991-92	53647	18180	8373	5559	224	2798	9.7	81.2	3.0
1992-93	57546	18261	9081	5839	235	2691	9.9	77.7	3.5
1993-94	63805	17035	9382	6285	261	2764	10.2	72.9	3.4
1994-95	68688	19481	10177	7028	271	3142	9.8	71.8	3.2
1995-96	72949	20122	10810	7415	322	3243	9.8	62.5	3.3
Growth rate	4.67	3.61	4.82	3.81	9.82	4.28	-	-	-

Note: Author's calculation of Energy Productivity.

Sources: *(i)* EPW "National accounts statistics of India 1950-51-1995-96". Mumbai 1997. p. 89.

(ii) Kerala State Electricity Board "power system statistics 1995-96"-Thiruvananthapuram p. 27.

use models have also been used to forecast energy requirement[3]. More advanced computing techniques like co-integration, genetic algorithm, and artificial neural network have also been employed in recent times[4]. However owing to various random factors and subjective prejudices, the accuracy of these methods are limited especially under conditions of high demand growth and fast socio-economic changes.

The projection models employed by us[5] is based upon time series analysis technique. Several standard regression models were tried with a view to identifying the most appropriate functional from for each sector. The regression models were verified using statistical software "Regression and Time Series" (RATS). Based on the above mathematical model, the energy demands for selected terminal years have been worked out in Table 6.12. The period taken for the analysis was 18 years from 1978-79 to 1995-96.

Based on the mathematical models given in Table 6.12 the energy demand for the terminal years of 2000, 2005, and 2010 has been worked out and the results are as given below. Domestic demand for energy will continue to increase at a compound rate of 11% annually. The anticipated consumption of this sector by the year 2010 is about 12,300 MU, which will be 43% of the total consumption. Commercial sector indicated a rapid growth in consumption at an annual compound rate of 16%. The study results project that during the period of forecast, the consumption in this sector will reach to 9200 MU.

Demand projection of industrial (LT) sector indicates a steady average growth rate about 6% in the past. But the results indicate that the growth rate will be retarded in d future and will be at an annual rate of 2% only. The demand forecast for 2010 from this sector

Table 6.12: Details of models employed[6]

Sectors	Model	Functional Form	R^2	Parameter estimate
Domestic	Hoerl Model	$Y = ab^x x^c$	0.99	a=0.473 b=-0.0028 c=0.008
Commercial	Geometric Model	$Y = ax^{bx}$	0.98	a=169.67 b=0.0346
Industrial (LT)	MMF Model	$Y = \frac{ab+cx^d}{b+x^d}$	0.99	a=211.76 b=2999219 c=719.78 d=5.52
Industrial (HTandEHT)	Geometric Model	$Y = ax^{bx}$	0.91	a=1452.97 b=0.0115
Agricultural	MMF Model	$Y = \frac{ab+cx^d}{b+x^d}$	0.98	a=82.88 b=4994.86 c=483.03 d=3.016
Total energy Consumption	Rational function Model	$Y = \frac{a+bx}{1+cx+dx^{d2}}$	0.94	a=253.8 b=1429.2 c=0.456 d=0.01015
Per capita Consumption	Exponential Association Model	$Y = a\,(b\text{-}c)^{-cx}$	0.99	a=-16.64 b=-3.19 c=-0.09

will be 720 MU. The energy demand from the EHT and HT sector will be 5480 MU and the average growth rate anticipated will be about 4.8% only. Per capital energy consumption is anticipated to grow at a considerable level, from 240 kWh in 1995-96 to 791 kWh in 2010.

The total energy demand arrived at from sectoral projection (6th raw of Table 6.13.) does not give allowance for T and D loss and energy shortages. In order to make

Table 6.13: Demand forecast for selected terminal years

Sectors	Demand in 1995-96 Actual (MU)	2000AD (MU)	2005 AD (MU)	2010 AD (MU)
Domestic	2777	4400	7400	12300
Commercial	689	2060	4290	9200
Industrial (LT)	532	660	700	720
Industrial (HTandEHT)	2771	3330	4250	5480
Agriculture	322	370	400	430
Total energy Demand	7415	11276	17600	29000
T and D Loss (% added) MU	N a.	@20% 2255	@18% 3168	@15% 4350#
Energy Shortage*	@25% 1854	@15% 2030	@10% 2077	@5% 1668^
Total Estimated Energy**	9269	15560	22845	35018
MW Required***	1764	2960	4347	6663
Existing Capacity	1505.5	1505.5	1505.5	1505.5
Additional Capacity to be Required	258.5	1454.5	2841.5	5157.5
Per capita Energy Consumption	240kWh	352kWh	523 kWh	791 kWh

* According to the Southern Regional Electricity Board Estimate (1997-98)

** Total estimated energy = Projected energy required + T&D Loss + Energy shortage.

***MW required is worked out on the assumption of 60% PLF.

Kerala State Electricity Board has targeted to bring down T&D loss by 15% by 2010AD.

^ 5% assumption is based on several literatures published by Kerala State Electricity Board, and that of observation of individual experts.

energy demand projection more realistic we have adopted T and D loss and energy shortage to the projected values of demand. The projected demand for energy would be 15560 MU, in 2000 AD, 22845 MU, in 2005 AD, and 35018MU in 2010 AD. The corresponding installed capacity works out to 2960 MW, 4347 MW, and 6663 MW for the respective years. This estimate of energy requirement, however does not consider the potential for energy saving.

Experts like Steven Nadel[7] have pointed out that about 20 –25% of energy consumption can be brought down, if all the 27 methods suggested by him are followed. Assuming 20% as lower case for energy saving potential, the total energy requirements for the terminal year 2010 would be 28015MU. Again assuming 0.6 plant load factor, the total installed capacity to be required is 5330MW. The existing capacity is 1505.5MW in 1995-96. Thus an additional capacity of 3825MW has to be installed by 2010AD to meet the energy requirements in the State. The investment expected to meet this much capacity is about Rs. 1, 53,000 Million. Assuming 1:1 proportion, an equal amount may have to be invested in transmission and Distribution network.

Notes and Reference

1. *(i)* CEA (1995) *"15th Electric Power Survey"* Government of India New Delhi.
   (ii) IRTC: Projection at the rate of 15% per annum.
   (iii) Kerala State Electricity Board: Official and Unofficial publications by the Board and that of Individual experts.
2. Raghavendra D. Rao and Parikh K. Jyoti (1996) *"Forecast and Analysis of Demand for Petroleum Products in India"*. Energy Policy, Vol. 24. No. 6 pp. 585-592.
3. Hign Liu Chan and Shu Kam Lee (1997), *"Modeling and forecasting the demand for coal in China"*, Energy Economics, Vol. 19 (271-285).

4. Irwin G. M Etal (1986) *"Statistical Electricity Demand modeling from consumer Billing Date"*. IEE Proceeding, Vol. 133 C. No. 6, pp. 328 – 385.

5. These models were suggested by Dr. P.S. Chandramohanan Nair and Parameshwara sharma.

6. Parameswara Sharma, D, Chandramohanan Nair P.S, Balasubramanian. R. *"Demand for Electrical Energy for the State of Kerala: A Subsectoral Forecast and Analysis"*, Proceedings of the All India Seminar on Electrical Energy System Management – India Scenario – University of Roorkee, India, Sept. 1998, pp. 212-217.

7. Nadel Steven et. al. *"Opportunities for Improving End Use Electricity Efficiency in India"* – Energy Planning and Policy Development Project, 936-5228. 1DEA; November 1991, USA ID. pp. 82-83.

7

Summary and Conclusions

Energy has been the sinequonon of economic development and human progress, from the days of Industrial Revolution. Being a universal input and its consumption being considered as an index of economic development, a phenomenal increase in the demand for energy took place in almost all countries, the world over. It was this unprecedented and increasing demand which culminated in the oil shock of 1973, in the wake of which all countries, particularly the developed countries adopted systematic and concerted efforts to economize on the use of energy through changes in the production and consumption, and energy conservation measures, as well as through resort to non-conventional sources.

Till recently when energy crisis became very acute, the approach to energy development adopted by the major countries of the world was that of supply based development paradigm. The persistent demand resulted in four types of crises – (a) Capital Crisis, (b) Performance Crisis, (c) Equity Crisis and (d) Environmental Crisis. This necessitated the pursuit of an alternative paradigm known as DEFENDUS. This paradigm gained prominence in the wake of persistent electricity scarcity experienced by developed and developing countries.

Electricity, whose commercial production began in 1878 in New York, became within a few decade, not only the most popular and convenient form of energy, but also an essential tool of development and a symbol of modernity, largely because of its unmatching ability to operate a variety of industrial equipments and household appliances. The possibility of generating electricity from multiple sources (as different from single source coal in the beginning) propelled electricity production into a gigantic industry in several countries. According to one conservative estimate, the annual revenue from electricity industry is of the order of $ 800 Billion, twice the size of world's auto industry.

In the developing countries both electricity generating capacity as well as actual production has been increasing during the last two decades, faster than the developed and newly developing countries. Among the developing countries, energy productivity has been lowest in Sri Lanka, Bangladesh and India, while the highest in South Korea, Malaysia and Singapore. In the developing countries electricity demand has been growing much faster than the developed countries, during the last two decades. In these countries electricity demand exceeded GDP growth. With rapidly growing demand per power, drastic changes in the technical process of power generation and the rising prices of power inputs, the power sector of most countries began to face several problems: (a) Power Shortage, (b) Cost Escalation in Power Generation, (c) High T&D Loss, (d) Environmental Issues, (e) Depleting Fuel Inputs Like Coal Oil and Gas and (f) Financial Crunch of the Utilities.

India has been facing almost all problems stated above during the last few decades, although the country had made significant strides in power capacity, generation, per capita consumption and electrification of villages. Available data indicated that during 1995-96 the peak capacity shortage was of the order of 18.3% and energy shortage of 9.2%. The commercial loss incurred by all the 19 SEBs in the country increased by 50%, during the short span of 1992-95. The persistent resource crunch faced by the SEBs have stood in the way of making additional investments in this sector, leading to perpetuation of power shortage in almost all states. The liberalisation policies launched by the government of India from 1991 provided a way out to escape from this predicament, by entering in to financial and technical collaboration with foreign firms and agencies.

Among the Indian States, Kerala possesses certain unique features and problems with respect to the power sector. The power system of Kerala is exclusively dependent on hydel projects. Once a surplus state, Kerala has been short of power for the last fifteen years. The unique features and the issues found in the power system of Kerala are:-

- Exclusive dependence on hydropower stations,
- Acute and chronic power shortage, despite being a surplus and power exporting state till a few years ago,
- Internal maximum demand of the state power system exceeding the installed power capacity,
- Lowest energy tariff,
- Zero fuel cost for power generation,
- T&D loss higher than the all India average,

- Pattern of energy consumption drastically different from all India,
- Lower per capita energy consumption as compared to the rest of the country.

Inspite of such peculiar characteristics and problems, the power sector of Kerala has not been subjected to any systematic and serious study by economists. The only study carried out from an economic perspective pertained to the period, when the state was surplus in power and the nature and dimensions of the problems of the power sector were widely different from what they are today. The present study is a comprehensive analysis of the power system of Kerala from a techno-economic angle.

Summary of Major Findings

During the seventies and the eighties, electricity generating capacity, actual generation, and demand grew faster in developing countries like India, as compared to the developed countries. Growth rate of demand for electricity in these countries by and large exceeded the growth rate of GDP, during this period.

Inspite of the great importance of the sector, the power sector outlay in India hovered around 18.5%. Till the sixth five-year plan, the relative share of this sector in the total plan outlay remained below that of the first five-year plan. The low relative share continued even during the post energy crisis period.

Taking the country as a whole, capacity addition in the power sector was found to have moved away from hydel to thermal stations, based on diesel, gas, and naphtha. This had serious implications in the form of environmental problems, (discharge of Co, Co_2, So_2, and

No_x) worsening of balance of payment position due to import of diesel and gas and aggrandisement of peak load shortage, as thermal stations are based load on stations in contrast to hydel stations.

Power consumption by the agricultural and domestic sector exceeded that by the commercial and industrial sectors, during 1950-96 at all India level. Power tariff for domestic and agricultural sectors being highly subsided in all the states, the more rapid growth of power demand by the two sectors had a highly adverse effect on the financial position of the state electricity board.

The power shortage faced by India since the turn of the 80s is the outcome of a host of factors like inadequate investment in power sector, insufficient capacity addition, large T&D loss, power system inefficiency (declining energy productivity due to low plant load factor) and poor financial position of the Utilities.

Examining the growth of the power system of Kerala, in terms of power system variables like installed capacity, generation, energy sales, maximum demand (both Internal and the System) number of consumers, connected load, per capita consumption, T&D loss, circuit kilometres of HT and LT lines, and number of distribution transformers, it was found that rate of growth of supply side variables lagged behind that of demand side variables during 1957-95 period. Internal maximum demand has been growing (8.33%) faster than the installed capacity (7.62%) and generation (7.51%). This discrepancy is the cause of power shortage and was partly met through power imports from other states. Import of power began to exceed export from the eighties.

Transmission and Distribution loss (energy loss occurred in the process of transmitting power from the generating point to the consumer end) increased steadily from 90 MU in 1950 to 1950MU in 1996-97. The main reasons for heavy T&D loss is due to insufficient high-tension lines as compared to Low Tension lines in the state. Technically the ideal ratio between HT and LT lines is 1:1. This ratio was never maintained in Kerala, and in recent years it has been declining. The number of transformers per 1000 consumers declined from 11.57 in 1950-51 to 5.10 in 1996-97. The number of transformers per MW of connected load remained almost static during the same period. Due to the insufficient growth of distribution transformers and HT lines, the power system was unable to maintain voltage level at the technically acceptable rate.

The per capita energy consumption (total energy consumption ÷ total population of the state) increased from 13 units in 1950 to 240 units in 1995-96. But energy consumption by actual power consumers (total energy consumption ÷ total power consumers in the state) steadily declined from 5000 units in 1950 to 1582 units in 1995-96.

The rate of growth of expenditure (19.58%) of the power system exceeded that of revenue (16.79%) during the period under review, leading to financial crisis of the Kerala State Electricity Board. Heavy tariff subsidy to domestic and agricultural consumers and uneconomic method of electricity tariffing are the two reasons for the declining rate of revenue of the state power system.

During 1979-97 period, it was found that installed capacity increased only 49.06%, while internal maximum demand at 171.26% and maximum system demand 44.95%. The tardy growth in installed capacity in relation to internal maximum demand appears to be the major reason for energy shortage. The reasons for slow growth in installed capacity are (1) inordinate delay in the completion of ongoing projects that were started years ago, (2) virtual absence of direct central investment till 1997, (3) inadequate and declining share of state's investment in power sector, (4) and total dependence on hydro projects to the virtual exclusion of other options till 1997. Experts maintained that even if all the available hydel stations are fully utilised, the state might not be able to meet the present demand in the immediate future. The present installed capacity is estimated to be 46% short of the desired capacity level. The desired capacity was estimated by us on the basis of Gompertz model, as it was found to be a better fit. According to this estimation, installed capacity has to be increased to a minimum of 2700 MW in 2000AD and 4006 MW in 2010. Therefore the state power system should install an additional capacity of 2498 MW within a decade to meet the power demand of the people of Kerala, [Without considering the choked demand and T&D loss].

Performance analysis of the ten major hydropower projects was conducted in terms of the parameters, capacity utilisation factor, plant load factor, and energy productivity. The analysis showed that the projects varied among themselves in terms of above criteria. Idukki and Sabarigiri together accounted for as much as 65% of installed capacity as well as design value of generation. But the two projects respectively come in the 9th and 5th positions in terms of plant load factor and 8th and 5th positions in terms of energy productivity. A significant finding from performance analysis is that during 1988-95 period, the actual generation exceeded the design value of generation. One is tempted to conclude from this that water availability was not a constraint for power generation during this period. In addition to this, an attempt has been made to examine the technical and economic efficiency of the state power system as a whole in terms of (1) Load Factor, (2) Demand Factor, (3) T&D Factor, and (4) the rate and structure of tariff.

The load factor, which is an indicator of the extent of demand, was found to be by and large declining. This abnormal behavior of load factor could be explained in terms of the failure of the system to meet peak hour demand, and escapist methods resorted to in the form of load shedding and power cut. The demand factor is the ratio of maximum demand to the total connected load of the system. The value of the demand factor tends to be one, if the efficiency of the power system is good, which implies that the system is capable to meet the demand in tandem with the increase in the connected load. The value of the demand factor in the state has declined from 0.37 in 1960 to 0.29 in 1995. This can be treated as a true reflection of power system inefficiency.

T&D loss in the state occurs in two ways, viz. technical and non-technical (commercial). About 70% of total energy loss are technical in character and 30% non-technical. Efficiency of transmission network is examined in terms of number of sub-stations, number of transformers and circuit kilometers of various lines. T&D loss in Kerala (23%) is greater than the national average of 21%, the World Bank norm of 15.5%, and the world target rate of 8.25%.

The annual compound rate of growth of T&D loss in Kerala works out to 8.85%, whereas the rate of growth of generation is 7.51%. As per our calculation, one percentage increase in energy generation leads to 1.18% change in the energy loss. If the power system of Kerala could reduce the energy loss at least by 1%, the state could add 19.5 MU of energy to the system. If this much of energy were to be generated, it would require an additional capacity of 3.71 MW, for which the installations cost would be around Rs. 150 million.

Since investment data relating to T&D network as such are not available, we had to resort to indirect methods to examine the trends in T&D investment. The indices used for this purpose were (1) consumers per circuit kilometers of 110kV lines, (2) consumers per transformers; (3) transformer per connected load and (4) transformer per consumption. In terms of growth of these indicators, investment in T&D network appears to have significantly declined over time.

An important determinant of T&D efficiency is the growth of substations of various capacities as they enable the transfer of power at stipulated ratings. For the evacuation of power from the generating point to the various substations located in different parts, 440 kV/ 220 kV sub stations are required. As per the proposal of Kerala State Electricity Board at least three 440 kV substations are required for the state, whereas there exists only one. Similarly eighteen 220 kV substations are required, whereas there are only five. Economic efficiency of Kerala State Electricity Board, which was already low, further deteriorated in recent years. During the nineties the tariff remained well below the average cost. Cost revenue differences per unit was 10.5 Paise in 1990. It increased to 18 Paise in 1995-96.

The sectoral demand analysis was attempted by grouping power consumers in to the following categories: - domestic, commercial, industrial (LT), industrial (EHTandHT), agriculture, public water works, public lighting and licencees. Sectoral analysis was done with reference to connected load, consumption, and consumers. The rate of growth of connected load in the domestic sector was 10.34%, commercial 7.8%, industry (LT) 7.7%, industry (EHTandHT) 5.9% and agriculture 7.8%, during the period 1970-95.

The relative share of domestic sector in connected load increased from 25% in 1970-71 to 45% in 1995-96, whereas in the industry (HTandEHT) it declined from 29% to 15%. In agriculture there was a marginal increase from 8.8% to 9.76%. Commercial sector remained unchanged. The shares of domestic and commercial sectors together constitute 55% of the total connected load, and this accounted largely for the peak power shortage. The decline in the share of industrial (EHTandHT) connected load is reflective of the stagnating industrial scenario of the state of Kerala. The big increase in the share of the domestic and commercial sector from 35% to 54% is reflective of Kerala pattern of development characterised by high rate of consumption.

Sectoral share in energy consumption shows that the share of domestic sector increased from 4.34% to 37.9%, that of commercial sector from 3.5% to 9.3%, industry (LT) from 5.8% to 7%, Industry (EHTandHT) from 60% to 37% and agricultural from 2.0% to 4.3%, between 1970-95. The observed decline in the share of the industrial sector was caused partly by the slow growth of industrial units in the EHTandHT categories, and partly by power cuts imposed on such units from 1982 onwards. Nearly 47% total energy sold in the state was consumed by the domestic and commercial sectors.

Even though the relative share of agricultural consumption has increased over time, it remains one of the lowest in India, the reason being, the topographical conditions and the peculiar-cropping pattern. The increase in the percentage share of energy consumption in the agricultural sector could be explained in terms of changing cropping pattern in favour of cash crops and the preferences, priorities and concessions extended to agricultural connections.

In terms of consumers, highest growth rate was registered by the agricultural sector, (11.38%) the next being the domestic sector (9.44%). Lowest rates were recorded by the industrial sectors. Among the three most significant variables of the state power system – viz., total energy consumption, total consumers and total connected load, the rate of growth of total consumers stands out the highest with 9.04% (consumption 4.91%, and connected load 8.52%).

Per capita energy consumption was found to have increased. But analysis of sector wise per capita consumption shows that only in domestic and commercial sectors, per capita consumption increased. Consumption by all other sectors, including agricultural declined. The rate of growth of per capita consumption was 4.93% and 3.67% respectively for the domestic and commercial sectors, during the period 1970-95. For the rest of the sector like industrial (LT) industrial (EHTandHT), agricultural and the total in the state, the growth rates were -0.67%, -3.02%, -4.59%, and -3.79% respectively.

Consumption per connected load increased in the case of domestic and commercial sector significantly. In the rest of sectors and for the state as whole, it declined. (Sector wise changes in the consumption per connected load have serious policy implications in regard to tariff subsidy and energy conservation policies). The reason for the decline is, non-availability of sufficient power. If system was to maintain 1970-71 level of energy consumption per watt of capacity installed, (load connected) energy supply had to be raised to 12187 MU in 1995-96 as estimated by us. Actual availability (including import) was 7415 MU, leaving a deficit of 4772 MU. (i.e. 39% of the required quantity). The possible economic impact of this deficit was also worked out in terms of energy productivity and output elasticity of energy. Energy productivity was of the order of Rs. 10/- during 1990-96, at constant price. The resultant decline in GDP worked out to Rs. 47720/- million in 1995-96.

An attempt was also made to forecast energy demand, by assuming observed trends in the sectoral demand for power. For projection we made use of time series analysis technique. For this purpose the statistical software called "RATS" was used. The period considered for the projection purpose was from 1978-79 to 1995-96. Energy demand was forecasted for the terminal years of 2000AD, 2005, and 2010. Our result showed that the annual compounded rate of growth of domestic, commercial, industrial (LT) industrial (EHTandHT), were 11%, 15%, 2%, and 4.8% respectively. The total energy demand in the state grew at the rate of 10% annually during the same period. Total energy demand forecasted for the year 2010 AD that comes to 29000 MU. This figure doesn't take into consideration the T&D loss and the existing energy shortages. Considering these two factors a 20% increase (15% for T&D and 5% for energy shortage) have to be added to the forecasted figures. Thus total energy requirement as per our calculation would come to 35018 MU. For generating this much of energy additional capacity to be installed would be of the order of 5158 MW. (On the basis 60% plant load factor). Energy conservation potential of the state needs to be looked into. Assuming an energy conservation rate of 20% the total requirement will be 28015 MU in 2010. The additional capacity for generating this much energy would come to 3825 MW, and the corresponding additional investment to be 1,53,000 Million.

Policy Suggestions

In view of the fast depleting energy inputs, the present trend in favour of the thermal stations at the all India level is to be discouraged and the installation of hydel stations encouraged instead. Since large hydel projects carry ecological hazards, it would be advisable to install medium range hydel projects (100-150 MW). The ideal balance between thermal and hydel stations may be maintained in the ratio of 60:40 for the country as a whole. As hydro potential is a perennial source of electricity, incentives may be given for setting up of small, mini and micro hydel projects in the country.

The recent tendency to depend on Independent Power Producers (IPPs) to build power plants using Diesel and Naphtha as fuels need to be discouraged in the larger interest of the nation. Power sector investment by the central government in generation, transmission and distribution has to be significantly enhanced with a view to ensuring equity in the distribution of power.

With a view to stabilising the financial position of State Electricity Boards, (SEBs) the power tariff has to be restructured taking into consideration the short run and long run marginal cost principal. The present classification of consumers into domestic and agriculture may be redesigned in such a way that the benefits of subsidy accrue to the really deserving sections. As the cost of electricity is on the increase in all the states, possibilities of using 'price' as an instrument for energy conservation may be worked out.

In order to ensure reliable and dependable supply of quality power in Kerala, the state has to create an additional capacity of 3350 MW by 2010AD. For achieving this target the state has to accomplish several things immediately. The micro, mini and small hydro potential, which the state possesses in abundance, may be fully exploited. The enormous scope that exists for non-conventional energy sources like solar and wind also may be tapped to the maximum extends possible. In view of the financial crunch of the state governments, efforts should be made to make use of the resources of IPPs who can raise funds and fuels inputs internationally, and also of the self financing power producers who can raise money and fuel inputs from internal sources. It would be more advisable to bank on the latter as the dependence on the former may give rise to certain negative effects in the long run.

Performance of hydel projects like Pallivasal, Panniar, Sengulam, Idukki, and Sabarigiri was found to be comparatively poor. A study on the technical aspects of low plant load factor of these projects may be carried out soon.

To reduce the T&D loss to 15.5% (the norm stipulated by the World Bank), it is essential that a number of substations, transformers of various capacities and length of HT lines be enhanced. Since hue investments will be required for this, a T&D Corporation may be floated under Kerala State Electricity Board.

The energy demand forecast carried out by different agencies at the state and national level suffer from a serious limitation, as such forecast is exclusively dependent upon secondary data relating to energy consumption, which do not reflect the real energy demand of consumers, because of power failures, existence of choked demand and non-accommodation of end use service of energy. Hence it is suggested that demand forecasting based on end use analysis be carried out, preferably by Kerala State Electricity Board. For this purpose, it is necessary to develop a techno-economic model to identify energy demand of each consumer based on his connected load, hours of consumption, use of electrical appliances, and possibilities of load staggering during peak hours. Such a model will be helpful in the formulation of energy conservation policies in the state. As the demand for power of domestic and commercial categories of consumes are on the increase in the state, it is highly helpful for the power system to apply the concept of Demand Side Management (DSM). The DSM options include (i) increase the off peak use of power by the domestic and commercial consumers, (ii) use of high efficiency equipments, (iii) differential tariff based on the time of use, and (iv) encourage the use of captive power during the peak hours. A related point may also be suggested here. Use of power electronic devices such as Compact Fluorescent Lamp (CFL) and electronic regulators would help to significantly conserve energy in the state.

The technological advancements occurred in generation; transmission and distribution areas of electrical engineering have not yet been introduced in Kerala. In advanced countries, for instance electronic meters are used in all types of electrical connections. High quality conductors and under ground cables of high voltage ratings are used to curb T&D loss. Similarly computers net work is extended in all segments of power system, including billing, data compilation, and load forecasting. Such technological innovations may be included in the power system of Kerala, at the earliest, either indigenously, or through technical collaboration. The recently established Kerala Power Finance Corporation is to be converted into nodal agency for investments in power sector of Kerala. A separate economic division may be created in the Kerala State Electricity Board for taking up works relating to data computation and analysis, cost benefit studies of alternative energy options, determination of environmental costs as well as fixation of economic tariff.

Bibliography

Books

Allen R.G.D. (1938). *"Mathematical Analysis for Economists"*, Macmillan, New York.

Asian Development Bank (1994). *"Energy Indicators of Developing Member Countries of ADB"* ADB. Manila.

Ayres R.U. (1978). *"Resources, Environment and Economics"*. John Wiley and Sons, New York.

Benjamin LEV (Ed) (1987). *"Strategic planning in Energy and Natural Resources"* Elsevier Science Publishers B.V. The Netherlands.

Brown Lester (Ed) (1994, 95, 96). *"The State of the World"* World Watch Institute. Horizon Books, New Delhi.

Chartier. P. (Ed) (1981). *"Energy from Biomass"* D. Reidel Publishing Co; USA.

Desai, V. Ashok (Ed) (1990). *"Energy Demand – Analysis, Management, and Conservation"* Wiley Eastern Ltd. New Delhi.

Devi, Ganga, S. (1996). *"Energy perspectives of Kerala"* M.Phil Dissertation (Unpublished), Pondicherry Univeristy, Mahe Centre

Energy Conservation Society: *"Year Book, 1996, 97 and 98"* Thiruvanandapuram.

Frisch J.R. (1986). *"Future Stress for Energy Resources – Energy Abundance: Myth or Reality?"* Graham and Trorman. UK.

Giriappa, S, (1986) (Ed). *"Rural Energy Crisis"* Himalaya Publishign House, New Delhi.

Goldemberg, J. et al. (1989). *"Energy for Sustainable Development"* Wiley Eastern Ltd.

Government of India, (1993). *"Energy Modeling for India – Towards a Policy for Commercial energy"*, Planning Commission, New Delhi.

Gujarati, Damodar. (1995). *"Basic Econometrics"* Mc Graw Hill. Book Company.

Hemlata Rao (1990). *"Rural Energy Crises, A Diagnostic Analysis"*, Ashish Publishing House, New Delhi.

Henderson PD, (1975) *"India's Energy Sector"* Oxford University Press, New Delhi.

Hill Robert, et al. (1993) *"The Future of Energy Use"*, Earth Scan Publication London.

Hydari Aneez, K.P (1994). *"Energy Efficiency and Conservation in Kerala—A Techno Economic Policy Analysis"* M.Phil. Dissertation, (Unpublished) University of Kerala, Thiruvanandapuram.

Japan Energy Conservation Center. (1997). *"Japan Energy Conservation Hand Book-1997"*, Japan.

Jyothis, S. (1995). *"Environment Friendly Technology in Energy Sector—An Economic Analysis of Solar Photovoltaic Cells"*, M.Phil Dissertation, (unpublished) University of Kerala, and Thiruvanandapuram.

Kaplan Seymour (1983). *"Energy Economics; Quantitative Methods for Energy and Environmental Decisions"*, Mc Graw Hill. Co.

Mahajan, V.S. (Ed) (1991). *"Studies in Energy and Economic Development", Deep and Deep Publications,* New Delhi.

Monga, G.S, and Sanctis, V.J (1994). *"India's Energy Prospects"*, Vikas Publishing Co., New Delhi.

Munasinghe, M. (1980). *"The Economics of Power System Reliability and Planning"*, John Hopkins Press.

National Council of Applied Economic Research (1992). *"Demand for Energy in Southern India"*, NCAER, New Delhi.

Neff, L. Thomas (1981). *"The Social Costs of Solar Energy—A Study of Photovoltaic Energy System"* Pergamon Press, United Kingdom.

Pachauri, R.K. (1975). *"Energy and Economic Development in India"* Praeger Publishers New York.

Pachauri, R.K. (Ed) (1986). *"Energy Planning and Economic Development"* TERI – New Delhi.

Panday G.N. (1994). *"A Text book of Energy System Engineering"* Vikas Publishing House, New Delhi.

Parikh. K. Jyothi (1981). *"Modelling Energy Demand for Policy Analysis"* Planning Commission, New Delhi.

Parikh. K. Jyothi, Reddy Sundara B., and Banarjee Rangan (1994). *"Planning for Demand Side Management in the Electricity Sector"* Tata McGraw Hill. New Delhi.

Pillai. P.P. (1980). *"Dynamics of Electricity Demand and Supply—An Econometric Analysis"* Agricol Publishing Co. New Delhi.

Raiky P.S. (1990). *"Energy consumption in India—Pattern and Determinants"* Deep and Deep Publications New Delhi.

Rao Govinda M., et al. (1998). *"The Economics of Electricity Supply in India"* Macmillan. New Delhi.

Reddy Sudhakara B. (1992). *"The Energy Sector of the Metropolis of Bangalore"* Ph.D. Thesis-Indian Institute of Science, Bangalore. (unpublished).

Richardson W. Harry (1997). *"Economic Aspects of the Energy Crises"* Lexington Books. U.K.

Roy Joyasree (1992). *"Demand for Energy in Indian Industries"* Daya Publishing Co. New Delhi.

Sarkar, S.S. and Bhatnakar (1996). *"Law of Electricity in India"* (4th edition) India Law House, New Delhi.

Shaw T.L., Lennard, D.E., and Jones P.M.S. (1984). *"Policy and Development of Energy Resources"* John Wiley and Sons, New York.

Singh Inderjeet (1994). *"Input-Output Analysis of Energy Conservation in India"* Anmol Publications New Delhi.

Tata Energy Research Institute (1995, 96 and 97). *"Tata Energy Data Directory and Year Book"* TERI New Delhi.

The Hindu (1996). *"Survey of Indian Industry"* Hindu Publication.

The World Commission on Environment and Development, (1988). *"Our Common Future"* Oxford University Press.

Turan Gonen (1986). *"Electric Power Distribution System Engineering"* McGraw Hill.

Reports

Baji V.T. (1996). *"Wheeling Power Application in a Industrial Belt."* M.Tech Thesis. R.E.C. Kozhikode.

C.E.A. (1996). *"Power Performance Budget—Power Sector Reforms"* Power Finance Corporation New Delhi.

Central Electricity Authority (1992-93, 93-94). *"Public Electricity Supply—All India Statistics—General Review"* C.E.A. New Delhi.

Centre for Monitoring Indian Economy (1996). *"India's Energy Sector-July—1996"*, C.M.I.E. Mumbai.

Economic and Political Weekly (1997). *"National Accounts Statistics of India-1950-51 to 1995-96"* E.P.W. Research Foundation. Mumbai.

Energy Research and Development Authority (1990). *"Lessons Learned Learned—A Review of Utility Experience with Conservation and Load Management Programs for Commercial and Industrial Customers"*, State of New York.

Government of India (1996). *"The India Infrastructure Report: Policy Imperatives for Growth and Welfare"*, (3 Volumes) Ministry of Finance, New Delhi.

Government of India (1995). *"Annual Reports on the Working of the State Electricity Boards and Electricity Departments"* Planning Commission New Delhi.

Government of India (1995-96). *"Annual Reports 1995-96"* Ministry of Power. New Delhi.

Government of India (1995-96). *"Economic Survey"* Ministry of Finance, New Delhi.

Government of Kerala. (1994-95, 1995-96, 1996-97). *"Economic Review"* Planning Board, Thiruvanandapuram.

Integrated Rural Technology Centre (I.R.T.C) (1996). *"Exercises for Integrated Resource Planning for Kerala End Use*

Analysis—An Empirical Study" – Technical Report-1 Electricity. (Unpublished), Palakkad.

Kerala State Electricity Board (1996). *"Kerala Power Sector Reforms Solutions for Tomorrow"* Mimeograph.

Kerala State Electricity Board. *"Power System Statistics"* Various Issues, KSEB, Thiruvanandapuram.

Kerala State Electricity Board. *"Power System Operations"* Various Issues. KSEB, Thiruvanandapuram.

KSEB PG Engineers Association (1997 and 1998). *"Proceedings of the Third National Seminar on Modern Trends in Power Engineering and Development"*, Thiruvananadapuram.

Mohanan Chandra. P.S. and Menon. R.V.G. (ed.). *"ISTE Summer School—Lecture Notes on Energy Conservation and Management"* College of Engineering, Thiruvanandapuram.

Nadel Stevan et al. (1991). *"Opportunities for Improving End Use Electricity Efficiency in India"* USAID Study.

Tata Energy Research Institute (1995). *"Environmental Considerations and Options in Managing India's long term Energy Strategy (ECOMILES)"* TERI, New Delhi.

TNEB (1995). *"Statistics at a Glance"* TNEB Chennai.

World Bank (1994). *"World Development Report—Infrastructure for Development"* O.U.P.

Journals

Al-Garni, Z. Ahamed et. al. (1994). *"A Regression Model for Electric Energy Consumption Forecasting in Eastern Saudi Arabia"* Energy, 19 (10).

Al-Garni, Z. Ahamed et. al. (1997). *"Model for Electric Energy Consumption in Eastern Saudi Arabia"* Energy Sources 19.

Al-Garni, Z. Ahamed et. al. (1994). *"A Regression Model for Electric Energy Consumption Forecasting in Eastern Saudi Arabia"* Energy, Vol. 19, No. 10.

Al-Garni, Z. Ahamed et. al. (1997). *"Model for Electric Energy Consumption in Eastern Saudi Arabia"* Energy Sources 19.

Banerjee. R. and Parikh, J. (1993). *"Demand Side Management in Power Planning: An Exercise for H.T. Industries in Maharashtra"* Economic and Political Weekly, August 7.

Banks E. Ferdenand. (1996). *"Economics of Electricity Deregulation and Privatisation: An Introductory Survey"* Energy Vol. 21, No. 4.

Bhattacharyya, S.C. (1996). *"Applied General Equilibrium Models for Energy Studies: A Survey"* Energy Economics (18), Elsevier U.K.

Bhattacharyya, S.C. (1995). *"Power Sector Privatisation in Developing Countries: Will it Solve all Problems"* Energy Sources Vol. 17.

Bhattacharyya, S.C. (1996). *"Applied General Equilibrium Models for Energy Studies, A Survey"* Energy Economics, No. 18.

Bhushan Bhanu. (1997). *"Competitive Bidding for Private Power Projects with Two Part Tariff"* Energy Management, July-September.

Byrne John, Shen Bo, and Wallace William. (1998). *"The Economics of Sustainable Energy for Rural Development: A Study of Renewable Energy in Rural China"* Energy Policy Vol. 26. No. 1.

Byrne John, Shen Bo, and Wallace Williams. (1998). *"The Economics of Sustainable Energy for Rural Development: A Study of Renewable Energy in Rural China"* Energy Policy Vol. 26. No. 1.

Centre for Monitoring Indian Economy (CMIE). *"India's Energy Sector – July 1995"* Mumbai 1995.

Chathopadhya. D. Banarjee Rangan, and Parikh Jyoti, (1993). *"Integrating Demand Side and Supply Side Resources in Electrical Utility Planning—A Multi Objective Approach"* IGIDR Discussion Paper No. 99.

Damodaran V.K. (1995). *"Policies for Implementation of Least cost Power Planning"*, Seminar Proceedings, Government College of Engineering, Kannur.

Das J.K. and Bhattacharjee. S. (1994). *"New Trends in Energy Management in India"* Electrical India, 15th May.

Davis Mark. (1998). *"Rural Households Energy Consumption: The Effects of Access to Electricity: Evidences from South Africa"* Energy Policy Vol. 26, No. 3.

Deshun Liu, Youhong Wang, and Aiming Zhou (1997). *"Cost-Benefit Analysis on IRP/DSM Applications—A Case Study in Shanghai"* Energy Policy, Vol. 25, No. 10.

Devadas. V. (1997). *"Micro Level Planning, Part-1 Forecasting Future Scenario"* Energy Sources, 19.

Devadas. V. (1997). *"Micro Level Planning, Part-2 Impact Analysis Through Scenarios"* Energy Sources, 19.

Fesharaki Fereidun, KEEVILL's heather, and Dorain P. James (1996). *"Recent Trends in Domestic Energy Prices of Asia: Impacts of Deregulation and Changing Policy Directions"* OPEC Review, June.

"Hitech Voice". The Journal of KSEB Post Graduate Engineers Association. Thiruvanandapuram. (Various Issues).

"Hydel" The Journal of KSEB Engineers Association, Thiruvanandapuram. (Various Issues).

Islam. M.N. (1995). *"The Role of Renewable Energy in the Energy System: An Issue in the Philosophy of Renewal of National Resources"* Energy Economics Vol. 17 No. 2.

Jalees Kanwar. (1997). *"Hydel Power: Potential and Problems"* Chemical Engineering World, Vol. 12. No. 9. September.

Jawaharlal. G. (1994). *"Impact of Agriculture Tariff on the Financial Resources of State Electricity Boards—A Case Study of Andhra Pradesh State Electricity Baord"* Electrical India, 15th Sept.

Jin son, Hyung and Min Jo. K (1988). *"Capital Budgeting Process for Electric Power Utilities—An Analytic Hierarchy Process Approach."* International Journal of Energy Research 22.

Karbuz sorbuz, Birol Fairh, Gurer Nadir. (1997). *"Electricity Demand in Turkey"* Pacific and Asian Journal of Energy, 7 (1).

Kats Gregory, *"The Earth Summit—Opportunity for Energy Reforms. (1992)"*. Energy Policy. June.

Kumar Vijoy et al. (1997). *"Bulk Power Tariff in North Eastern Region in Line with ECC Recommendation"*, Vidyut Bharati, October-December.

Malik. S.B. and Satsangi P.S. (1997). *"Data Extrapolation Techniques for Energy System Planning"* Energy Management, Vol. 38, No. 14.

Mani Sunil. (1996). *"Economic liberalisation and Kerala's Industrial Sector—An Assessment of Investment Opportunities"* Economic and Political Weekly, August 24-31.

Mongia Nandita et al. (1994). *"Energy use and Carbon Implications in India—Focus on Industry"* Energy Policy Vol. 22. No. 11.

Morris Sebastain. (1996). *"The Political Economy of Electric Power Development in India"* Economic and Political Weekly.

Munasinge. M. (1985). *"An Integrated Framework for Energy Pricing in Developing Countries"* Energy Journal Vol. 10, No. 3.

Nene. P.L. (1994). *"Future Perspective for Power Grid Corporation"* Electrical India, 15th May.

Nene. P.L. (1994). *"Privatisation of Power Sector—Need for a Fresh Look"* Electrical India, 30th April.

Ott Gerhard, (1994). *"The World Energy Scene"* Proceedings of IMC-WEC International Conference on Energy, November 17-18, New Delhi.

Pal M. and Maiti P. (1997). *"An Econometric Model of Exploration and Exploitation of Hydrocarbon"* Journal of Quantitative Economics, Vol. 13. No. 2. July.

Parikh. J., et al. (1991). *"IGIDR—HT Industries Survey in Maharashtra."* IGIDR Discussion paper No. 43.

Parikh. J. (Ed) (1992). *"DSM Matters: Demand Side Management in the Electricity Sector"* IGIDR Working paper Reprint No. 26.

Parikh. J.K. and Chaitanya. A.K. (1980). *"Are our Industries Energy Efficient"* Economic and Political Weekly, March 15.

Pillai. M.G.K (1995). *"Supply Side Options"* Seminar Proceedings, Government College of Engineering, Kannur.

Pokharel Shaligram and Sekar Chandra. M. (1998). *"A Multiobjective Approach to Rural Energy Policy Analysis"* Energy Vol. 23, No. 4.

"Power Line" (Various Issues.) New Delhi.

Purkayastha. P. and Ghosh Arun. (1997). *"Power policies: Need for a national Debate"* Economic and Political Weekly, Vol. 32, No. 3.

Ramanathan. R. and Ganesh. L.S. (1995). *"Energy Alternatives for Lighting in Households: An Evaluation Using an*

Integrated Goal Programming—AHP Model" Energy, No. 20.

Reddy, Sudhakara. B. (1995). *"Modeling of Competing Technologies in Residential Sector"* IGIDR Working paper Reprint No. 165.

Reddy, A.K.N. and Prasad, K. Krishna. (1977). *"Technological Alternatives and the Indian Energy Crisis"* Economic and Political Weekly, Special number.

Reddy, A.K.N. Gladys Sumithra, D. Balachandra. P. Antonette D'sa. (1991). *"A Development Focussed End Use Oriented Electricity Scenario for Karnataka"*, Economic an Political Weekly, April 6th and 13th.

Reddy, A.K.N. and Gladys Sumithra. (1997). *"Power System of Karnataka—some Revelations"* EPW Vol. 32, No. 32. March 20-28.

Reddy Sudakara. B. (1995). *"Econometric Analysis of Energy use in Urban Households"* Energy Sources, Vol. 17.

Reddy Sudhakara, B. (1995). *"The Concept and Evaluation of Demand Side Management"* International Journal of Global Energy Issues. 7 (1/2).

Reddy Sudhakara. B. (1995). *"Electricity Pricing and Load Management in Maharashtra"* Energy Sources 17 (3).

Reddy, Sudhakara. B. (1996). *"Economic Evaluation of Demand Side Management Options Using Utility Avoided Costs"* Energy Vol. 21 No. 6.

Sanghvi, P. Arun. (1982). *"Economic Costs of Electricity Supply Interruptions: US and Foreign Experience"* Energy Economics Vol. 4 No. 3.

Sanghvi, P. Arun. (1984). *"Least Cost Energy Strategies for Power System Expansion"* Energy Policy, March.

Sanghvi, P. Arun. (1991). *"Power Shortages in Devewloping Countries: Impact and Policy Implications"* Energy Policy Vol. 19. June.

Sankar, U. (1997). *"Pricing of Electric Power in India: Problems and Prospects."* Madras School of Economics (Mimeo).

Sankar, U., Mythli, G, and Anuradha (1997). *"Environmental Problems in India's Energy Sector and Policies for Corrective Action"* Report Submitted to World Resources Institute, Washington, July.

Sant, Girish and Dixit, Shantanu. (1993). *"Least cost power Planning: Case Study of Maharashtra"* International Energy Initiative, Bangalore.

Sarkar, A.U. and Karagoz, Serkan. (1995). *"Sustainable Development of Hydroelectric Power"* Energy, Vol 20, No. 10.

Sarkar, Ashok. (1996). *"Reliability Evaluation of a Generation a Resource Plan Using Customer Outage Costs in India"*, Energy Vol. 21 no. 9.

Sarkar, Sahok and Sreestha M. Ram. (1996). *"Integrated Analysis of Customer Value of Generation System Reliability in India"*, Energy Sources. Vol. 18.

Schramm, Gunter (1993). *"Issues and Problems in the Power Sector of Developing Countries"* Energy Policy July.

Subrahmanyam, K.V.S, (1997). *"Small Hydro Development—A Vibrant Scenario in Karnataka"* First International Conference on Revewable Energy–Small Hydro. Feb. Hyderabad.

Sumithra, Gladys, *"Economics of Energy Conservation"*, Lecture Notes on Energy Conservation, R.V.G. Menon and P.S. Chandramohanan (ed.) College of Engineering, Thiruvanandapuram.

TIDE—The Journal of Tata Energy Research Institute New Delhi. (Various Issues).

Tripathy. S.C. (1997). *"Demand Forecasting in A Power System"* Energy Conservation Management. Vol. 38. No. 14.

Union Minister of Power, Government of India. (1994). *"Private Investment in Power Sector"* Electrical India, 15th June.

Urja, the Journal of Central Electricity Authority, (Various Issues).

Wene C.O. (1996). *"Energy—Economy Analysis: Linking the Macro Economic and Systems Engineering Approaches"* Energy, Vol. 21, No. 9

Wu Kang and Li Bingseng. (1995). *"Energy Development in China: National Policies and Reginal Strategies"* Energy Policy Vol. 2 No. 2.

Zang, Zong, Xiang. (1995). *"Energy Conservation in China: An International Perspective"* Energy Policy, Vol. 2 No. 2.